Windows® Home Server
Protect and Simplify Your Digital Life

Rick Hallihan

Wiley Publishing, Inc.

Windows® Home Server: Protect and Simplify Your Digital Life

Published by
Wiley Publishing, Inc.
10475 Crosspoint Boulevard
Indianapolis, IN 46256
www.wiley.com

Copyright © 2008 by Wiley Publishing, Inc., Indianapolis, Indiana

Published simultaneously in Canada

ISBN: 978-0-470-18625-1

Manufactured in the United States of America

10 9 8 7 6 5 4 3 2 1

Library of Congress Cataloging-in-Publication Data
Hallihan, Rick, 1977–
  Windows home server : protect and simplify your digital life / Rick Hallihan.
    p. cm.
  Includes index.
  ISBN 978-0-470-18625-1 (pbk.)
1. Microsoft Windows server. 2. Operating systems (Computers) 3. Home computer networks — Computer programs. I. Title.
  QA76.76.O63H34346 2008
  005.4'476 — dc22
                     2007045590

No part of this publication may be reproduced, stored in a retrieval system or transmitted in any form or by any means, electronic, mechanical, photocopying, recording, scanning or otherwise, except as permitted under Sections 107 or 108 of the 1976 United States Copyright Act, without either the prior written permission of the Publisher, or authorization through payment of the appropriate per-copy fee to the Copyright Clearance Center, 222 Rosewood Drive, Danvers, MA 01923, (978) 750-8400, fax (978) 646-8600. Requests to the Publisher for permission should be addressed to the Legal Department, Wiley Publishing, Inc., 10475 Crosspoint Blvd., Indianapolis, IN 46256, (317) 572-3447, fax (317) 572-4355, or online at http://www.wiley.com/go/permissions.

Limit of Liability/Disclaimer of Warranty: The publisher and the author make no representations or warranties with respect to the accuracy or completeness of the contents of this work and specifically disclaim all warranties, including without limitation warranties of fitness for a particular purpose. No warranty may be created or extended by sales or promotional materials. The advice and strategies contained herein may not be suitable for every situation. This work is sold with the understanding that the publisher is not engaged in rendering legal, accounting, or other professional services. If professional assistance is required, the services of a competent professional person should be sought. Neither the publisher nor the author shall be liable for damages arising herefrom. The fact that an organization or Website is referred to in this work as a citation and/or a potential source of further information does not mean that the author or the publisher endorses the information the organization or Website may provide or recommendations it may make. Further, readers should be aware that Internet Websites listed in this work may have changed or disappeared between when this work was written and when it is read.

For general information on our other products and services please contact our Customer Care Department within the United States at (800) 762-2974, outside the United States at (317) 572-3993 or fax (317) 572-4002.

Trademarks: Wiley, the Wiley logo, and related trade dress are trademarks or registered trademarks of John Wiley & Sons, Inc. and/or its affiliates, in the United States and other countries, and may not be used without written permission. Windows is a registered trademark of Microsoft Corporation in the United States and/or other countries. All other trademarks are the property of their respective owners. Wiley Publishing, Inc., is not associated with any product or vendor mentioned in this book.

Wiley also publishes its books in a variety of electronic formats. Some content that appears in print may not be available in electronic books.

For Tammy
whose loving support made this book possible

Credits

EXECUTIVE EDITOR
Chris Webb

DEVELOPMENT EDITOR
Kelly Talbot

TECHNICAL EDITOR
Mark Justice Hinton

PRODUCTION EDITOR
Kathryn Duggan

COPY EDITOR
Mildred Sanchez

EDITORIAL MANAGER
Mary Beth Wakefield

PRODUCTION MANAGER
Tim Tate

VICE PRESIDENT AND EXECUTIVE GROUP PUBLISHER
Richard Swadley

VICE PRESIDENT AND EXECUTIVE PUBLISHER
Joseph B. Wikert

PROJECT COORDINATOR, COVER
Lynsey Osborn

COMPOSITOR
Craig Woods, Happenstance Type-O-Rama

PROOFREADER
C.M. Jones, Jones Editorial Services

INDEXER
Melanie Belkin

ANNIVERSARY LOGO DESIGN
Richard Pacifico

About the Author

Rick Hallihan is an industry expert with a wide range of experience in technology, networking, and software development. Over the years he has developed software using Java, C, C++, and C#. Rick also has experience managing servers running Linux, Windows 2000 Server, and Windows Server 2003, including Active Directory and Group Policy management, and building networks with Cisco routing and networking hardware.

In addition, Rick has been an active technology enthusiast for many years. He has been blogging about Microsoft technologies and the Internet since March 2004. His blog can be found at `http://onemanshouting.com`. In January 2006, Rick was selected by Microsoft to participate in "Search Champs," a collection of industry participants that meet in Redmond, WA, to learn about, discuss, and provide feedback on Microsoft's Internet-oriented products and services.

Rick began his involvement with Microsoft's Windows Home Server unknowingly with a blog post in January 2005, where he outlined a vision for a "Windows Server, Home Edition" that would leverage Microsoft's Small Business Server platform. Little did Rick know that Microsoft was already hard at work building something similar. Soon after Windows Home Server was announced to the public, Rick was afforded the opportunity to discuss the product in-depth with Charlie Kindel, Microsoft's general manager for Windows Home Server, mostly because of that predictive posting that he had made two years before.

Because of his involvement with the community, Rick was granted Microsoft's MVP Award for Windows Home Server. Rick looks forward to being part of the emerging community that is developing around Windows Home Server.

About the Technical Editor

Mark Justice Hinton has worked as a computer professional for more than 25 years, including 20 years of teaching computer classes for the University of New Mexico. Mark has helped thousands of students and clients get more out of their computers in areas from DOS to Windows Vista, as well as (X)HTML and Web development.

Working for clients and students — and just out of curiosity — Mark digs deeply into understanding and explaining how things work and why they don't always.

Mark has been the technical editor for six books for Wiley. He is the author of *PC Magazine Windows Vista Solutions* (Wiley, 2007). His blog is `www.mjhinton.com/help/`.

Contents at a Glance

Acknowledgments xiii
Introduction xv

Chapter 1	Introducing Windows Home Server	1
Chapter 2	Your Digital Life	13
Chapter 3	Selecting Your Home Server	29
Chapter 4	Setting Up Your Home Network	39
Chapter 5	Getting Started with Windows Home Server	57
Chapter 6	Creating and Using Accounts	79
Chapter 7	Creating and Managing Backups	99
Chapter 8	Digital Spring-Cleaning	121
Chapter 9	The Center of Your Digital Home	141
Chapter 10	Recovering Lost Data	163
Chapter 11	Remotely Accessing Files and Computers	187
Chapter 12	Taking Care of Your Home Server	215
Chapter 13	Security and Your Home Server	235
Chapter 14	Expanding Your Windows Home Server	249
Appendix A	Finding More Information	271

Index 279

Contents

	Acknowledgments xiii
	Introduction xv
Chapter 1	**Introducing Windows Home Server** 1
	Simple Backups 1
	Your Files, Anywhere 2
	Seamless Expansion 5
	Network Health 5
	Who Needs a Home Server? 7
	Understanding What WHS *Isn't* 8
	Summary 11
Chapter 2	**Your Digital Life** 13
	Developing a Strategy 14
	Key Ideas for Organizing Your Digital Life 14
	Committing to Using Centralized Storage 15
	Understanding Metadata 16
	Creating Your Categories 17
	A Warning about Unsorted Categories 18
	Organizing Your Categories 19
	How Can Windows Home Server Help? 24
	Centralized and Easily Accessible Storage 25
	Predefined Shared Folders 25
	User-Defined Shared Folders 25
	Personal Shares 25
	Search Technology 26
	A Living Strategy 26
	Summary 27
Chapter 3	**Selecting Your Home Server** 29
	Buying or Building Your Server 29
	Choosing a Prebuilt Server 29
	OEM/Retail Machines 30
	System Builder 30
	Support 30
	Other Considerations 31
	Building Your Own Server 31
	Risk 31
	Cost 32
	Customization 32
	Satisfaction 33

	Selecting Your Server	33
	General Considerations	33
	Special Considerations for Prebuilt OEM/Retail Servers	36
	System Requirements	36
	Summary	37
Chapter 4	**Setting Up Your Home Network**	**39**
	Designing Your Network	39
	Parts of a Home Network	40
	Planning It Out	45
	Environmental Concerns	48
	Setting It Up	49
	Broadband Modems	49
	Routers	49
	Switches	50
	A Note on DHCP and Subnets	50
	Network Adapters	51
	Wireless Security	52
	WEP or WPA?	52
	Additional Wireless Considerations	54
	Summary	55
Chapter 5	**Getting Started with Windows Home Server**	**57**
	Finding Your Home Server a Home	57
	Technical Requirements	57
	Environmental Concerns	59
	The Newest Member of Your Household	60
	Setting Up Your Home Server	61
	Setting Up Windows Home Server on PC Hardware	61
	Setting Up a Retail/OEM Windows Home Server	74
	Connecting Your Home Network	75
	Summary	77
Chapter 6	**Creating and Using Accounts**	**79**
	Basics of User Accounts	79
	Authentication	79
	Authorization	80
	Creating Accounts	80
	Creating an Account on Windows Home Server	81
	Creating an Account on Your PC	86
	Using the Update Password Tool	91
	Changing a Password	91
	Updating the Rest of Your PCs	91
	Should You Enable the Guest Account?	93
	What Is the Guest Account Used For?	93
	Enabling the Guest Account	94
	Managing Permissions	96
	Changing Folder Permissions	96
	Enabling and Disabling Remote Access	97
	Summary	98

Chapter 7	**Creating and Managing Backups** **99**	
	Backup Defaults 99	
	Managing Your Backup Schedule 100	
	Constraints 100	
	Considerations for Your Backup Schedule 100	
	Deciding on a Schedule 101	
	Setting the Schedule 102	
	Managing Backup Retention 104	
	Considerations 104	
	Deciding on Backup Retention 107	
	Setting Backup Retention 108	
	Disabling Backups for a Computer 109	
	When to Turn Off Backups 109	
	How to Turn Off Backups for a Computer 110	
	Turning Backups Back On 110	
	Managing Volumes and Exclusions 112	
	Considerations for Volumes 112	
	Considerations for Folders and Files 113	
	Other Thoughts on Volumes and Exclusions 113	
	Running the Backup Configuration Wizard 113	
	Turning Off Computers 119	
	Summary 119	
Chapter 8	**Digital Spring-Cleaning** **121**	
	Revisiting Your Strategy 121	
	Before You Begin 122	
	Setting Up 124	
	Creating User-Defined Shares 125	
	Creating Subfolders 127	
	Data Collection 129	
	Finding Your Data 130	
	Moving Files 133	
	Staging 135	
	Checking for More Files 135	
	A Caution about Search 137	
	Learning New Habits 137	
	Setting a Good Example 137	
	Creating Shortcuts 137	
	Reminding Others of Benefits 139	
	Revisiting Spring-Cleaning 140	
	Summary 140	
Chapter 9	**The Center of Your Digital Home** **141**	
	Centralizing Your Printer 141	
	Limitations 142	
	Setting Up Your Printer 142	
	Connecting the Printer 143	
	Logging in to Your Home Server 143	

	Adding Your Printer 145
	Logging Off from Your Server. 152
	Connecting Clients to Your Shared Printer 153
	Sharing Media with Windows Home Server 155
	Setting Up Media Library Sharing. 155
	Accessing Media from Your Xbox 360 157
	Accessing Media from Other Devices 161
	Summary 162
Chapter 10	**Recovering Lost Data 163**
	Recovering Data from Backups. 164
	Opening Backups. 164
	Restoring Files on WHS Shares. 169
	Restoring a Deleted File 169
	Restoring a Previous Version of a File 171
	Recovering from a Hard Drive Failure. 173
	Other Reasons for Using System Restore. 174
	Starting Recovery 175
	The Restore Computer Wizard 178
	Summary 185
Chapter 11	**Remotely Accessing Files and Computers 187**
	Enabling Remote Access on Your Server 187
	Configuring User Accounts for Remote Access 193
	Configuring Your Broadband Connection. 197
	Basics of IP Addresses and Routing. 197
	Setting Up Port Forwarding for UPnP Routers 198
	Manually Setting Up Port Forwarding 200
	Connecting to Windows Home Server Shares. 207
	Enabling Remote Desktop Access on Home Computers 209
	Enabling Remote Desktop Access. 210
	Configuring Your Firewall to Allow Remote Desktop 210
	Security Considerations 211
	Connecting to Home Computers 212
	Summary 214
Chapter 12	**Taking Care of Your Home Server 215**
	Common Problems and Alerts 215
	Failed Backups. 216
	Missing or Disabled Security Elements 216
	Missing or Unhealthy Drives 217
	Low Disk Space 219
	Adding and Removing Hard Drives 220
	Adding a Drive. 220
	Removing a Drive. 222
	Monitoring and Preventative Maintenance 225
	Reviewing Operations of Windows Home Server 225
	Physical Maintenance 229
	Summary 233

Chapter 13	**Security and Your Home Server** **235**	
	How Windows Home Server Helps with Security	235
	Monitoring and Managing Home Network Health	236
	Understanding Security Suites	238
	Antivirus	238
	Antispyware	239
	Firewall	239
	Other Features	240
	Defense in Depth	240
	Trade-offs	240
	Antivirus for Windows Home Server	242
	Patches and Updates	243
	Automatic Updates	244
	Enabling Automatic Updates on Client Computers	244
	Keeping Other Programs Updated	245
	Automatic Updates and Your Windows Home Server	246
	Other Backup Tools	248
	Summary	248
Chapter 14	**Expanding Your Windows Home Server** **249**	
	The Sky Is the Limit	249
	Media Hub Enhancements	250
	Security and Home Automation	250
	Personal Publishing	250
	Data Security and Information Sharing	251
	Installing Add-ins	251
	Buying or Downloading the Software	251
	Installing an Add-in	251
	Uninstalling an Add-in	255
	Current Add-ins	256
	ASoft AutoExit 2008 for Windows Home Server	257
	ElectricPocket LobsterTunes	257
	KeepVault Windows Home Server	258
	Jungle Disk for Windows Home Server	259
	PhotoSync for WHS	260
	Whiist Website Management Plug-in	261
	Windows Home Server Program Launcher	263
	Windows Home Server Website Manager	266
	Xbox Community Feeds	266
	Evolving Add-ins	269
	Diskeeper Corporation's Diskeeper 2008	269
	Embedded Automation mControl for Windows Home Server	269
	Lagotek Corporation's Home Intelligence Platform	269
	SageTV for Windows Home Server	269
	Summary	270

Appendix A	**Finding More Information** **271**
	Windows Home Server Communities. 271
	Microsoft's Windows Home Server Forums 271
	WHSBook.com. 272
	Blogs 273
	Microsoft's Windows Home Server Blog on TechNet. 273
	Charlie Kindel's Blog—cek.log 274
	We Got Served 274
	MS Windows Home Server. 275
	Home Automation 276
	Embedded Automation 276
	Lagotek 276
	Smarthome Home Automation Superstore 276
	Other Information 276
	Underwriters Laboratories Consumer Section. 276
	Other Questions? 277
	Index **279**

Acknowledgments

I want to thank my wife, Tammy, and my three kids for allowing me the time to write this book. Every hour I spent tinkering with my Windows Home Server box or typing away at the computer was an hour that I was not available to them.

I want to thank Seagate Technology for providing me with some loaner USB hard drives so that I could try different drive configurations and keep my data safe while I was experimenting with the Windows Home Server Beta and RC1 software. Likewise, I want to thank Robert Scoble for setting me up with a point-of-contact at Seagate to get the ball rolling.

Thanks also to Microsoft and their Edelman Xbox Public Relations group for providing me with a loaner Xbox 360 so that I could experiment and generate screenshots showing how to use the Xbox 360 to access content on Windows Home Server. Thanks to Larry Hyrb (a.k.a. Major Nelson) for pointing me to the right folks to contact about this.

Finally, I want to thank Microsoft's Windows Home Server team, especially Todd Headrick, for being very responsive to technical questions while I was developing content for the book.

Introduction

As a new category of product, Windows Home Server may be a bit confusing to some computer users. Many people will see the word "Server" and assume that bringing a Windows Home Server machine into their home will be complicated and difficult. The main purpose of this book is to show users that setting up and using Windows Home Server can be easy and, more important, that it can be used to simplify their digital lives by protecting their important files and making them available in a variety of different ways.

I am very excited by the idea that technology can actually be used to make people's lives better. Unfortunately advances in technology sometimes make life better for only a small subset of people, the technology elite who live and breathe computers and networking. One of the most common criticisms for Windows Home Server is that many of the features could be cobbled together using a low-cost Linux-based server, network attached storage device, or other products. The problem with this criticism is that it assumes that everyone is comfortable stitching together a bunch of disparate technologies in order to build a solution for their home network. If it really were easy, then everyone would have already done it! Windows Home Server makes a huge stride to close the technology divide. With the first release of Windows Home Server, Microsoft has focused on leveraging their server technology to build a solution that is usable by everyday computer users.

Through the course of this book, I hope to provide easy-to-follow instructions and recommendations that will allow you to bring a Windows Home Server into your home, connect it to your home network, and make the most of your digital life by leveraging the features of Windows Home Server.

How This Book Is Organized

This book is designed to lead you through the process of obtaining, setting up, and utilizing Windows Home Server in your home. Some people may already have home server or may have made up their mind already about the machine they plan to use. Each chapter is designed to convey a different aspect of integrating Windows Home Server into your home network. If you are already comfortable with a particular topic, then you may choose to skip that chapter, but keep in mind that Windows Home Server brings distinct capabilities to you network and also places unique demands on your network's infrastructure. For example, Chapter 4 discusses home networks in detail. While you may already have a very functional home network, you may want to take the time to read Chapter 4 because it discusses some of the specific demands that will be brought to your home network because of Windows Home Server, and it will also highlight recommendations for dealing with these demands.

One main theme that runs through the book is the idea that Windows Home Server should be used as a tool to simplify your digital life. The process of planning how to best utilize Windows Home Server begins in Chapter 2, and the execution of the plan occurs later in Chapter 8. In between, this book covers many of the mechanics of setting up networking, user accounts, and computer backups. The later chapters focus on different ways that you can expand the usefulness of Windows Home Server, as well as ways that you can maintain the effectiveness and security of your home server. The book concludes with a chapter covering add-ins, which are modules that can be added to your Windows Home Server in order to expand its functionality beyond the feature set that Microsoft delivered.

The following list describes the contents of the chapters in more detail.

- **Chapter 1, "Introducing Windows Home Server":** Chapter 1 introduces users to Windows Home Server as a product. Because it is so vastly different from typical consumer desktop computers and also very different from the servers that are run by businesses, Windows Home Server requires some explanation to define exactly what its purpose is and how it is useful. Chapter 1 provides you with a clearer understanding of how Windows Home Server can fit into your home network.

- **Chapter 2, "Your Digital Life":** Chapter 2 begins the process of developing a plan for making the most of Windows Home Server in order to protect and simplify your digital life. You are guided through the process of evaluating how to protect your important data, where to store it, and how best to keep it organized. Basic ideas behind data protection, including evaluating the risk of loss against the importance of the data are covered. By the end of Chapter 2, you should have some good ideas about how to leverage the features of Windows Home Server in order to keep your data protected and available. You should also be ready to develop a plan for organizing your data in a logical and useful way.

- **Chapter 3, "Selecting Your Home Server":** Chapter 3 provides information that will help you to evaluate your options for obtaining a Windows Home Server. First, it covers the decision whether to buy or build your home server. The different components that make up a server are covered, as well as descriptions about how they contribute to the performance of a Windows Home Server machine. This understanding helps you to evaluate different options for purchasing or building a server. Some of the pitfalls of building your own server are also covered, because Microsoft is not offering the Windows Home Server operating system as a regular software release, but rather are making it available through their OEM System Builder channels.

- **Chapter 4, "Setting Up Your Home Network":** Chapter 4 covers the basics of setting up a home network. As a product, Windows Home Server is only really useful as part of a network with one or more client computers. Some features of Windows Home Server are only available if it can be connected to a broadband Internet connection as well. Chapter 4 also discusses the unique demands that Windows Home Server can place on a network, as well as some ideas to plan for these demands. Setting up wireless Ethernet security is also covered.

- **Chapter 5, "Getting Started with Windows Home Server":** Chapter 5 covers the process of getting Windows Home Server running on your home network. Topics include selecting an appropriate location for your Windows Home Server, setting up a prebuilt home server or installing Windows Home Server on new or existing hardware, and connecting your client computers to your new server.

- **Chapter 6, "Creating and Using Accounts":** Chapter 6 shows you how to set up accounts in order to make use of Windows Home Server for centralized storage and remote access. Basics of user authentication are covered, as well as some ideas for how to ease the transition for households that are not used to the idea of using separate usernames or passwords. Windows Home Server has some unique requirements if you want to be able to seamlessly utilize shared folders from your client computers, and these requirements are explained. Lastly, the process of setting and managing permissions for shared resources is covered.

- **Chapter 7, "Creating and Managing Backups"**: Chapter 7 covers the process of managing Windows Home Server's backup functionality. The default settings for schedule and retention are covered, and then situations that may make you want to change the settings from the defaults are covered. Next, the process of configuring backups for individual computers, including setting up folder exclusions is discussed. Lastly, Chapter 7 covers some specific concerns for mobile computers.

- **Chapter 8, "Digital Spring Cleaning"**: Chapter 8 covers the process of utilizing your Windows Home Server to execute the plan that was originally developed in Chapter 2. You are guided through the process of creating a backup of your client computers in order to guard against accidental loss of data, and then you review the process of moving data to a central storage location on your Windows Home Server. In addition to the mechanics of moving data to the home server, this chapter also covers the idea that organization of data is an ongoing challenge, and it covers some suggestions for making it easier for members of the household to help keep things in order.

- **Chapter 9, "The Center of Your Digital Home"**: Chapter 9 highlights the ideas that Windows Home Server can be more than just a backup and storage machine, but can also act as a hub for other functions on your home network. The first topic covered is using Windows Home Server as a centralized print server, providing access to a printer to all of your clients. The second part of the chapter describes in detail how to make use of Windows Home Server as a media server in order to deliver media files to televisions or sound systems using Media Extenders, or an Xbox 360.

- **Chapter 10, "Recovering Lost Data"**: Chapter 10 walks you through the process of recovering accidentally deleted files, retrieving previous versions of files, or restoring a computer after a hard drive crash. This chapter covers the different types of data loss that Windows Home Server can resolve, and provides step-by-step instructions for bringing back lost files or restoring a computer to the state that it was at before a hard drive crash or data corruption occurred.

- **Chapter 11, "Remotely Accessing Files and Computers"**: Windows Home Server provides a great deal of capability for remotely accessing files and computers, and Chapter 11 shows the reader how to configure and use this functionality. First, this chapter covers the process of setting up remote access on the server, on the networking equipment, and also setting permissions for user accounts in order to allow remote access. The chapter also covers the process of setting up remote desktop access on supporting operating systems. Chapter 11 then shows you how to connect remotely, how to access shared folders, and how to remotely connect to your home client computers.

- **Chapter 12, "Taking Care of Your Home Server"**: Chapter 12 covers several topics that center on the idea of keeping your Windows Home Server operating in a reliable manner for years to come. Common notifications and alerts are described, and corrective actions are discussed. This chapter also discusses some steps that you can take to confirm that the Windows Home Server software is operating properly, and some preventative maintenance that can be done in order to keep your home server operating smoothly.

- **Chapter 13, "Security and Your Home Server":** The addition of a Windows Home Server brings with it both new tools for maintaining the security of your home network as well as new responsibilities. Chapter 13 discusses how Windows Home Server will help you monitor the health of your home network, and also covers some of the unique security challenges that Windows Home Server might introduce.
- **Chapter 14, "Expanding Your Windows Home Server":** One of the best features of Windows Home Server is that in addition to solving very specific problems for home users, it is also a fully functional server operating system and Microsoft has developed specific features that let third-party developers provide special software packages called *add-ins* that can be installed to Windows Home Server. The general process for adding and removing add-ins is covered, and several currently available add-ins are highlighted.

Who Should Read This Book

This book is written to be useful to anyone who is comfortable using Windows home computers and who is interested in setting up a Windows Home Server machine on his or her home network. Readers should be familiar with basic ideas such as launching programs and browsing folders. Server and network related terminology is explained when introduced, and part of the purpose of this book is to demystify the networking concepts that make Windows Home Server useful.

Technology-savvy individuals or power users may also find the book useful as it provides step-by-step instructions and explanations of some of the more complicated aspects of setting up and using Windows Home Server.

Lastly, anyone who wants to leverage the features of Windows Home Server to protect and simplify his or her digital life will appreciate the organizational framework that is developed throughout the course of the book.

What You Need to Use This Book

To make the most of this book, the reader should be planning to purchase or build a Windows Home Server machine, or should have one installed on his or her home network already. Beginning in Chapter 3, many of the step-by-step tutorials can only be utilized with a Windows Home Server. In addition to a Windows Home Server, at least one client should be available on the home network.

For the purpose of planning, readers do not necessarily need access to a Windows Home Server or client machines. Tutorials include step-by-step screenshots, so readers can get a sense of the processes even if they cannot follow along on their own hardware.

What's on the Website

The website for the book can be found at `http://whsbook.com`. This website is intended to be a location where resources for the book can be found. It is also a place where readers can ask questions and discuss the various aspects of the book and the Windows Home Server product.

Any files referenced in the course of the book can be found at `http://whsbook.com/files`. Files referenced in the book are organized by chapter.

Discussion forums can be found at `http://whsbook.com/forums`. Separate forums are available to discuss hardware options, security, remote access, backup, third-party add-ins, as well as a forum specifically for asking questions about or discussing this book.

The author also maintains two blogs on the site. The first blog, Simplify (at `http://whsbook.com/blogs/simplify/`), is an extension of this book and will be a place for the author to post relevant updates and related content. The second blog, Lessons Learned (at `http://whsbook.com/blogs/writing`), will be of more interest to current or aspiring authors and will cover some of the lessons that the author learned while writing this book.

Additional information related to the publishing of this book, as well as other books on related topics can be found on the publisher's website at `http://wiley.com`.

Summary

The first release of Windows Home Server does a very good job of bringing many of the benefits of a modern server operating system into the home network. This book will help you to do more than just utilize Windows Home Server. By understanding more about Windows Home Server, you will be able to maximize the benefit that you can realize by bringing it into your home.

As you read this book you should gain a thorough understanding of how to select a Windows Home Server machine that will meet your needs. You develop a plan to simplify your digital life, and you gain an understanding of how you can utilize Windows Home Server as an integral part of your plan. You learn how to manage backups and user accounts on Windows Home Server, and gain an understanding of how specific facets of your home network might drive you to change some of the default behaviors of Windows Home Server. As you progress through the book, you learn how to take control of your data through a *digital spring-cleaning* process and how to encourage other members of your household to participate in a more organized digital life. You find out how Windows Home Server can be used to recover deleted files, previous versions of files that have accidentally been changed, or even restore a computer to a known good state following a hardware failure. You also learn how to maintain the security of your home network and how to best maintain both the software and the hardware that comprises Windows Home Server. Lastly, you learn how to leverage Windows Home Server as a flexible platform that can be expanded to meet specific needs in your home.

As you read and learn, I hope that you discover that you can truly *protect* and *simplify* your digital life by building a strategy that makes the most of Windows Home Server.

Chapter 1

Introducing Windows Home Server

Windows Home Server was introduced by Microsoft in the second half of 2007 to fulfill unmet needs of home users. Everyone knows that they should keep their important files backed up, but home computer users are rarely vigilant about backups unless they have recently suffered a loss. People often use multiple computers in the home, and keeping data accessible where you need it can be a challenge. Microsoft realized that they could leverage their existing technologies and build an entirely new kind of device: a server for the home. The team set out with several well-researched and ambitious goals, all focused around providing simple-backup to an appliance-like device that would be inexpensive, expandable, and accessible.

A server is a computer that serves a special purpose. It may not look like a typical desktop or laptop, but it is built on the same technology. A server *serves* other machines, also known as clients, by providing services to the network. Windows Home Server is a server for your home network. It provides backup services and file storage for the local network and remote access services over the Internet. A Windows Home Server device may be an appliance, which means it is simply a box with no display, keyboard, or mouse, or it may look like a regular computer. Appliance-like machines (described in Chapter 3) may be styled and designed in such a way that they will blend in with audio-video equipment, or they may be small boxes that can run quietly on your desk or on a shelf. Your Windows Home Server will run 24 hours a day in order to back up your other machines, and make other services available to them. Windows Home Server is one part hardware and one part software, used together to protect and serve your network.

Simple Backups

Most people understand how important it is to back up their files. Many of us can remember a time that we managed to delete an important file, or suffered a hard drive crash that took with it important files. Those of us who like to tinker with computers probably even have more than our fair share. My wife jokes that being married to a computer engineer means that most of the computers in the house will be partially broken at any given time.

The reality is that computers, while generally reliable, are not perfect machines. Most of the components of a PC are pretty resilient, but unfortunately the hard drive is all at once the most important and the most fragile. At the core of your hard drive is one or more thin platters, spinning at somewhere between four thousand and ten thousand revolutions per minute (RPM). For comparison, most car engines redline between five thousand and seven thousand RPM. Ten thousand RPM is almost certain death for a car engine, but for many modern hard drives, this rotational speed is normal. This means that the outer edge of a hard drive platter is probably traveling somewhere between 50 and 100 miles per hour. While this is going on, several tiny electromagnetic heads float over the surface of the hard drive on a microscopic cushion of air, reading and writing data to specific locations on the disk with amazing precision.

The hard drive manufacturers do an excellent job of creating hard drives with very tight tolerances, and hard drives are usually pretty reliable. Occasionally something occurs that causes things to go awry. In my house, one of our older laptops suffered not one, but two drops from a height of about five feet. The first time this happened, I picked up the laptop, and was amazed and relieved that it was still working. I opened a few files and programs and breathed a sigh of relief that we had narrowly escaped a major loss of data because we had not performed any backups for at least six months. The next morning, the laptop could not boot, and was complaining loudly about the hard drive being inaccessible. The second drop several months later actually left the new hard drive intact, but the machine suffered a failed memory module, and an unseated graphics module that required almost a complete disassembly of the laptop to correct.

The moral? Bad things happen. Computers are composed of electrical and mechanical devices that can and will fail, and unless you are extremely proactive with a backup solution, you will lose data at some point.

In addition to the fallibility of the hardware, we often cause our own loss of data. Most people have experienced situations where they accidentally delete important files or overwrite an older file with changes and later wish they still had the original version.

Many computers come from the manufacturer with backup technology included. Microsoft has even included fairly robust backup capabilities in Windows Vista, although some functionality is removed from the less expensive Home editions. Unfortunately even with this backup technology available, most people won't use it. Even when it is used correctly, you have to make sure that the backups have enough disk space and that the files are being backed up properly.

The good news is that Windows Home Server makes backups simple and easy. It's no longer necessary to understand information technology jargon like *incremental*, *differential*, and *full backups*. Windows Home Server presents backup and restore functionality in a manner that provides a sensible and usable default experience, and also offers flexibility to handle varying user needs as shown in Figure 1-1.

Your Files, Anywhere

The number of homes with multiple computers is on the rise, and those that use more than one PC face unique challenges. If you don't always use the same PC, you often have to remember to copy files to removable media, or my personal favorite, e-mail yourself the document as an attachment. Depending on which computer you happen to be using, you may not have the latest copy of a file, or you may not have it available at all. In multiuser homes, you may not always be able to use the same computer, and you can't always plan in advance where you might need files to be located.

Many people have learned that they can address this problem by using file shares, but setting them up is a cumbersome process that home users usually don't want to deal with. It can be difficult to set up usernames and permissions, and when things don't work right, it's easy to get frustrated and just go back to keeping your files on the local hard drive.

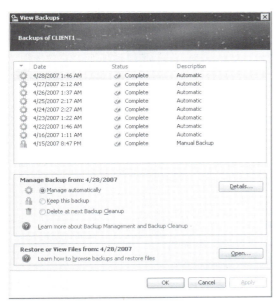

Figure 1-1

In addition to the problem of keeping files available when you are home, as more and more of your important information becomes digital, it is increasingly important to be able to access that information when you are away from home. Many businesses have recognized that providing easy access to information can make their workers more productive. Likewise, providing easy remote access to your home-based digital lives can make you more productive with your personal information.

Windows Home Server attempts to address these needs by providing centralized reliable storage in the home, and remote access to files and computers while away from home. The centralized storage is implemented as several default shares, as shown in Figure 1-2, that are available to all connected computers. Users each get their own share for personal files, and you can also set up customized shares to address specific needs.

Windows Home Server also makes files accessible from outside of the home network, as shown in Figure 1-3. Again this is something that many tech-savvy users have been able to set up on their own, but Windows Home Server makes it easy enough that it is accessible to all home users. Through a simple wizard, users can set up a website that gives them access to all the file shares on their home server, and that also lets them connect to PCs that are running Windows Vista Business, Enterprise, or Ultimate edition. These features mean that you no longer have to worry about making copies of any file you might possibly need when you travel or go on vacation. As long as you can get to an Internet connection, you will have access to the files you need or want. This will also cut down on the problem of having multiple copies of files scattered across your many computers, memory sticks, and e-mail accounts.

Chapter 1: Introducing Windows Home Server

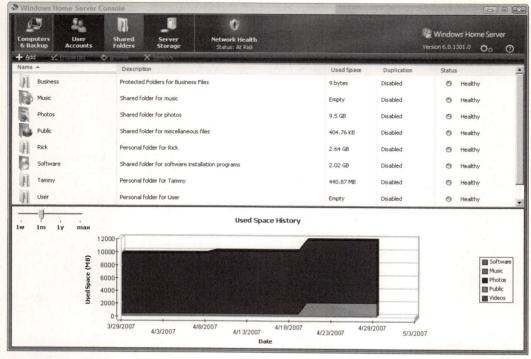

Figure 1-2

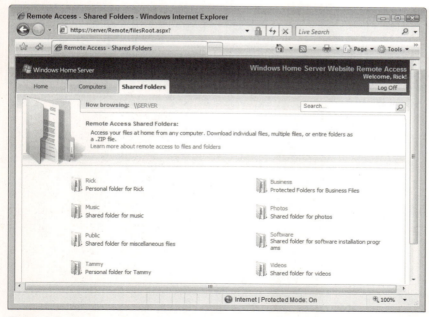

Figure 1-3

Seamless Expansion

The use of PCs in the home for storage of all kinds of data means that we all face a space crunch. Newer cameras capture sharper pictures, but these picture files take up significant space on your hard drive. A typical image from a modest digital camera can take up 2 megabytes of space, and photo aficionados that use the "raw" format on their cameras might be using upwards of 25 megabytes per picture!

As an example, my wife and I are casual digital camera users. Starting in 2003 (we had a digital camera for many years before this, but lost our archives to a hard drive crash in early 2003) we took 300 megabytes of digital pictures. In 2004 this expanded to 929 megabytes. Partway through 2005 we bought a newer digital camera and our photo storage requirement grew to 3.4 gigabytes for that year. 2006 saw 4.2 gigabytes of pictures taken. This example is just addressing still pictures. When you start bringing in audio files, home videos, mp3s, downloaded movies and television shows the storage horizon approaches very rapidly.

In the old days this meant adding a hard drive to your PC to make room for your growing storage needs. After adding a new larger hard drive, users would have to reorganize their files to make use of the new space. This could mean moving a category of files to the new drive, or possibly transferring everything from the old drive to the new one. Computer cases are also limited in the number of physical drives that can be installed, so adding more drives may not even be an option. Furthermore, many computer users simply aren't comfortable opening up their PCs.

Windows Home Server's unique storage engine makes adding storage simple. Through a user-friendly interface, shown in Figure 1-4, you can get an overall view of the storage on your server. When you need to add more space, Windows Home Server's Drive Extender technology makes it easy. Depending on the specifics or your Windows Home Server's manufacturer, the exact method may change a bit, but the basic process will include powering down the machine, either adding an internal drive or plugging in an external USB 2.0 or FireWire drive, and turning the server back on. The user can then use a wizard in the Windows Home Server console to make the space on the new drive available for use. All drives in a Windows Home Server are part of a storage pool, and the server spreads files across them, without the user having to think about which physical drive a particular file will be stored on. As an added bonus, if you have multiple hard drives attached to your Windows Home Server machine, you can turn on duplication for specific shared folders. When duplication is activated, Windows Home Server makes sure to have copies of every file stored on at least two hard drives, thus protecting your data in the event that one of your physical drives fails.

Network Health

With multiple PCs in the house, it becomes more difficult to keep track of how PCs are performing, and how they are protected. The addition of a Windows Home Server device might sound like it adds complexity to the network, and most users already feel overburdened by the task of keeping their machines up to date with patches, monitoring security settings, and maintaining antivirus software. Instead of being an additional burden, Windows Home Server adds integrated network health monitoring to the home users' arsenal for keeping track of their network. For Windows Vista computers and Windows XP machines with Service Pack 2, Windows Home Server interacts with the Windows System Security Center, and provides alerts to any machine with the Windows Home

Server console software. This means that you won't miss important alerts that other computer users in your household may be inclined to ignore or that they may not understand. Figure 1-5 shows an example of a problem viewed in Windows Home Server's *Home Network Health* view.

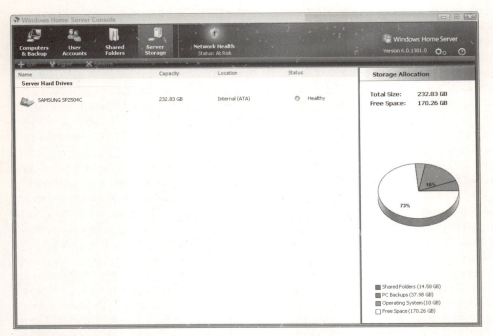

Figure 1-4

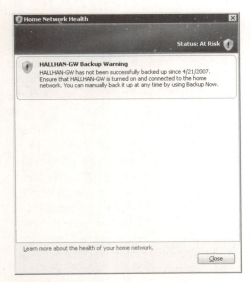

Figure 1-5

Who Needs a Home Server?

Microsoft is obviously hoping that the answer to this question is "everyone," and the truth is not far off. The typical target household for Windows Home Server is a home where two or more PCs are used for either business or personal computing. To make the most of Windows Home Server, the house should also have a broadband Internet connection.

The term *server* may tend to scare people away from Windows Home Server, but potential customers should realize that while the machine is a server in its functionality, it is easier to set up, administer, and utilize than a normal Windows PC. Users are not asked to answer questions that they may not understand. Default settings are very reasonable, and significant effort has gone into providing a simple user interface that gives users the exact information they need, without excessive or confusing computer jargon.

Now it's simple to say that everyone with multiple PCs needs a home server, but the real question is "Why should *you* want a home server?" At the core, the backup functionality is important enough to earn Windows Home Server a prominent spot on my wish list. Microsoft's Windows Home Server team likes to use the term *Divorceable Offense* for any event where irreplaceable yet important data is lost through negligence. This might include pictures of a newborn baby, or your kid's first T-ball game, or perhaps a wedding video. In the past, our memories were generally scattered across a number of analog formats such as paper print photographs, VHS or Hi8 videotapes, slides, audio tapes, and mailed letters. Each year sees more of our life digitized, and that digitized life resides on our computers.

We're also entering a time where many industries are starting to cut out the middlemen. Disintermediation is what they called it in business school. With the advent of connected homes and digital media, we can now purchase digital content and have it delivered directly to our home PCs. Now it's not just the media we create, the communications we participate in, but also the digital media that we purchase that is stored on those rapidly spinning platters of our hard drives.

Everyone agrees that all of this data should be periodically backed up. In many households, one person is designated as the "Computer Guy/Gal," and the duty of keeping all the family's computers running and data protected falls on his or her shoulders. This individual may or may not have any training in computers, but he or she is entrusted with these responsibilities. I'm the computer guy in my house, and when something goes wrong, I'm supposed to be able to fix it.

I noted earlier that my wife and I lost several years of digital photos to a hard drive crash. This was a considerable loss for us as the photos included much of our early married years. The only saving grace was that we had uploaded many of our favorite pictures to a website, so we were able to retrieve some of our digital memories, although the pictures had been scaled down for the web, so they aren't suitable for creating prints. Before the hard drive crash, I knew that I should be backing up our files, and even had backups of many of our documents (about three months old at the time of the crash), but I had not backed up the photos for more than a year. Following the crash, I wish I could say that I had learned my lesson, but it wasn't until three years later that I finally implemented a daily backup program. I tried to be vigilant for a while, but remembering to manually back up files is battle that is seldom won.

As my family's "Computer Guy" I am excited about Windows Home Server because it allows me to protect my family's files the way I know they should be protected. Some of the other features of Windows Home Server are interesting, and I'm particularly intrigued by the fact that Microsoft has released an Applications Programming Interface (API) that allows third-party developers to extend Windows Home Server to cover almost any task, including home security and automation. I was sold on the idea when I read about the backup functionality, and everything else is icing on the cake.

Understanding What WHS *Isn't*

At this point it is important to begin to understand some of the limitations of Windows Home Server. As a version 1 product in an entirely new product category, the Windows Home Server team faced a monumental challenge in defining the scope of their task. They chose to focus on three key areas: simple automatic backup, reliable and expandable storage, and remote access. Many other obvious features could eventually find their way into future versions of Windows Home Server. (For more information about Microsoft's decision-making process, see the "Why Doesn't Windows Home Server Do Foo?" sidebar.)

Windows Home Server doesn't do e-mail. This is probably more of a disappointment to power users than anyone else. While some people dream of running a Microsoft Exchange e-mail server out of their home, most people are very happy with the functionality that they get from online services like Hotmail, or from their Internet Service Provider. The limited appeal of a Windows Home Server e-mail solution is likely the reason it was left off the list.

Windows Home Server does not do Active Directory. Active Directory is the computer and user management engine that Microsoft's main line of server products uses to manage accounts, computers, and settings in the business environment. Although it would be advantageous to be able to centrally manage users and computer settings in the home, Active Directory is considerable overkill for this purpose and would have required a great deal of modification to make it work in the simple manner that Windows Home Server's end users would require. There are also some other technical hurdles because Windows XP Home edition, and the Home versions of Vista do not allow computers to utilize Active Directory. Although centralized user management would have been a nice addition, it's understandable that this was not feasible for version 1. Windows Home Server includes a Password Synchronization tool that provides most of the benefit of a central user store, without all the complexity of Active Directory.

One piece that is obviously absent from Windows Home Server's backup strategy is the ability to ship backups to an off-site location. Businesses usually send backup tapes to another location, or utilize their networks to duplicate data to a remote location. This is a good idea because it protects the data if something happens that affects the entire building, such as a flood or fire. This missing link in the backup strategy is being filled by third parties, but it is not built-in to Windows Home Server for this version. You should consider making use of a third-party off-site backup solution (one is highlighted in Chapter 14), or you should consider performing periodic manual backups of your most important data and shipping CDs or DVDs to an out-of-state family member so that you don't lose everything if your home suffers a catastrophe. It is reasonable to make manual backups of this nature once or twice a year.

Another frequent request that has not yet been addressed is the ability to centralize parental controls for Internet usage. Again, the third-party market for these types of tools is pretty expansive, and it's likely that some of these companies will integrate their systems with Windows Home Server to provide centralized management.

While Microsoft is providing pretty impressive solutions with Windows Home Server, it's important to realize that Windows Home Server is also a platform, and just like Windows, third-party developers are free to provide solutions that meet user's needs.

Why Doesn't Windows Home Server Do Foo?

When someone asks "Why doesn't Windows Home Server do *Foo*?" a response of "because" goes just about as well as it does when my son asks, "Why can't I just eat chocolate for dinner?"

This post is an attempt to generically answer the "why not" questions by explaining the process my team used to plan Windows Home Server.

. . .

As is the case with most new product ideas, we had a "jewel of an idea" that would serve as a cornerstone for everything we did. The nucleus of our vision if you will:

> *A* home server *is an always available smart node on the home network dedicated to providing services to other nodes on the home network and the Internet.*

This is an insanely broad definition. Clearly you can't build a product around something so broad, but you can develop a long-term vision.

. . .

Early in the planning process, we used a combination of brainstorming, secondary research, and our prior experiences to create a taxonomy for categorizing all of the things a home server could do. Because we are solution and scenario focused, it makes sense for this taxonomy to start with "Scenario Areas" as the highest-level bucket. We identified 11 scenario areas where a home server would be valuable (valuable to customers, end users, Microsoft, third parties, and so on):

- PC and Network Management
- Home Network Infrastructure
- Storage
- Data Protection
- Publishing and Sharing
- Anywhere Access
- Communications
- Entertainment
- Family Applications
- Third-Party Platform
- Enthusiast Playground

Within each of these scenario areas, we identified 10–20 end-to-end scenarios resulting in several hundred total scenarios. We spent just enough time talking about each scenario to be able to have a succinct description (one short paragraph max). For example, within the Anywhere Access scenario area, we wrote down the following scenario:

> *When you are outside of the home, you can search for specific files stored on your home server, even if you can't remember the specific name(s) of the files.*

Continued

Why Doesn't Windows Home Server Do Foo? *(Continued)*

To provide a solution for a given scenario, one has to build software features and technologies. So we also identified the features and technologies that would be required to provide a solution for each scenario. This "book of scenarios" painted a pretty clear picture of just about everything anyone could imagine a home network doing. It was a lot of fun creating it because we all got to basically dream up every cool idea possible.

It would take decades to build a product that delivered solutions for every scenario we documented. Our ambitions were huge, but to be successful we knew we had to get extremely focused. To get the list of things to do down to a size that was believable, we used a combination of the following:

Secondary research, primary research, industry trends, available technologies, available resources, engineering competencies, knowledge of other Microsoft product's strategies, visions and plans, business model, schedule, results of prototypes, estimated costs (people and time) to develop and test features and technologies.

We spent about six months in this process, going from several hundred scenarios (a 360° view) to a list of a few dozen scenarios (a 30° view). To do this we decided to completely ignore whole scenario areas and hundreds of scenarios; we drew a line in the sand and said:

> *We have decided to climb these mountains in v1 and leave the others for another time.*

"These mountains" are:

- An easy-to-use consumer experience on top of the most powerful operating system on the planet
- Automatic multi-PC backup and simple restore
- Easy-to-expand, reliable centralized storage
- Anywhere access

The common theme for these are reflected in our mission for v1: *...helping families with multiple PCs connect their digital experiences, providing a familiar and reliable way to store, access, share, and automatically protect what is most important.*

It was at this point in time that we could start to really formulate an actual product plan. But even that 30° field of view is too great for a single release. So as we finalized our multiyear, multirelease product roadmap we made even more "cuts." Comparing the literally hundreds of possible scenarios we could have focused on with the few we will actually deliver in v1, I'd say our field of view is around 15°. And given the amount of passion, hard work, and dedication all members of the team have poured into the product and our progress, so far I'm confident that we've found just about the right balance.

I started this post with the question "Why doesn't Windows Home Server do foo?" Hopefully, if you've read this far I was able to show you the process we used to decide what Windows Home Server will do in the first version. And as a corollary, this explains why certain capabilities will have to wait for subsequent versions. —cek (Charlie Kindel, Microsoft's General Manager for Windows Home Server)

Excerpted with permission. Originally posted to the Windows Home Server Blog by Charlie Kindel. To read the entire post, see `http://blogs.technet.com/homeserver/archive/2007/02/13/why-doesn-t-windows-home-server-do-foo.aspx`.

Summary

In this chapter you learned that Windows Home Server is basically a new category of computer, a server that is designed to fill several needs in your home network. You now understand that having a Windows Home Server on your network will automate the task of backing up all of your computers on a daily basis, so that you no longer have to worry about losing data because of hardware failure or accidental deletion. You also learned that Windows Home Server can make your data available to all of the computers in your home, and that it can also make files available when you are away from your home network. The last major area that Windows Home Server will assist with is keeping track of the health of all of the computers on your home network.

You reviewed the target market for Windows Home Server, so that you can better understand what it can do for you, and you saw some things that Windows Home Server doesn't do now, so that you know what to expect.

With this understanding, you're ready to start thinking about how Windows Home Server can help you protect and simplify your digital life.

Chapter 2

Your Digital Life

The first step in learning to simplify and protect your digital life is developing an understanding of what your "digital life" actually is. This answer will be a little different for everyone, so you will have to spend some time thinking about all of the media, data files, or other digital information that is important to you.

This chapter will help you develop an understanding of your digital life, and then help you develop a plan for how to better organize your digital life in order to make the most of Windows Home Server. There is no requirement that you be organized in order to use Windows Home Server. Windows Home Server will back up your files on every computer, no matter how they are organized. Learning and planning a strategy to keep things better organized will enhance your computing experience, and Windows Home Server makes several resources available to make this easier. By providing centralized storage and remote access, you no longer need to keep files on multiple computers where they might be needed. Keeping your digital life centralized on Windows Home Server will make it accessible across your network, and even remotely if you configure Windows Home Server's remote access features as described in Chapter 11.

One other important point to remember is that this chapter is about *planning*. At this time it wouldn't really be a good idea to start moving files around. During this chapter you should focus on getting a grasp of the scope of your digital life. Chapter 8 covers the *digital spring-cleaning* process, including using Windows Home Server to create initial backups to make sure that you don't accidentally lose data during your cleanup process. Also remember that if you currently have an organizational scheme that works, it should simply become part of your plan, although you may want to tweak it in order to make better use of Windows Home Server.

Some typical components of a digital life include digital pictures, e-mail, school reports, MP3 files, and financial records. It's not important to develop a comprehensive list at any point in your life. Occasionally, you will come across a new piece of digital information that is important to you, and it won't fit into any of the categories that you have already nailed down. It is more important to learn the process for organization, and develop a mindset that will allow you to gather and organize digital information as it comes into your life. Figure 2-1 shows a view of some devices that might be part of your digital life.

Your digital life is anything that *can* be stored on a computer and is important to you. It's important to remember that the qualification is that it *can* be stored on a computer, not that it currently *is*. The files on the memory card in your camera that you haven't downloaded for three months are part of your digital life. The music on your MP3 player is part of your digital life, even if you don't have copies on your hard drive. The contact list on your phone might also be part of your digital life. If information is digital and important, then it is part of your digital life.

14 Chapter 2: Your Digital Life

Figure 2-1

Developing a Strategy

It is important to develop a strategy for keeping your digital life organized, accessible, and protected. Many of us go through life without protecting our data, and the only time we actually think about it is when we have just lost an important file, or worse yet, an entire hard drive!

The following sections can help you develop your strategy for organizing your digital life. First, some overall tenets are described that will help keep your strategy on track. Next, you will learn about some of the functional ideas that will assist you in keeping your data accessible and *organized*.

Key Ideas for Organizing Your Digital Life

Your strategy should focus on several key ideas.

The first is that information should be protected to a level that is proportional to both the value of the data, and the difficulty in recreating that data. This combination of value and replicability will help you to determine the priority that you place on a given category of data. For example, with digital photos of your newborn child, high emotional value and the fact that they are irreplaceable would give them a very high priority in my evaluation. A Word document or a one-page letter to a local utility about a billing error might have a medium priority until the error is resolved, and become lower after that. While it is possible to assign specific priorities to individual items, this is a tedious and fairly fruitless exercise. Again, the object here is to learn to think about protecting your data with the right mindset.

The second key concept is that machines are fallible. Hard drives crash. Recorded CD-RW's can become unreadable if they are left in direct sunlight (or for any number of other reasons). You should develop your strategy around the assumption that you will have hardware failures in the future, and you want to be prepared.

The third and most important concept that you should grasp is that if your strategy is complicated or difficult to follow, it will not be successful. Unless you are an extremely dedicated individual, organization and protection of your data will be one of the things that will get ignored when your life gets busy. This is just a fact of human nature. This idea is doubly important for houses with multiple computer users. If you want to have any hope of getting an entire family on-board with your strategy, it needs to be simple and easy.

Committing to Using Centralized Storage

If you are reading this book, then you are probably hoping to utilize Windows Home Server to help you organize your digital life. A key part of making this work well is committing to keeping your important files stored in a central location, on your Home Server. By keeping your files in a central location, you enable a number of important benefits. It will be easier to keep files accessible to all of your computers, and you will not have to worry about which version of a file is on a given machine. You will also be able to utilize Windows Home Server's remote access feature to retrieve files if you are away from your home network. Also, it will be easier to protect your data, with Windows Home Server's drive extender, or with third party tools like KeepVault's Windows Home Server Online Backup Service (covered in Chapter 14), since your important files will already be gathered into one place.

There are downsides to centralized storage, and they should be understood as part of this commitment. When data is stored centrally, you may not have access to it when you are away from your home network. With Windows Home Server's remote access features, this won't be a problem as long as you have Internet access, but if you are operating totally disconnected, you will have to plan ahead in order to have the files you need available. While I was working on this chapter I was reminded of this. I had to take my sister-in-law to tennis lessons this evening, and I decided that it would be a good time to sit and type for a while. Unfortunately I'm so used to keeping my working files on my Windows Home Server, I didn't even think about the fact that my working copy of Chapter 2 was sitting on the server. When I powered up my laptop at the park and double-clicked the shortcut on my desktop, it took me several seconds to realize why the document wouldn't open. I tried in vain to see if there was an open WiFi hot spot at the park where I was, but no such luck.

You can plan for situations like this by enabling Windows Vista's Always Available Offline option. Just right-click on any network folder and select the Always Available Offline option, and Vista's Sync Center will automatically manage a local copy of all the files, and synchronize changes whenever you are connected. This feature should only be utilized for folders that you might realistically need when working disconnected, because it uses both disk space, and resources to keep local copies of the files in sync. If multiple changes are made to the same file, Vista will prompt you to select which version of the file you want to keep, and give you the option of keeping both versions so that you don't lose any changes.

Note

Offline Files is also available under Windows XP, but it is simply known as *Offline Files* since the Sync Center is new in Windows Vista. Files are still automatically synchronized, and XP will prompt the user to manually resolve conflicts.

Understanding Metadata

The next section discusses how to categorize your data, but first I want to introduce the concept of *metadata*. Metadata is anything that can help describe or identify what information is in a file. Most files have some common metadata, including the date the file was created and the date it was last modified.

Some people also consider the filename to be metadata, but this generally depends on what information is put into the filename. In Windows operating systems, the filename extension is also metadata that indicates what format the file is, and it is used to determine what program is used to open a file.

For image files, especially digital photos taken with a digital camera, there is extended metadata that is defined by standards known as EXIF (Exchangeable Image File) and IPTC (International Press Telecommunications Council). Image metadata can indicate additional information about the camera that took the picture, the date and time the picture was taken, and the dimensions of the files.

Figure 2-2 shows some image metadata in columns in Windows Vista. (Note the prompts to add various metadata, like Rating, for a selected picture in the Details pane at the bottom of the Window.) Because Vista uses these metadata standards, tags and information will actually stay with the picture, even if it is copied, e-mailed, or moved to your server. Some third-party image management tools actually use a separate database, which can be very powerful, but they lack the simple utility of the built-in metadata.

Many file types include different kinds of metadata. Word documents have fields that contain information about the author and title of a document. Metadata is a bit of a wild frontier, with different camera manufacturers supporting different fields and software manufacturers choosing what kind of metadata they will include in their own file formats.

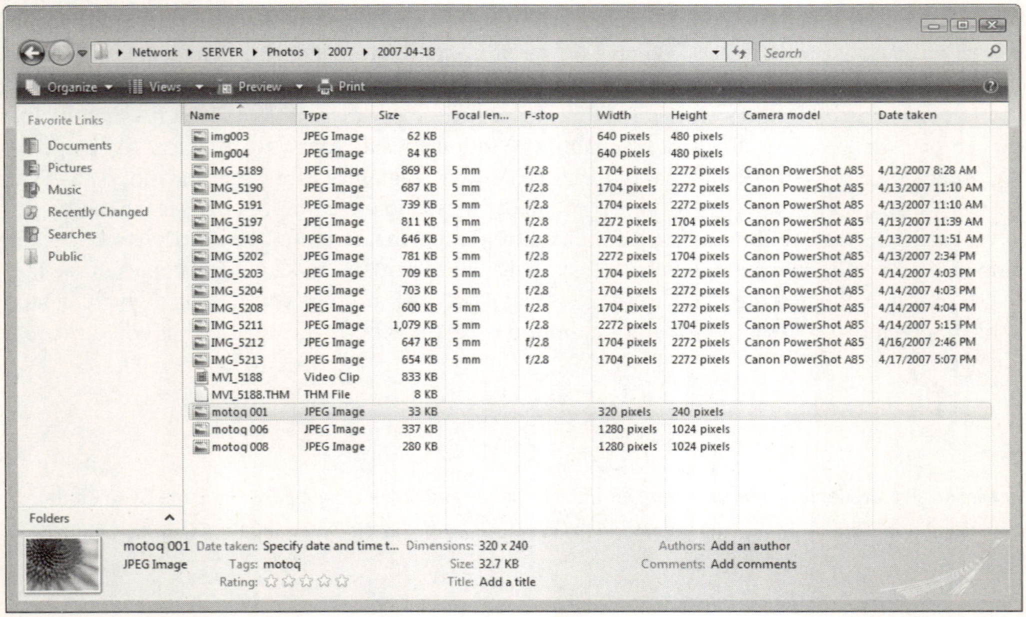

Figure 2-2

Metadata by itself is not particularly useful, but when coupled with search technology, metadata can help users find files easier and faster. When you start to create an organizational scheme for your information, you must balance the complexity of your plan with the fact that searching metadata will often enable you to find what you need.

Using the metadata your camera writes to each picture, you can search using that metadata and a tool that sees it like Windows Vista. Although you're not likely to search by f-stop, searching by camera model can help you separate photos taken by different family members with unique cameras or cell phones. This automatic metadata is useful for sorting and grouping images in Vista and Windows Photo Gallery, or it can be used during your *digital spring-cleaning* (described in Chapter 8) to help bring some order to your collection of files. The usefulness of metadata also increases greatly if you utilize Vista's built-in features to add metadata such as tags to describe the subjects and locations of your photos. For example, you could add the tags Matt, Mary, Riley, Chloe, Rafting, and South Carolina to a photo, and later you could find it via any of those key words.

Creating Your Categories

The next step in creating a strategy is to develop categories for your files, and to list out the other information that you want to protect. This exercise should be one in which you balance organization against the fact that tools and metadata can help you find data. Figure 2-3 shows the default folders/categories of files that are created in a user account in Windows Vista. These exact categories may or may not be a good fit for the data that is important in your digital life. Keep in mind that the concept of *categories* is how you want to logically think about your organizational strategy, and that the tool that you will use to categorize information will be *folders* on your computer and on Windows Home Server.

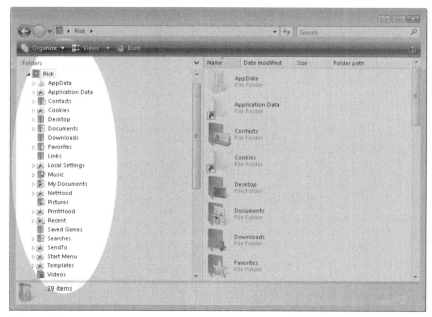

Figure 2-3

For most people, the number of categories should be between eight and fifteen in order to be manageable. If you create more than this many top-level categories, you will likely find overlap between categories, which will make it more difficult to organize files, and will lead to confusion when you are trying to locate files. For example, if you create a *correspondence* category, a *finances* category, and a *bills* category, where do you store the letter that you have drafted to send to your credit card company? Likewise, when you return to finish the letter, where do you find it? Try your best to keep things simple so that answering each of these questions will be simple and quick.

These are not hard-and-fast rules, but rather guidelines. If you find yourself creating more or fewer categories than this, then you should really think about if the categories you are creating are going to make it simpler and easier to organize and retrieve your data.

Figure 2-4 shows a sample planning worksheet with some example categories. You can use it as a starting point, or you can start from scratch if these categories don't apply to you. (You can download a blank form from `http://whsbook.com/files`.) Just start with the categories and your planned storage locations for now; the remaining columns will be addressed later in the chapter.

	Category	Location	Priority (High, Medium, Low)	How Organized	How Protected
	Digital Life Planning Sheet				
1	Digital Photos	\\Server\Photos			
2	Home Business	\\Server\Business			
3	Financial / Tax	\\Server\Finance			
4	Kid's Stuff	\\Server\Kids			
5	Music	\\Server\Music			
6	Home Movies	\\Server\Videos			
7	Email	Laptop / Desktop			
8	Address Book	Laptop / Desktop			
9					
10					
11					
12					
13					
14					
15					
16					
17					
18					

Figure 2-4

A Warning about Unsorted Categories

Many people like to include an *unsorted* category when they first create their list. The idea with an unsorted category is that anything that you don't have time to sort gets saved here. Although this seems like a great idea, in practice it tends to end up as a catchall that rarely ever actually gets sorted out. The main reason for having an unsorted category is to give you a location to quickly place files when you don't feel you have time to put them into their proper location. The other reason is to give you a place to dump all of the files that you are collecting from various computers when you first set up a centralized storage location.

If you feel you need to use an unsorted category when you first get started, try to make a goal of emptying it out and deleting it within a month. In that time, you should work to refine your organizational plan and learn to place files where they belong when you first download or save them.

Organizing Your Categories

Underneath your categories, you should try to have at most three additional levels of organization, and for most categories, one additional layer will be sufficient (for the reasons discussed in the previous section, "Creating Your Categories"). These additional subcategories will result in the creation of subfolders underneath your main category folders. As discussed earlier, categories are the organizational concept, and folders are the tool that you use to implement categorization. These additional tiers should help you to refine the categories and keep files logically grouped as to their specific contents.

Just as you can create complexity and confusion by having too many overlapping categories, creating multiple tiers of subcategories can make organization difficult. One of the key tenets described earlier was that overly complex organization schemes are difficult to follow and will often be ignored. Although it may seem logical to create a complex structure of subfolders to keep files precisely organized, it is often better to have a simpler scheme that will be easy to use.

Next you will go through several common media types and learn how best to keep them organized.

PHOTOS

Photos are some of the most important, irreplaceable files that we all keep on our PCs. There are many different solutions to managing and organizing files. I'm going to cover the method my family uses to keep photos organized. I like this method because it does not rely on any additional software. It utilizes Windows's basic folder capability and still keeps files accessible and organized in a usable manner.

Many people have gotten used to using the software that came with their cameras or printers to categorize and organize their photos. I prefer to use a more generic method, because it allows me to upload and access files from any computer and I know it will always be supported.

The following methods work very well for my family, but they should be viewed only as an example of a system that is simple and usable. Your preferences may be different, but this example should help you to develop your own organizational plan.

Chronological Organization

The backbone of my family's photo organization is the idea of storing photos in chronological folders. We use a two-tier setup, and we name the folders in such a way that Windows' default view of the folders will keep the files in chronological order.

The first tier is simply a group of folders for each year that you have digital photos from. The folders should simply be named 2005, 2006, 2007, and so on. This first tier helps to keep things less cluttered, and it allows you to drill down to a specific year when you are looking for a photo. The first tier of the folder hierarchy is shown in Figure 2-5.

The next tier is a set of folders that are named for the date when we download the pictures from the camera. We choose to use this scheme because it simplifies the process of managing our photos. If we tried to go strictly by month, we either have to do extra work (sorting the files manually), or we have to accept that files taken in late May might get lumped in with some other photos downloaded in June. Also, we download photos several times a month, so keeping all of a month's pictures in one folder gets cumbersome. We name the folders according to the full date, including year, and we name them in such a way that alphabetical sorting will also keep them in chronological order. This is important because the dates assigned to a folder might change if you copy the folders from one machine to another, whereas the filename will stay constant. So, for a set of photos that were downloaded on May 1, 2007, we would create a folder named 2007-05-01. The inclusion of the year in the folder name is somewhat redundant, because this folder is contained in a parent folder called

2007, but we choose to keep it this way because it means that we can copy the folders directly to a CD or DVD, and the *date label* that is contained in the folder name is complete. Also remember that it is important to keep the leading zeros on the month and day numbers in order to maintain the chronological/alphabetical relationship. An example listing of subfolders is shown in Figure 2-6.

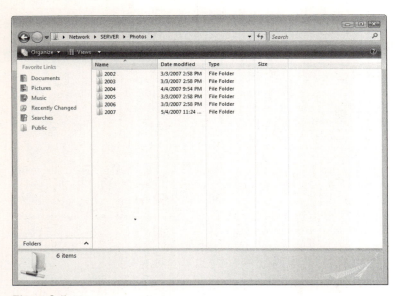

Figure 2-5

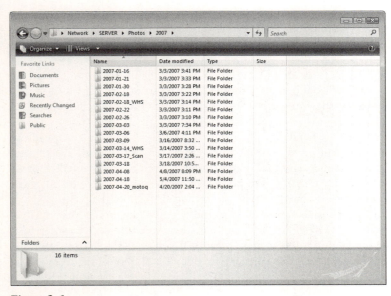

Figure 2-6

In Figure 2-6, you may notice that some folders have additional words or abbreviations attached to the end. The overwhelming majority of our photos are family photographs: pictures of the kids, animals, our house, and our lives in general. Whenever we do something that is out of the ordinary, we add an underscore and a tag of some kind to identify that folder as being different. The folder with _motoq at the end indicates that I downloaded all the pictures from my Motorola Q cell phone. The _scan folder contains a bunch of photos that I ran through our scanner. You can use this basic tagging to identify folders that contain something that is a little different from your normal folders. Some photo organization tools may use different naming or tagging schemes, or you may prefer to add more or less info to your naming scheme. The key is to keep it simple and usable while still creating a logical way to find your photos.

Tagging

Previously I talked about adding a single tag to identify folders, but the concept of tagging can actually be much more powerful. In Windows Vista, you can add as many tags as you want to files in order to help you find what you need in the future. Unfortunately tagging is still a manual process, so you will have to weigh this effort with the benefits it provides. The most useful tags for photos will identify the subject of the photos in a meaningful way. For example, I might want to apply the tag Rick to any pictures that I appear in. To do this I would follow this process. Open a picture folder. Select Large Icons from the views menu. Now scroll through the images and for every file that I appear in, hold down the CTRL key and click on the picture. This will multi-select all these pictures. Next click the Add a tag link in the Details pane at the bottom of the window as shown in Figure 2-7, and type **Rick**. If you want to add multiple tags to a file or group of files, you separate them with a semicolon (;). In Windows Vista you can make use of Windows Photo Gallery, which allows you to drag and drop pictures onto tags, among other methods. Many other tools exist that will assist with this process, but it is a good idea to stick with tools that use the photo's built-in metadata fields so that the tags will be permanently associated with the pictures.

Figure 2-7

The power of tags is that they cross other organizational boundaries, such as folders. My basic method of using chronological folders helps me find pictures by date (obviously). However, if I apply the tag `Rick` to every file that I appear in, I can quickly find all these photos, regardless of location, using Windows Photo Gallery or search.

> **Note**
>
> If you want to learn to make better use of Windows Vista's bundled photo organization tools, including Windows Photo Gallery, *Windows Vista Solutions* by Mark Justice Hinton (Wiley, 2007) in the PC Magazine series covers this and other Windows Vista topics (ISBN 978-0-470-046869).

Other Organization Options

While I have found chronological organization to be a great fit for the way my family thinks about our photographs, this method will not meet everyone's needs. This works well for us because when we're looking for a photo, it's fairly logical to think about whose birthday or what holiday it was. Depending on the types of photos you take and how you are likely to recall your photos, there are many other schemes that might work better for you.

For example, if you frequently travel you may want to organize your photos primarily by the location where the picture was taken. A person who takes many artistic photos might organize by the type of subjects he or she is shooting, such as landscapes, stills, and portraits. Someone who takes photographs for-profit would probably do best to organize by client. Other people might find it easier to organize photos by events, such as `Dave's Birthday 2007`, `Company Picnic`, and so on.

These different schemes can also be blended if it makes sense, as long as the added complexity this adds does not overwhelm you or others in your home that assist with organizing pictures. The important ideal to strive for is *natural organization*. This means that the folder structure should feel natural and should match how you mentally catalogue pictures in your mind.

If your spouse or kids have totally different opinions of what *natural organization* should be, you may have to strive for a compromise, or it may just be best to maintain two different organizational schemes. It is better to have multiple schemes of organization than to have one rigid scheme that only one member of the household is willing to follow!

ENTERTAINMENT

Entertainment is any media that you keep on your computer strictly for fun. These could be television shows, MP3 music files, DVD movies, or e-books. Entertainment files that you download for free, or MP3 files that you rip from CDs that you own may have a lower priority, whereas Television shows downloaded from iTunes, or digital music files that you pay for may have a higher priority.

Entertainment files should be organized first by media type, and then by topic. This should hopefully line up with the way you will think about retrieving the files. Usually, consuming entertainment media is a conscious process. You think "I'm going to watch a TV show," and then you select a show. Other times you may decide you want to listen to music, and then proceed to picking some songs for a playlist. This two-tiered scheme should make it easy to categorize and find your entertainment related files.

Most tools, including Windows Media Player, will also create folders for the artist and album title for ripped CDs. Keeping this default organization underneath your categories will help you to further differentiate between different elements of a music collection.

If you only keep one or two genres of music on your computers, then you may opt to forgo having a genre tier, and just use the artist name as the tier directly below `Music`. Again, you should tailor this to your own personal needs, and focus on keeping your organization simple, usable and maintainable.

Note
Naturally, if you are a serious movie or music fan with an extensive collection, you might want a more carefully tailored system. The same thing would be true if you are a professional photographer, videographer, or DJ.

DOCUMENTS
Documents are the last type of file that this chapter addresses. Documents might include letters, school reports, resumes, business files, spreadsheets, PDF files, Flyers, or pretty much any information that uses words or pictures to convey information.

For my documents folder, I like to use the first tier to categorize documents by topics, like `House Stuff` and `School`. I use a second tier here more sparingly. For many topics, leaving all of the documents directly in the folder works well. For some documents I like to use project-based organization. When I worked on my master's degree, I added additional tiers to keep things logically organized. One tier indicated which class the files were for. The next tier indicated which week of class they belonged to. Because most of our assignments were due on a weekly basis, I viewed each week as a separate *project* that needed its own folder. This allowed me to gather my notes, reading material, and assignments in a manner that kept everything accessible while I was doing my work. Figure 2-8 shows an example of this organization.

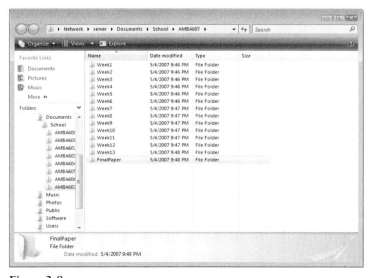

Figure 2-8

Different types of data might call for different organization. Once again, simple, logical, and natural organization should be your goal. The following shows a sample of a few different types of data and how you might choose to organize them within your Documents category:

- Finances
    - 2004
    - 2005
    - 2006
- Letters
    - Mom M.
    - Mom B.
    - Grandma B.
- Careers
    - Resumes
    - Correspondence
    - Company Research

Once again, these are merely examples that can help you to decide a scheme that will work for you!

Note

Some application programs like to maintain tighter control over the files with which they interact. iTunes and AOL are just two examples. These programs may not store their data in the typical locations in your user profiles, and they may in fact break if you move the data files.

When dealing with integrated packages like AOL or programs that have digital rights management (DRM) like iTunes, be cautious about what you move. You can always do a trial by moving one or two files and then seeing if they are still accessible, and just be prepared to move the files back if the move breaks functionality.

If you end up needing or wanting to leave data on your local computers, it will still be backed up and protected by Windows Home Server's backup technology; the only thing that you miss out on is centralized access to the data, and if it is closely tied to the application software, this centralized access will probably not work anyway.

How Can Windows Home Server Help?

Windows Home Server offers a wide variety of tools to help you simplify your digital life, and the availability of these tools should factor in to your organizational strategy, including centralized storage, and integration into Windows Vista's search on your client machines.

Centralized and Easily Accessible Storage

Windows Home Server's Shared Folders feature provides you with a reliable centralized location to store your files. By keeping your files on your Windows Home Server, you make them accessible from any computer on your network, and with Windows Home Server's remote access feature, you can retrieve any of your files from any internet-connected computer.

Predefined Shared Folders

Windows Home Server ships with some basic shared folders predefined. There are shares for Music, Photos, Software, and Videos. A predefined Public share can also be used to share files with unauthenticated users in your home, like visitors. Each user also gets their own share in which to keep personal files. The predefined shares can offer a basic starting point for your organizational scheme. The predefined shares may not fit into your organizational plan, but they are a good starting point.

Note
Predefined shares cannot be removed, deleted, or hidden. They will always appear on the Windows Home Server Console's Shared Folders screen, and they will show up in the folder list if you access the server through the network neighborhood. There is no harm in having unused shares on your server.

User-Defined Shared Folders

Windows Home Server also allows you to define any number of user-defined shares. This is the place where you will want to create any top-level categories in order to facilitate your organizational strategy. Using the previously defined categories, I would create shares for Documents and Entertainment, and I would use the Photos folder as is.

Personal Shares

Each user that is set up on Windows Home Server receives his or her own personal shared folder. By default he or she is the only one allowed to read or write to that folder. Personal shares provide a location for individuals to store the data they would otherwise keep in their client profile's *Documents* folder or on their desktop. The added benefit is that they will have access to all of the files in their private share no matter what computer they log in to, and if you have enabled remote access (as shown in Chapter 11), they will also be able to access their personal files remotely via the Internet.

You should encourage the members of your network to put files that are useful to all users into the appropriate shared folders so that everyone can have easy access.

The same ideas for organization that apply to the common shared folders can be applied to individual private shares. You can encourage use of a good organizational scheme, and each person will probably have his or her own unique idea of what that is.

In general, information can be more useful if more people have access to it. When discussing your organizational plan with your household, try to include this idea that the entire household should put important non-personal data into the common shared folders.

In most homes, everyone shares the traditional real-world tools. The hammer lives in a drawer in the kitchen, or a toolbox in the garage, and everyone knows where it is and can use it when they need it. You should remember that Windows Home Server is itself a type of tool, meant to make it easier to manage your digital life. Likewise, some of the information that you keep on your home server is useful for everyone, just like a tool. By keeping information centralized and accessible to all, your home might end up being a bit more open and productive.

Search Technology

Windows Home Server also includes search technology, derived from Microsoft's Windows Desktop Search. Files that are stored on the server will be indexed so that they can be quickly searched by keyword, title, file type, or even on common metadata like tags, titles, and so forth. It is this ability to search metadata through WHS or Vista that makes the manual effort of tagging files worthwhile. This search functionality is even available over the remote web interface, so you should be able to quickly locate the files you need, even when you are away from your home network. On a client computer that has the Windows Home Server Connector software installed, you will even get search results from the server when you use Windows Vista's search box from the Start menu.

A Living Strategy

The most important element for a Digital Life Strategy is that it needs to be simple and usable. In order to work well, it must match well with how you logically think about finding things. If you are the kind of person who always puts your car keys on a hook by the door, your organization will be different from someone who randomly puts them on the kitchen table, or counter, or wherever.

Your plan should be intuitive, and for file storage that is shared by multiple users, it should be simplified to the point where everyone can easily see where files should be found and where new files should be placed.

After you have considered your categories, priorities, and organization, you should be able to develop a simple written plan. Figure 2-9 shows a completed planning worksheet shows and example of what a plan might look like at this stage. (You can download a blank form from `http://whsbook.com/files`.)

Once you settle on an initial category list and organizational scheme, it will almost immediately begin drifting out of sync with your needs. Flexibility is important because even the most organized planner will not foresee all of the different things that will eventually need to be sorted.

When you run across a file that just doesn't fit, you should consider adding a new category or subcategory to your system. At the same time, you should be wary of your category list growing out of control because this adds complexity that will make your organization more difficult to maintain in the future.

As technology changes and more parts of our lives become digital, you may have to adjust your strategy. You will find that some parts of your plan work well, while others are either too cumbersome to adhere to, or just aren't useful. You may find that even though you are perfectly happy with 25 categories, split out by subcategories, your significant other or your kids need a much more simplified scheme in order to be willing to actively take part in the plan. You have to strike a balance between sticking to it and being flexible enough to react to the changing demands of your digital life.

	Category	Location	Priority (High, Medium, Low)	How Organized?	How Protected?
1	Digital Photos	\\Server\Photos	High, Irreplacable	Chronological	WHS Folder Duplication
2	Home Business	\\Server\Business	Medium	Subcategory / Project	WHS Folder Duplication
3	Financial / Tax	\\Server\Finance	High	Subcategory	WHS Folder Duplication
4	Kid's Stuff	\\Server\Kids	Medium	Subcategory	WHS Folder Duplication
5	Music	\\Server\Music	Low	Media Type / Genre	Not Protected
6	Home Movies	\\Server\Videos	High	Chronological	WHS Folder Duplication
7	Email	Laptop / Desktop	High	Default for Program	Full Computer Backup through WHS
8	Address Book	Laptop / Desktop	High	Default for Program	Full Computer Backup through WHS
9					
10					
11					
12					
13					
14					
15					
16					
17					
18					

Figure 2-9

Summary

Throughout this chapter you have learned several topics that should help you to develop a strategy for organizing, simplifying, and protecting your digital life. This strategy will be the basis of the digital spring-cleaning process that is covered in Chapter 8.

You learned that you should protect your data in a way that is proportional to its value and in a way that considered how difficult it would be to reproduce. You revisited the idea that computers are fallible machines, and that important data really should be protected. Next, this chapter discussed the idea that complicated organization schemes are recipes for failure and disorganization, and you learned that it is best to keep your categorization of data simple and easy to follow.

Next you learned some ways that you can categorize your data, and ways that you can further organize these files. You read some examples of organization schemes for several different categories of data, and hopefully you have developed some opinions about what type of organization will feel natural to you for your data.

Lastly you learned about the tools that Windows Home Server provides to help you keep your data organized and safe. You learned that utilizing default and custom shares gives you your top-level categories of data. You also learned that Windows Home Server's search engine is integrated with client computers so that they can automatically search for data contained on the server from their desktop.

This initial look at organizing your data is just that, an initial look. You should not try to start moving around your files, because this is a good way to misplace and accidentally delete important data. Later in Chapter 8, you actually begin the process of cleaning up your digital life, but not until you make sure that your data is all backed up!

Chapter 3

Selecting Your Home Server

Deciding to use a Windows Home Server on your home network is an important first step in simplifying and protecting your digital life, but the decisions don't stop there. Many original equipment manufacturers (OEMs) such as Gateway, HP, LaCie, Medion, and others are offering plug-and-play systems that will be offered through their regular retail channels. In addition to the big OEMs, other computer manufacturers can utilize Microsoft's System Builder program to obtain licenses in order to build generic Windows Home Server machines, or even highly specialized servers with unique hardware. Lastly, hobbyists can purchase these System Builder licenses in order to put together their own Windows Home Server system, using new or salvaged computer parts.

The decision about what kind of server you want, the specific model, and any options will rest on a variety of factors. You will have to consider cost, features, expansion options, and risk. Given these factors, you should be able to evaluate what kind of server will be best for your home.

Buying or Building Your Server

Most people will likely buy prebuilt servers either from retail stores, online stores, or traditional computer manufacturers. This approach will carry less hassle and risk. Computer hobbyists may choose to build their own Windows Home Server machines in order to save money, include specific hardware, or simply for the satisfaction of building something useful.

There are positives and negatives to each method, and understanding the wide range of considerations will help you to make a selection no matter which path you choose. Whether you choose to build or buy, you should carefully consider your options so that you end up with a server that will meet your current needs and serve you well into the future.

This chapter will cover the various factors that will affect your selection of either a prebuilt server or a custom-built one. Then you will see some general considerations that apply to both options, and finally you will dig deeper into the specific elements that apply to both prebuilt and custom-built servers.

Choosing a Prebuilt Server

The most compelling argument for choosing a prebuilt Windows Home Server is that you will get a machine that you can take out of the box and plug it in, and it will just work. The Windows Home Server team along with the original equipment manufacturers have done a great deal of work to make sure that the installation experience is as painless as possible, and the only way to get this streamlined experience is to buy a prebuilt machine.

OEM/Retail Machines

Prebuilt machines come in two different flavors. Special-purpose home servers are built specifically by OEMs and conform to guidelines that Microsoft has developed. These are the most polished Windows Home Server machines. They are available from online retailers like Amazon.com, Buy.com, and also in brick-and-mortar stores like Target, Wal-Mart, and Staples.

If you are a computer novice, this option will probably be the best for you. Retail machines are relatively inexpensive, and setup will be as simple as plugging in power and a network cable and following some very simple instructions. While the upgradeability of these machines may be limited, any upgrades that are available will be simple to perform, with little or no knowledge necessary of how to work on computers, and often without requiring any tools.

Many retail channel Windows Home Server machines will also be more aesthetically pleasing and more compact than the other options. These models can be left on the corner of your desk or on a shelf somewhere to quietly do their job.

However, if you are the type of person who likes to upgrade your own PCs, or tinker with installing new hardware, then you may want to consider getting a server that is built in a more standard chassis, either from a system builder, or by assembling your own.

System Builder

Another category of prebuilt machines will be available through Microsoft's System Builder channel. Through this program, any PC manufacturer can build machines and preload the Windows Home Server software. This type of machine could be a great option, but users should carefully consider the reputation of the manufacturer before making this choice. Any company that does a good job of building desktop PCs should be able to put together a reliable Windows Home Server machine.

System builder machines may not have as clean of an appearance as OEM machines. They also may require tools, or general PC hardware knowledge in order to upgrade or expand storage. On the plus side, it may be easier to get the specific options that you want this way, because system builders usually offer custom configuration options (like how Dell lets you configure a desktop machine online).

Most home servers from the System Builder channel look like regular PCs or Servers. Many make use of smaller form factors, but in general they are very similar to desktop PCs that the System builder sells.

System builder machines may also be available from local computer builders. If you choose to purchase from a local computer shop, most of them provide good technical support to assist with any difficulties or hardware failures. Most cities also have small businesses and entrepreneurs who can also provide support to supplement this. You can rely on recommendations from friends, or even check with the local office of the Better Business Bureau to help select a provider.

Support

With both OEM/retail and system builder machines, you will have a manufacturer that you can rely on for installation and setup instructions, troubleshooting, and support. Just as with desktop PCs and laptops, different manufacturers are better at supporting their products after they go out the door than others. Many manufacturers also provide great documentation including quick-start guides, user's guides, and maintenance manuals. You may also have access to technical support through e-mail, websites, or phone for a period of time after you purchase your machine. All of these things are benefits of purchasing your Windows Home Server machine either through the retail channel from a manufacturer that you trust, or from a system builder that has a good reputation for supporting their products.

Other Considerations

The main drawback to buying a prebuilt machine is that you have less control over how the system is configured. This is more of a concern for OEM machines, where the configuration is fixed by the manufacturer and mass-produced. By purchasing an OEM machine, you trade some flexibility in order to obtain a polished and predictable experience.

Most prebuilt machines will ship without the capability of hooking up a monitor, keyboard, and mouse. In theory, you should never need to hook up a display to your home server, but there may be scenarios where it would be helpful to interact directly with the server instead of having to access it remotely. For example, this might be useful for setting up a shared printer, as discussed in Chapter 9. If you are a hobbyist developer or if you plan to use your home server for nonstandard applications, the ability to connect a display and input devices may also allow you to tinker and experiment more easily.

Building Your Own Server

Another option that might be attractive to hobbyists and computer enthusiasts is to build their own server from new or used parts. Similarly, you can repurpose an old desktop machine that meets the minimum specifications (shown in the "System Requirements" section at the end of this chapter) to be used for Windows Home Server. These options can sometimes be cheaper than many prebuilt options, and they give you full control over exactly how your server is built. Many people get a great deal of satisfaction from selecting parts and piecing them together into a working machine. In addition, Windows Home Server's relatively mild hardware requirements might allow an older machine to have an extended life as a server, with little or no additional cost for upgrades.

Microsoft is not offering the software license for Windows Home Server at retail. If you decide to go this route, you will have to purchase the software from a reseller that supplies OEM software products. Software that is purchased in this manner comes with very limited support options from Microsoft should you run into trouble, so weigh this option carefully.

Risk

Before you decide to build your own Windows Home Server machine, you should carefully consider the importance of having a reliable machine. One of the most significant features of Windows Home Server is that it keeps your data safe. Unless you are very confident in your ability to build a reliable machine, then you may want to consider buying a prebuilt home server, buying a prebuilt desktop machine to run Windows Home Server, or getting the assistance of someone who is more experienced and confident building PCs.

In a similar vein, although it is possible to reutilize older hardware, if you want a truly reliable machine you should consider purchasing new hardware in order to minimize the risk of a faulty component causing data loss or unreliable performance. The Windows Home Server team at Microsoft likes to call repurposed older hardware *frankenmachines*, and during the beta program they tried to warn testers away from using these types of machines. Although it is possible to pull together a reliable machine from older hardware, this route introduces additional uncertainty. Windows Home Server is intended to be able to be run on desktop-quality hardware, but the fact that it is a server operating system means that it will sometimes place more demands on the hardware than typical desktop use. A piece of hardware that behaved reliably under desktop conditions may become unreliable with the added stresses of being used in a server.

If you decide to use an older machine, you can reduce risk in several ways. You can replace parts that typically have a limited working life, like hard drives and fans. You can add additional hard drives in order to make use of Windows Home Server's built-in redundancy. You can also decide to periodically perform a manual backup of the data on your server or use a third-party online backup service, as described in Chapter 14, to keep your data safe in case you suffer a severe failure of your Windows Home Server.

Caution
If you are comfortable and experienced with building or modifying your machines, this can be an interesting project. However, if you have little experience in these matters, this is probably not the ideal project for you to start with to learn how to build your own machines, because the reliability of your Windows Home Server can affect your entire digital life.

Cost

When PCs first became popular, you could often save a good amount of money by purchasing parts and building your own PC. Current pricing trends have lowered margins on PCs, and PC manufacturers tend to get very competitive pricing on components because they purchase parts in such large quantities. If you are an extreme bargain shopper, you may be able to beat the curve, but for most consumers it will be very difficult to come out ahead. Purchasing a low-end desktop PC from a company such as Dell or Gateway is another option, but you often get stuck paying for a desktop operating system and productivity software that you won't need to use for a Windows Home Server machine. On the other hand, if you are the type of person who enjoys modifying your PC, chances are good that you might already have a few computers and related hardware at home, which can reduce some of your startup costs.

Another source of decent and inexpensive machines to consider is the outlet stores that many major PC builders run. They often offer scratch-and-dent and refurbished machines at a significant discount. Dell has their outlet easily available at `http://outlet.dell.com` and Gateway's outlet is easy to find by typing "Outlet" into the search box at `http://gateway.com`.

Bargain hunting aside, you should consider whether the marginal savings of building or installing your own Windows Home Server is worth the trade-off of reliability and support. For some folks the only option may be to reuse an older PC with minor upgrades. Although having *any* server backing up your data is certainly better than trying to keep up with manual backups, if the cost of your *frakenmachine* is going to approach the cost of a retail-purchased Windows Home Server, then you should probably seriously consider just going the prebuilt route so that you have a streamlined and supported solution. On the other hand, if you are the kind of Dr. Frankenstein who likes to loosen up the bolts and work on your *frankenmachine*'s brain, these issues might be secondary concerns to you anyway.

Customization

Another good reason to go the build-your-own route is the level of control you get over exactly what goes into your home server. If you want three different home-automation PCI boards, and 4TB of storage, and you want sound and video capabilities to run your custom-built HAL emulation program, then this might be the kind of fun project for you to roll up your sleeves and get started with.

Satisfaction

Along with the ability to put the exact components you want into your server, it can also be very satisfying to build something useful and important, and once you rely on your home server for your first full PC restore, you will agree that a working Windows Home Server machine is both very useful and very important. Again, an adequately backed up Windows Home Server will help ensure that your satisfaction doesn't turn to frustration when something goes wrong.

Selecting Your Server

After you have decided what category of Windows Home Server you will be comfortable with, you still have options to consider. The guidelines for hardware for Windows Home Server are pretty basic, and retail/OEMs and system builders have a good variety of different systems with different levels of capability.

Some factors will be more important to people who are purchasing at retail, others will only apply to individuals building or configuring custom machines. Reading through this chapter will help you to better understand the options and how they affect the utility of your Windows Home Server.

General Considerations

Whether you are going to build or buy your server, you need to have a basic understanding of how the different components will affect the performance of your server. For retail machines this will help you to compare the specifications for different systems. For custom-built or home-built systems, it will allow you to decide which components and upgrades will give you the best system for your money.

CPUS

The CPU, or central processing unit, is the nerve center of a Windows Home Server machine. CPU speed is especially important for remote access, and for speeding up operations such as adding and removing hard drives from your Windows Home Server system.

As a differentiator, don't worry about the CPU too much. Most modern CPUs have more than enough horsepower to handle basic Windows Home Server functionality. In general, faster is always better, but don't waste upgrade dollars on getting a screaming CPU.

Many current CPUs are being built with multiple cores. You can think of each core as being an independent CPU that can handle a job. In traditional single-core CPUs, the operating system has to divide the time the CPU has available and schedule tasks to run sequentially. Basically a single core can only do one job at a time, so it will spend a little bit of time on each task, switching back and forth. Each time it switches between tasks, some extra work has to be done to keep track of what it is working on. This is called a *context switch*. If you have multiple CPUs or a CPU with multiple cores, each core can do a job or a set of jobs, and you basically divide the number of required context switches by the number of cores that you have, reducing overhead and getting everything done faster. The operating system can also schedule important low-level tasks to run on a dedicated core, so that they can complete without interruption. Because servers often perform a multitude of jobs simultaneously, having multiple cores will often provide a significant increase in performance.

If you plan to use Windows Home Server for just the basic functions, then don't worry about your CPU too much. If you plan to do anything unique with your home server, or if you plan to have a larger number of PCs attached (more than six), then you'll want to consider selecting a server with a faster dual-core or multi-core CPU.

HARD DRIVES

Hard drives are needed to permanently store programs and data. Because one of a Windows Home Server machine's main jobs is storing data, this component is the most important.

You will want to make sure that the hard drive in your system is reliable. There are many different measures of reliability for hard drives, but the two most important to consider are the mean time between failures (MTBF) and the manufacturer's warrantee. The MTBF is a statistical measure of how long a drive can be expected to last in hours. The manufacturer's warrantee is the practical measure for how long you can truly count on the hard drive to last. Most hard drives will work well beyond their warrantee coverage, but it is a good measure of the manufacturer's faith in the quality and longevity of the drive. For warrantees, 1 year is standard, 3 years is good, and 5 years is great. You can find information about MTBF and warrantees on most hard drive manufacturer's websites. Warranties are typically called out on a product's general information page, and the MTBF can usually be found under *detailed technical specifications*, or in a section dedicated to reliability.

Another consideration is the speed of the hard drives. While most of your file transfers will be limited by the speed of your network, not the hard drive, Windows Home Server's bookkeeping functions such as folder duplication and defragmentation will require less time if you have faster hard drives. The two biggest factors in the performance of hard drives are rotational speed and the size of the on-drive cache. Rotational speed is measured in revolutions per minute (RPM), and cache is measured in megabytes (MB). Faster rotation is better, with typical drive speeds ranging from 4200 RPM (slow) to 12000 RPM (very fast). On-drive cache ranges from 1MB to 16MB and beyond, with higher amounts of cache contributing to higher performance. You should consider 7200 RPM and 2MB of cache as a minimum if you don't want your hard drive to slow down your server.

A fast reliable 300GB hard drive is a good place to start. If you have large libraries of media files, MP3s, digital photographs, and home movies, then you may want to consider a larger hard drive, or plan on adding additional hard drives to your server.

If you want to enable Windows Home Server's built-in redundancy, then you will need to have at least a second hard drive. Ideally this drive should be as large as the first drive, but the new Drive Extender technology can make use of any size drive to help keep your data safe.

You don't need to worry as much about your long-term storage requirements, because Windows Home Server's Drive Extender technology makes it easy to add additional storage later. Unlike traditional computers, new drives in your home server machine can be added to a single logical storage pool, making the space available for files without worrying about drive letters, or complex configurations such as those used in RAID (Redundant Array of Inexpensive Disks) systems in business servers.

RAM

Random access memory, or RAM, is what the computer uses to store information and programs that are currently in use. Every job that your server is doing at a given point in time will require a chunk of memory, some for the actual computer code that describes the job, and more for the data that it is working on.

The minimum requirement for Windows Home Server is 512MB. Running just the basics on Windows Home Server, it rarely will require more than this. If you plan to run extra functions or add-ins on your server, 1GB is a more reasonable amount of RAM. If later on you start noticing that operations on your server are slowing down, take a moment to watch and listen to your server. Most machines will have a light labeled "HDD" that indicates when the hard disk is busy, and the hard drive generally makes noise when it is reading and writing data. If your server does not have enough RAM to perform its work, it will have to *swap* some information from RAM to the hard drive in order to make room for other things in RAM. When it needs the first chunk of information again, it has to move something else out of RAM and copy the original chunk from the hard drive back into RAM. When this happens a lot, it's called *thrashing* and it can significantly slow down your server.

Although adding more RAM to a desktop machine is often seen as a good way to increase performance, a Windows Home Server machine rarely performs tasks that require larger amounts of RAM. 1GB is a good place to start, and if you think that you may want to add memory-hungry add-ins to your server in the future, you should try to buy a system that has room for additional RAM, or one where you can remove the existing RAM chips in order to make room for chips with more capacity. You can read about add-ins in Chapter 14, and the memory requirements can usually be found on the developer's website.

NETWORK CONNECTIONS

Everything that Windows Home Server does is accomplished over the network, so a fast, reliable, and secure network interface is essential to your server system.

Microsoft has decided not to allow wireless connections in the first version of Windows Home Server because of several factors including the complexity of setting up secure wireless connections without a display and keyboard, and the fact that wireless connections have a tendency to have intermittent interference and are typically much slower than wired connections.

Your Windows Home Server system must have a wired Ethernet adapter, either built in to the motherboard, or included as a PCI card, or external USB adapter. Most current adapters are capable of at least 100 megabits per second (Mbps), but some adapters are capable of running at 1 gigabit per second (Gbps). Most home network routers include a switch that operates at either 10 Mbps or 100 Mbps, so you will probably not be able to take advantage of adapters that support higher speeds without replacing your home networking gear.

In general for networks, faster is better. In my home network my server is connected to a wireless router with 100 Mbps wired Ethernet, but everything runs over wireless connections that average about 30 Mbps. Initial backups take a fair amount of time, but subsequent backups usually complete in a matter of minutes. Working on larger files directly on the server can be a little bit slow though. If you have the option to build your home network with 1 Gbps wired Ethernet, it will make your experience with Windows Home Server more enjoyable. If you can use 100 Mbps wired Ethernet, your experience will be very acceptable. Anything slower than this and you will notice the delays and transfer times when you are moving files to and from the server, or opening files directly from the server. If you plan to stream large movie files over your network, you should seriously consider upgrading to 1 Gbps wired Ethernet. Otherwise you may experience slowdowns on other parts of the network when someone is watching a movie or other video. If you have any gamers in your house, you will want to be careful not to overload your network. Gaming itself usually does not require a great deal of bandwidth, but games require quick network response times, and if the network is saturated, the gamer may experience lag. If a large part of your network runs over wireless, then you should still make sure that the link between your wired home server and your wireless router is as fast as possible, because the server may be sending data to multiple clients at the same time, and you don't want the server's network interface to be the bottleneck.

CHASSIS/EXPANSION

The Windows Home Server operating system is extremely capable of expanding to meet your growing storage needs in the future. To take advantage of this, the physical machine needs to be able to expand as well. Many retail Windows Home Server machines have easy storage expansion options, with empty drive bays that are accessible without tools.

If you are interested in using your Windows Home Server for any specialized tasks, such as home automation, you should make sure that you select a machine that has the right kind of expansion to support this. Slimmed down retail machines may lack PCI slots, serial and parallel ports, and other typical types of expansion that you would find on regular PCs. Home automation is discussed further in Chapter 14.

Most modern types of expansion are available as USB devices, and all retail and system builder Windows Home Server machines will have four or more USB slots. If you need to attach more devices than this, you can use USB hubs. One important point to remember is that hooking multiple high-performance devices into a USB hub can degrade their performance because all traffic must go through a single controller inside the server. If you plan to rely on external USB drives for your expansion capability, you should make sure that you will have enough free USB version 2.0, Firewire, or eSATA ports to support this.

It is impossible to know exactly how you are going to want to use your server in the future, but you should try to make sure you have reasonable options going forward. If you are a PC novice who never opens his or her PC case, then you probably just want to make sure that you have a good number of USB ports available, with some no-tools-required options for installing additional hard drives. If you like to tinker with PCs, then you might want to consider a larger, more expandable machine that can handle whatever types of additional hardware you may want to use in the future.

Special Considerations for Prebuilt OEM/Retail Servers

Many OEMs are producing Windows Home Server machines, and the specifications of these servers will vary. Because they are targeted at the retail market, the configuration of these machines will basically be fixed. Evaluating a retail machine will be a simple matter of considering consumer reviews, company reputation, and reading the specifications to determine if the server's strengths and weaknesses are a good fit for how you want to use your home server.

Retail machines may also ship with specialized functionality that is installed or enabled by the manufacturer. For example, HP is including a feature on their MediaSmart server that allows the owner to utilize their HP Photosmart Share services directly from the server. These offerings will vary widely from different manufacturers, so you should evaluate if they are useful to you, and if it's possible to get access to them without buying that manufacturer's brand of server.

System Requirements

The actual process of building your own server is beyond the scope of this book, but if you decide to go this route or if you are purchasing a customized machine from a system builder, you must consider how suitable the machine is for your intended use of it as a home server.

The basic requirements as published by Microsoft are shown in the following table.

System Requirements	Minimum Requirements	Recommended Requirements
CPU	1 GHz Pentium 3 (or equivalent)	Pentium 4 or AMD x64
RAM	512MB	512MB ECC memory
Hard drives	80GB internal (ATA, SATA, or SCSI) hard drive for the primary drive	Two or more internal (SATA or SCSI) hard drives with a primary (system) hard drive of 300GB
Network interface card	100 Mbps Ethernet network interface card from the Windows Server Catalog (http://go.microsoft.com/fwlink/?LinkId=88123)	1 Gbps Ethernet network interface card from the Windows Server Catalog (http://go.microsoft.com/fwlink/?LinkId=88123)

Note

Additional hard drives of at least 8GB capacity can be added, but the primary system drive should be the largest drive.

Building a Windows Home Server machine is almost identical to assembling a desktop PC. If you have experience with this kind of assembly, then it should be no challenge to gather parts that will meet or exceed the preceding requirements. If you can only go above the specs on one item, it should be the hard drive, and the next would be the RAM.

Although a video adapter is not listed in the requirements, you will need a video adapter in order to perform the initial installation of Windows Home Server. Even the appliance-style Windows Home Server devices include a video adapter internally even though they do not provide a way to connect a monitor to that adapter. Many motherboards will simply refuse to boot without a video adapter, and portions of the Windows Home Server software rely on its presence even if it is not actively used. The process of actually setting up the software is covered in Chapter 5.

Whether you assemble the server, buy a refurbished desktop, or have a machine custom built, the information in this chapter should help you to acquire a machine that will perform well as a Windows Home Server.

Summary

Now that you understand the different ways that you can buy or build a Windows Home Server machine, you should be able to decide what method will serve your needs best. Whether you decide to buy a retail home server machine, order a custom machine from a system builder, or build your own, the knowledge of how the different components can affect server performance will help you to make an informed decision.

If you purchase a retail system, you know that they will be capable of performing well as a basic home server, and you understand the types of expansion they might allow, and how the server will be able to grow to meet your needs in the future.

If you decide to order a custom home server from a system builder, you know what upgrades will enhance your home server experience, and which ones would likely be a waste of your hard earned money.

For the brave hobbyists who decide to build their own server from new parts, or who plan to build a *frankenmachine* from their PC graveyard, you have an understanding of the necessary components, and you hopefully understand the importance of building a reliable machine.

Overall, you now have a better understanding of the building blocks of a Windows Home Server machine, and that knowledge will help you to make an informed decision about what choice will be best for you.

Chapter 4

Setting Up Your Home Network

If you already have a working home network, then most of this chapter may not be necessary for you. It still will be useful to read through so that you understand the unique demands that Windows Home Server can place on a network, and how best to set up a home network to make the most of Windows Home Server.

Many people already have simple home networks that work very well for sharing a broadband connection, but they may not be well suited for enabling all of the functionality of Windows Home Server. Broadband connections are typically limited to 2 Mbps or less, with higher cable modem plans running around 10 Mbps. Almost any functioning home network will have enough bandwidth to effectively share a broadband connection.

Windows Home Server will work decently on most networks, but its utility will increase as you increase the bandwidth available between your home computers and the server. Bottlenecks such as slower wireless connections, or older Ethernet switches or hubs will make operations such as opening files or copying them to the server take a long time.

From the perspective of trying to be effective at simplifying and protecting your digital life, you should remember that any point of frustration, especially in a household with multiple users, can derail even the best laid plans. In my beta testing of Windows Home Server, my wife complained about the amount of time that it would take to move files off our digital camera's memory card up to the server. Further, she manually rotates pictures that were taken in a portrait orientation, and this simple editing operation that used to take less than a second for files on the local hard disk would take twenty or thirty seconds. As a temporary solution, we altered our process so that we now do any preliminary edits to the photos while they are still on the memory card, and then copy the files to the server. My long-term solution is that I plan to run wired Gigabit Ethernet between the server and our main desktop machine. Running Ethernet wire through an existing house can be a big hassle, so you have to weigh the benefits before deciding to do something like this yourself. In my experience, Gigabit Ethernet can transfer files quickly enough that you hardly ever notice that you are working over the network.

Designing Your Network

The idea of designing a network may be a little intimidating to some readers. Hopefully after going through this chapter you will realize that designing a home network to make the most of your Windows Home Server really just involves learning some basic technical concepts, and understanding the trade-offs that can be made regarding performance, cost, complexity, flexibility, and convenience.

Can You Use More than One Windows Home Server?

Windows Home Server currently supports up to ten computers per server. If you attempt to add an eleventh computer to a server, the Windows Home Server will refuse.

Windows Home Server does allow for multiple servers to coexist on the same network; you just have to choose different server names for each machine. If you happen to have more than ten client machines on your home network, you can simply add an additional Windows Home Server machine to back up the additional machines. If you use the same usernames and passwords on each server, you will also be able to simply access shared files from either server without having to enter a password.

Another reason you may want a second server is to support a home-based business. Although many people use their personal computers for work-related stuff, if you run a business out of your home, it is a good idea to maintain separate computing resources to keep your business data isolated from your personal data. It also means that if you ever decide to move your business out of the home, you will have a server that you can take with you that contains all of your business data.

Parts of a Home Network

There are three basic parts that all home networks have. Sometimes two of these will be combined into a single box, simplifying your network further. Most home networks have a broadband access modem to connect them to the Internet. They also have a switch or hub to connect the computers together and to the broadband modem. Lastly, a home network has one or more computers that can be used to access local resources or the Internet.

BROADBAND ACCESS MODEMS AND ROUTERS

A broadband access modem is the connecting point between your home network and the Internet. Different kinds of access include DSL, cable Internet, and fiber-optic broadband like Verizon's FIOS. Most of the time, the broadband access modem is supplied by the company that provides your Internet service.

Whether you have DSL, cable modem, or some other type of broadband modem, the design of these devices is pretty similar. They have a connector on the box for whatever media is used to deliver broadband to your house. For DSL, this is a standard phone line connection. For cable Internet, this is an F-Type connector such as the one you find on the back of a television set. The other connector on the box is typically an RJ-45 connector, also known as a standard Ethernet connector. Ethernet has many different flavors, so you may see these connectors labeled 10BT, 100BT, or 10/100. Whatever the label says, you can recognize this connection because it looks similar to a telephone jack except that it is wider and has eight contacts inside, whereas a telephone jack has two or four contacts.

Figure 4-1 shows several types of broadband devices. The first is a basic cable modem with a single Ethernet interface. The next is a simple DSL modem with a single Ethernet interface. The third is a DSL modem with an integrated switch. The type of device you use will largely depend on your Internet Service Provider (ISP). Models that include an integrated switch might allow you to run your entire network from one box. Some models also include a wireless Ethernet access point. Still others might have a USB connection in addition to the Ethernet connection. The USB is just another way to connect a broadband device to a single computer. While the USB interface is sometimes easier to configure, the

Ethernet interface provides more flexibility for expanding your network. The variety of broadband devices is very large, so this book can't cover all of the possible combinations. It is important to understand that they are all very similar functionally, and the differences are focused around how they connect to your ISP, and how you can connect your home network and computers.

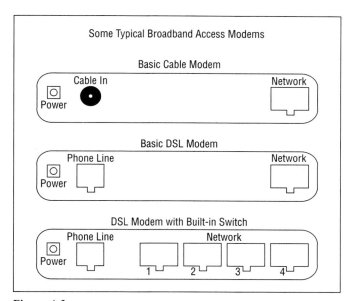

Figure 4-1

Most broadband access modems also contain a router. The router serves several functions. The exact features that each router supports can vary. In general they employ a technology called Network Address Translation, also known as NAT. NAT effectively hides your computers from the Internet and does not allow strangers to connect directly to your machines. NAT also allows you to connect multiple computers to the Internet through the router, even though your ISP only provides your Internet connection with a single IP address. Besides this simple method of hiding your computers from the Internet, many broadband routers also employ more advanced firewall technologies, blocking specific types of traffic, and giving you the option of allowing some types of traffic into your network. An example of how a router can be set up to allow inbound traffic is shown in Chapter 11, as you learn how to enable access to your home server from the Internet.

Another function that most broadband routers include is that they provide Dynamic Host Configuration Protocol (DHCP) services to your home network. The DHCP service provides addresses to any machine that connects to your home network. Each machine will automatically be provided an unused IP address so that it can connect to the network without requiring manual configuration of a compatible address.

If you have a broadband modem that does not also include routing functionality, you can purchase a home network router from a retail store like Best Buy, or even Wal-Mart. The cheaper models can sometimes be found on sale for less than thirty dollars, with more expensive models approaching two hundred dollars. Selecting a cheaper model from a well-known manufacturer such as Linksys, D-Link, or Netgear is usually a good option.

Comparing Broadband Options

Many people only have one option for Internet service. If you have multiple options, understanding the differences among them can help you decide what will be best for you.

- **Cable Internet:** Provided by cable companies like Comcast, cable Internet can provide higher-speed downloads than other options. Many cable providers will provision accounts to allow download speeds of 10 Mbps. Although this may seem like a huge advantage, the speed of cable Internet services is shared between all of the customers on a given network segment. That means that your entire neighborhood may be sharing the 10 Mbps connection, so if several other people are heavily using their Internet connections (downloading files, for example), your connection speed may be degraded significantly.

- **DSL:** Digital subscriber line, or DSL, is provided by local phone companies and third parties known as competitive local exchange carriers (CLECs). These companies install equipment at the phone company's buildings that uses higher frequencies to send and receive data via normal copper phone wires. DSL connections are typically provisioned at 768 kilobits per second (kbps), 1.5 Mbps, or 3.0 Mbps. At first glance, DSL is losing to cable in the speed war. DSL's advantage is that the bandwidth is dedicated to a single customer, so that bandwidth is available no matter what your neighbors are doing.

- **Satellite Internet:** Companies such as HughesNet (formerly DirecWay) offer a high-speed Internet solution that appeals primarily to customers that do not have any other options available. All that is required is that you have an unobstructed view of the southern sky from your home. Satellite Internet service generally offers speeds comparable to DSL, but the monthly charges are roughly double the cost of a similar DSL plan. One important thing to remember is that although the throughput is similar to DSL, Satellite Internet suffers from a problem known as latency. Because it takes time for the signals to travel to and from the satellites in orbit, it can take roughly a quarter of a second before you actually get a response to an action such as a clicking a web link. This generally is pretty tolerable for most Internet usage, but people who like to participate in online gaming can find this delay to be a huge detriment when they are playing games that rely on quick responses, such as first-person shooter games.

- **Residential wireless:** A relatively new option that is available only to select locations is known as residential wireless. One of the larger companies offering this service is Clearwire (`http://clearwire.com`), but many smaller companies are offering similar services. Residential wireless leverages technologies such as 802.11 wireless Ethernet, 802.16 wireless metropolitan area networks, or proprietary technologies to provide broadband access without requiring a physical connection. Speeds typically range from 2 Mbps to 25 Mbps, but the higher speeds are typically only available if you are very close to the service provider's location. Prices are similar to DSL, but the required equipment can be a bit more expensive.

SWITCHES

Switches are used to connect multiple devices together on a network. Switches are smart devices that can direct data from one device to another using standard Ethernet protocols.

Switches are recognizable because with the exception of a power connection, all the rest of the ports are standard Ethernet ports. A switch that is built into a broadband router simply looks like a bank of between four and eight Ethernet ports arranged in a row (see Figure 4-1 for an example). Each device on your network must be connected to your switch via a standard Ethernet cable. Modern computers almost always have a built-in Ethernet connector, but older machines may require a network interface card (NIC) that plugs into the computer's expansion bus.

The switch or switches in your network determine how fast information can travel from one device to another. Older switches run at 10 megabits per second. This is sometimes written as 10 Mbps, or more informally as 10 megabits. Typical home-network switches operate at 100 megabits. Current top-of-the-line switches operate at one gigabit per second. The following table gives examples of how long certain operations would take over various types of connections:

Examples of How Network Speed Affects Computing Tasks (in Seconds to Complete)

Task	10 Megabit Ethernet	802.11g Wireless (~30 Mbps)	100 Megabit Ethernet	Gigabit Ethernet
Opening a 10-page Word Document	0.10	0.03	0.01	0.001
Copying a 5 Megapixel RAW Digital Picture	12	4	1.2	0.12
Ripping a 10-song CD to MP3	50	17	5	0.5

If you need to expand your home network, you can also connect switches together. If one of your devices has an uplink port, you can use this port to connect to the other switch using a standard Ethernet cable. If neither device has an uplink port, you can connect the two with a crossover cable, which should be available at any computer store. Switches can be connected into a long chain, or in a star pattern. You can choose whatever design you want, but you should avoid creating loops as this can confuse the logic that the switches use to keep track of the physical connections that lead to each network device.

Many broadband access routers also include a small built-in switch. This will allow you to connect a small number of devices without the need for a separate switch.

COMPUTERS AND SERVERS

The computers and servers are where the real action on a network takes place. Each computer or server will connect to the network via a network interface card, or NIC. Just like with switches, your NIC will be rated for a certain speed. Most computers purchased today include a built-in 10/100 (Megabit) NIC. NICs that are capable of Gigabit Ethernet are usually labeled 10/100/1000, and they are capable of operating at any of these speeds.

The speed at which a given device can interact with the network is limited by its NIC. If you decide to spring for a higher-speed switch that supports Gigabit Ethernet, then you will also have to equip your server and any clients that require the additional bandwidth with NICs that support the higher speed.

Special Considerations

There are certain activities that you may use your home network for that would indicate that you should invest in higher-speed networking equipment, like a Gigabit Ethernet switch.

- **Streaming video:** Streaming small video files will not be a major load on your network, but if you have Media Center PCs or other devices such as network-enabled digital video recorders (DVRs) that you will use to stream video to computers or media extenders (described in more detail in Chapter 9), you should consider increasing the speed available on your network. Transferring video consumes a great deal of bandwidth, and if part of your network is congested with video traffic, other activities such as accessing the Internet or just opening small files on your server may be slowed down.

- **Gaming:** The resource demands of different games vary greatly, but in general, games do not perform well if the home network is congested. Network congestion can reduce the throughput that is available for downloading visual elements of the game, and it can increase the latency of the connection to the Internet, putting the player at a disadvantage in games where reaction times are important.

- **Frequently working with large files:** If you are storing important data on your server and if you frequently use or edit large files, you may want to upgrade your network to Gigabit Ethernet. Digital home movies and high-resolution photographs are two types of files that can be cumbersome to work on via a slower link. Pretty much any file larger than about 5MB falls into the large file category and could be bothersome to work with via a wireless link, or even a 100 Megabit Ethernet connection.

SOME NOTES ABOUT WIRELESS

Wireless connections are present in many modern homes. Setting up a wireless connection is a little more complicated than setting up wired Ethernet. After a wireless connection is set up properly, you can consider it an extension of your wired network. Depending on whether you are using a wireless access point that is integrated into your broadband access router, or if you are using a standalone access point, the configuration of these devices can be either very simple or very challenging.

Once set up, wireless offers an amazing amount of convenience. I rarely plug my laptop into its wired connection because almost everything I do on it is tolerant of the slower speeds that wireless provides. I do have a wired connection set up for when I want to copy larger files, perform backups, or restore from backups.

The speed of wireless networks can be very deceiving. The wireless technology marketers like to talk about the top speeds, but realistically the actual throughput is much lower. For older 802.11b networks, the top speed of 11 Mbps is rarely seen. 5 Mbps is a more reasonable expectation. For my home network's 802.11g wireless, I typically see around 30 Mbps on my laptop when I keep it one room away from the access point. My wife's desktop also has a wireless connection, and although it is capable of 54 Mbps, I can't seem to get it to go more than about 11 Mbps. I'm fairly certain this is because the antenna is buried in the computer desk near the power cables and lots of other sources of interference.

Wireless is great for convenience, but you should remember that you are trading a fair amount of speed and reliability for that convenience. If you choose, as I have, to rely on wireless for some or all of your home network, you need to manage your expectations about the time it will take to work with files directly from the server. In addition, it's a good idea to have a wired network connection available for any wireless computers so that you can plug them in if you need to transfer large amounts of data to or from your server. The ideal setup would be to have a docking station available where the computer can recharge overnight and perform backups via a wired Ethernet connection through the docking station.

Planning It Out

Now that you understand the parts, you should look at how they fit together. Your home network will be unique and hopefully not too complicated.

This exercise is best done visually, so grab a pencil and some paper. If you want to use a computer to draw your network, Microsoft Visio has network objects included and can be used to make professional looking drawings. For a free alternative to Visio, check out http://gliffy.com. Gliffy has simple network shapes and connectors that will let you build, save, export, or print a drawing of your network.

A typical single-PC home network is shown in Figure 4-2.

Figure 4-2

If you are implementing a Windows Home Server machine, your network is probably a little more complicated. Figure 4-3 adds some complexity. You can see that the home server and a desktop machine are connected via wired Ethernet, but that there is a laptop that is connected over a wireless connection.

The most important elements of your plan will include identifying the speeds that your computers and switches are capable of, and identifying the bottlenecks between your server and each of the devices that you plan to use with your server. Many switches and routers identify on the physical box what speeds they support, but for ones that do not, or for computers, you may have to check the manufacturer's documentation to determine what speeds they support. Remember that the speed that a device can communicate with the server will be determined by the NIC in the device, the NIC in the server, and the combination of switches and/or hubs between the two. The slowest device in this chain will limit the rate that data can travel between that device and the server. Having a slow device on the network does not degrade the entire network.

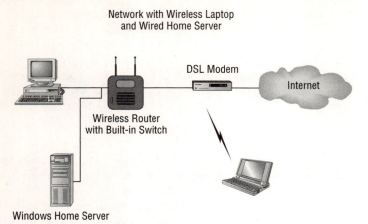

Figure 4-3

Figure 4-4 shows a network, with notes showing how fast each device can exchange data with the server. Notice that the family PC and the laptop in the docking station have 1 Gbps throughput to the server, but the wireless laptop is constrained by the speed of the wireless link at roughly 30 Mbps. An example of a bottleneck is shown at the home office PC. In this example, the network includes an old 10 Mbps hub (A hub is an older device that serves the same function as a switch) as a means to connect the home office PC with the office printer. Unfortunately, using this hub in the network restricts the speed at which the home office PC can communicate to the home server. To resolve this bottleneck, the user could either connect the home office PC and the office printer directly to open ports on the Gigabit Ethernet switch, or they could replace the 10 Mbps hub with a new 100 Mbps or 1 Gbps switch. If the home office PC is rarely used to access data on the server, it may be fine to leave it as is. Also, even with all of this talk of bottlenecks, even the slowest of the links at 10 Mbps is faster than most home broadband Internet connections, so replacing it won't do anything to improve Internet connection speeds.

If you are setting up your first home network, or if you are significantly reworking your network to make room for a Windows Home Server, this exercise will help you to plan how best to connect the various devices. Remember to keep it simple, and focus on maintaining the highest bandwidth between your Windows Home Server and any machines where you are likely to want to use and process large files, like digital photos, movies, and music. Eliminating bottlenecks by using wired Ethernet connections with 100 Mbps switches is a good start, and upgrading to 1 Gbps switches will give you the best speed that is currently available and will provide the best experience when working with data stored on your home server.

Armed with a drawing of your current or planned network, you can decide if there are changes that you want to make now, or you can keep it as a reference to use later to decide where you want to do server-intensive work. You can also use it to decide where you can improve your network in the future.

Wireless security is discussed further at the end of this chapter.

Chapter 4: Setting Up Your Home Network

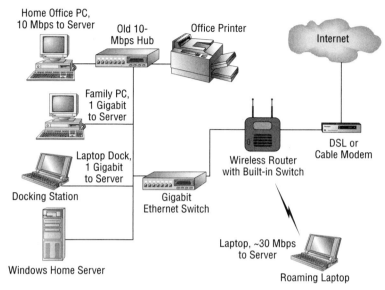

Figure 4-4

Apartments, Condominiums, and Old Buildings

If you are in a building that was built 70 or more years ago (or even more recently, depending on where you are), you might have additional considerations. For example, think about these questions:

- Have the outlets and wiring been brought up to current standards?
- Are the outlets properly grounded?
- Have the phone lines been updated to current standards?
- If you are in an apartment or condominium, what are the landlord's or association's rules regarding making such upgrades?
- Are there any local ordinances affecting your wireless network within a building that has other tenants?

Continued

Apartments, Condominiums, and Old Buildings *(Continued)*

- Is your surge protector good enough? There are several important considerations for surge protectors:

  - **UL tag:** The surge protector should have an Underwriters Laboratories tag that says "transient voltage surge suppressor" on it. This ensures that it has been tested by an independent nonprofit organization for quality and safety.

  - **Indicator light:** This indicates that the surge protector is functioning.

  - **Energy absorption/dissipation:** How much energy the surge protector can absorb before failing. 200-400 joules is common, but 600 joules is safer. Obviously, more is better.

  - **Clamping voltage:** Controls at what voltage electricity goes to the ground line. This should be under 400 volts.

  - **Response time:** How long it takes before the surge protector responds to a power surge. This should be 1 nanosecond or less.

Naturally, every situation is different, but these are good examples of some of the factors that you might want to explore.

Environmental Concerns

In addition to the logical layout, you must also decide physically where to locate your computers, server, modems, switches, and wires. Computer, servers, and networking equipment will generally work better, last longer, and be more reliable if you locate it somewhere where you have clean, temperature controlled and dry airflow. It may be tempting to try to tuck a server on a shelf out in the garage, but doing so could significantly impact the longevity and reliability of the system.

As a general rule, if the box has a fan that operates continuously when it is powered on, you should try to locate it in a room where you are comfortable yourself. You should try to keep all of the parts of your home network away from excessive heat or cold, away from sources of significant humidity, like showers and kitchens, and away from dirt and dust.

Boxes that do not have fans, typically switches and home routers, are generally a little more tolerant of the environment and are better suited for being tucked away in a basement, closet, or any other "uncomfortable" location. As long at the location is clean and dry, it should be fine for non-fan boxes.

For any home networking equipment, and most consumer electronics, you can perform a quick check to be sure that the device is getting adequate airflow for cooling. After the box has been operating continuously for at least several hours, place your hand on the box. If there are any locations where the box is so hot that you cannot hold your hand in contact with it for at least thirty seconds, you should consider moving the box to a place where it receives more airflow. Dust, heat, noise, accessibility, and general environmental concerns are covered in greater detail in Chapter 5.

… 49

Setting It Up

Now that you have a plan, you can go over some pointers for the various types of networking gear. Some basic requirements for all boxes are that they need power, adequate airflow, and accessibility for cabling.

Some good news is that most home networking equipment, switches, broadband modems, and wireless access points all ship with very usable default configurations. Some of the more complicated devices often include setup programs that you can run from a PC that will allow you to set up the device by answering simple questions. If you have the instructions for your device, it is best to use those and just refer back to this chapter for common pitfalls.

As a general rule, setting up home networking gear involves running the Ethernet cabling, attaching power, and if there's a power switch, turning it on.

Broadband Modems

There is enough variety in the setup procedures for broadband devices that it is best to refer to your manufacturer's documentation for specifics. Different providers have wildly different settings for security and access restrictions. If you plan to change anything on your modem, remember to write down your provider's tech support phone number before you start. If you manage to mess up a setting on your modem, you won't be able to get on the Internet to figure out how to fix it! If your modem has an integrated router or switch, then the following sections may apply as well.

Routers

If you are using a router that is separate from your modem, you have to connect the uplink port of your router to the network port of your modem. The uplink port may be labeled Internet, Uplink, or Web. It is usually separated from any integrated switch ports. The uplink port should be connected to the modem via a standard Ethernet cable.

You can either set up your router with its manufacturer's utility or manually review the configuration. Most routers include a set of configuration screens that you can access via a web browser. First you need to plug a computer into one of the Ethernet ports. If you have the IP address of the router, you can open a web browser and type `http://aaa.bbb.ccc.ddd` where the letters are the IP address of the router.

If you don't know the IP address, you can find it by running a utility called `ipconfig` from a command line on an attached computer. To start a command line window, you can use ⊞+R to open a run box, and then type **cmd** in the box that appears, and press Enter. Next type **ipconfig** and press Enter (Note: The command line under Windows is not case sensitive.) The resulting screen should look like Figure 4-5, and the address you need is circled.

Most routers purchased recently will have a good default configuration, but some older routers will have insecure defaults, or important features may be disabled. Some settings you should check include making sure that Network Address Translation (NAT) is turned on, confirming that WEP or WPA security (discussed later in this chapter) is enabled on wireless connections, and making sure that the built-in firewall is turned on.

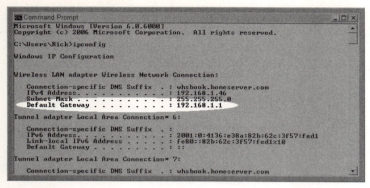

Figure 4-5

Switches

In a home network environment, switches typically just work. They require a power connection, and you have to run Ethernet cables to the switch in order for it to be useful, but beyond that no configuration is required.

For a switch to be truly useful, it must be connected to another piece of networking equipment like a broadband access modem or a router. If your switch has an uplink port, you can hook the uplink port to your modem or router using a standard Ethernet cable. If you don't have an uplink port, you must purchase a special Ethernet cable called a crossover cable. Crossover cables can be found at most computer stores or ordered from online retailers like Computer Discount Warehouse (http://cdw.com) or Amazon (http://amazon.com).

A Note on DHCP and Subnets

An important part of your home network is known as the Dynamic Host Configuration Protocol, or DHCP. Every computer on the network needs an IP (Internet Protocol) address. An IP address can be assigned manually, but things are easiest if automatic assignment is enabled. DHCP is used to automatically provide IP addresses to computers and servers on your network, eliminating the need for manually configuring IP addresses on all of your boxes. The device on your network that provides DHCP services is known as the DHCP Server, and although the word *server* is used, it can be a part of your modem, router, switch, or even located on a desktop PC.

A subnet is a logical grouping of computers that have similar addresses. Computers that are on the same subnet can communicate to each other through a switch without having to go through a router. The most important thing to remember about DHCP and subnets is that you only want *one* DHCP server on your network, and you want a *single* subnet. If you have multiple devices on your network that are capable of acting as the DHCP server, you should select one to use and disable this functionality on the others.

A common scenario where this happens is if you decide to add a wireless access point to a network that also has a broadband modem/router device. In this scenario, the best solution is to disable DHCP on the wireless access point and also to place the wireless access point in *bridge mode*. It is possible to use a wireless access point without doing this, but if you do so you may have addressing conflicts on your network and your wireless computers might be on a different subnet from your other devices. Many home networking services are limited to a single local subnet, and having your network split in two may limit the sharing and services that you can use. Placing the wireless access point in bridge mode logically "bridges" the two networks together so that they behave as one. With the wireless access point in bridge mode, wireless computers will obtain IP addresses from the same DHCP server that the wired devices use. This added complexity also highlights the benefit of using a single device that includes your broadband router, a built-in switch for wired Ethernet devices, and an integrated wireless router for wireless devices.

Network Adapters

If you want to add a machine to your home network that does not already have a built-in network adapter, then you can add one relatively easily. You can tell if your computer has a built-in network adapter by checking your user's manual, or by looking for an RJ-45 connector (which looks like a telephone plug, only wider) on the back of the computer.

If you are not comfortable working inside your computer, you should consider purchasing a USB 2.0 Ethernet adapter. These network adapters can be plugged into a spare USB port, and installation is often automatic, or simply requires insertion of a CD when Windows asks for a driver. The other option is to install an internal network interface card. Internal NIC's must be selected to match your computer's internal expansion bus. Your computer user manual may have information about installing expansion cards. There are really no drawbacks to using a USB 2.0 network adapter, so that is the recommended option. These adapters generally cost less than forty dollars, and are available at retailers like Best Buy and Wal-Mart, or can be ordered from online stores like Amazon (http://amazon.com) or Computer Discount Warehouse (http://cdw.com).

Adding a USB 2.0 Wireless Ethernet adapter is similar to the process for adding a wired Ethernet adapter. Depending on the type of data that you plan to use on your network and the difficulty involved in actually running Ethernet cables through your home, you may decide that this option is better for you, or that it can be a temporary solution to get computers connected while you work on wiring.

Note

If you want to learn more about working on the insides of computers, including adding and configuring network adapters, CompTIA A+ Certification All-In-One Desk Reference for Dummies by Glen E. Clarke and Ed Tetz (Wiley, 2007) (ISBN: 978-0-471-74811-3) covers almost every topic you could imagine regarding installing hardware and troubleshooting computers. It is targeted at those who wish to obtain CompTIA's A+ certification, which is a vendor-neutral certification for computer technicians, but the book is also an excellent reference for those who want to learn more about working with computer hardware.

As part of the driver installation under Windows, you will be asked if you want to use typical settings for this networking device, as shown in Figure 4-6. The default settings will work well assuming that you have a single subnet and a single DHCP server configured on your network.

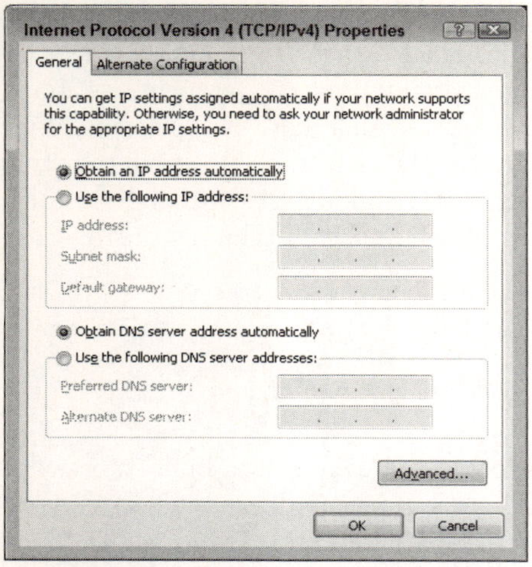

Figure 4-6

Wireless Security

Earlier in this chapter, the "Routers" section discussed enabling NAT and firewalls to protect your network from threats coming in from the Internet. Chapter 11 discusses specifics about securing Windows Home Server's remote access features. This section discusses some specific things you need to consider if you are running a wireless network.

If you use a wireless network in your home, you need to be proactive about securing your wireless access point. If you do not secure your wireless network, your neighbors, or even passersby, can make use of your Internet bandwidth. Although it may sound like a neighborly act to share your Internet connection, you do not want to be held accountable for what someone else does through your network connection. The jury is still out on this, but many people believe that leaving a wireless access point unsecured actually gives implicit permission for others to use your network.

The other important reason to secure your wireless is because unsecured networks enable casual eavesdropping on your network activities, and could also open up a hole for a malicious person to compromise your computers or server. In addition, if you enable the guest account on Windows Home Server, anyone with access to your wireless network will be able to access any content to which the guest account has permissions.

WEP or WPA?

Wireless security is configured at the router. This security involves encrypting data sent over the air to make it more difficult for someone who intercepts the broadcast signal to unscramble the data. The data sent is encrypted using a "key" and decrypted by the receiver using the same key. To make setup easier, some routers are unsecured by default. If they have security enabled by default, wireless routers will usually have a sticker or label that includes the default protocol and key that is required to connect to the router.

Chapter 4: Setting Up Your Home Network

As you configure security on your router, you may have a choice between an older, less secure standard (Wired Equivalent Privacy, or WEP) and the newer, more secure standard (Wi-Fi Protected Access, or WPA). There are several levels of WPA. Any will suffice for home networks. You should be sure that your wireless network adapter supports the level of security you choose on the router. Choose the highest level of encryption supported by all wireless devices.

For practical consideration, it does not matter considerably whether you use WEP or WPA. WEP has some weaknesses that will allow a determined attacker to crack the encryption and gain access to your data and network, but the protocol is widely available and still serves as a good deterrent against casual misuse of your wireless network. Some older devices only support WEP, and wireless routers only support using one security protocol at a time, so if you have one of these older devices you will be forced to use WEP on your network. WPA is a newer standard that provides greater protection than WEP.

The general process for setting up WEP or WPA is:

1. Enable WPA on your wireless access point. This is usually best done from a computer that is connected to your router via an Ethernet cable, but it can be done from a computer that is connected via wireless. When you change wireless security settings, you will have to reconfigure the wireless network settings on your client computers, so connecting via wired Ethernet will allow you to complete the configuration without disruption. To access the configuration screens, you connect to your router in the same way as described earlier in the "Routers" section. Once connected, browse your router's interface and locate a section that has a title similar to "Wireless: Security." Figure 4-7 shows this screen on a Westell 327W DSL Modem with Integrated Wireless Access Point. Different hardware will have different interface screens, but they should have similar titles and fields. Select WEP or WPA from the drop-down list. Remember that all wireless clients must use the same protocol.

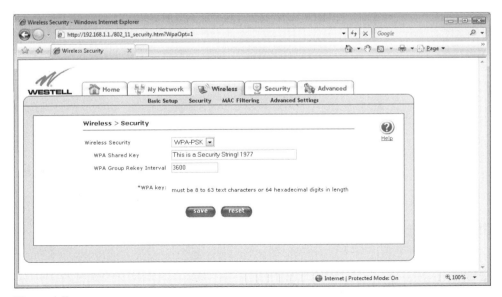

Figure 4-7

2. Generate a key for WEP or WPA to use. The interface should give you instructions telling you what is required for a key. For WPA it generally will require a string of between 8 and 63 characters of text. WEP will allow 5, 13, or 29 characters of text, with longer strings generating longer keys. The router then uses this passphrase to generate the actual key that will be used for wireless security. The interface and a sample WPA passphrase are shown in Figure 4-7.

3. Enable security on wireless client computers. Under Windows, wireless security is configured when you first connect to a wireless network. If you have recently modified the wireless security settings on your router, your wireless connection may still be connected but not working or displaying an error message. If this is the case, right-click the wireless icon in the system tray and select Disconnect. To set up the connection with the correct security settings, right-click the network icon near the date (one or two little monitors). If you have Windows XP, choose View Available Wireless Networks. For Windows Vista, choose Connect to a network. In the resulting dialog box, select the name of the wireless network from those available. In the next screen, confirm that the correct mode of security was detected, and enter the same passphrase entered on the router in step 2. The dialog under Windows Vista is shown in Figure 4-8. For WPA, you may have an option to select an encryption type, but the default TKIP (Temporal Key Integrity Protocol) should work as long as you did not manually change the encryption type on the router.

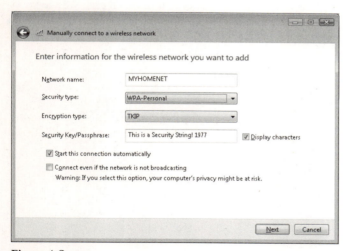

Figure 4-8

Additional Wireless Considerations

Most routers will maintain a list of the clients that have connected to the wireless access point. Sometimes it is shown under the My Network tab, and other routers will show it in the wireless security section under the MAC Filtering option. Locate where this information can be found on your router, and you can periodically check to make sure that unauthorized computers are not accessing your wireless connection.

If your home network is in a high-density neighborhood or in an apartment building, you should be aware that your wireless network's signal will be broadcast to your neighbors as well. Wireless signals typically travel anywhere from 100 to 300 feet. In an apartment building this will include the neighbors on floors above and below yours. When you have a signal spreading like this, you not only have to worry more about securing your wireless signal properly, but you also may run into interference. Wireless networks generally have 11 channels available, but adjacent channels actually overlap each other, so it is best to only use channels 1, 6, and 11. If you experience interference (evidenced by poor wireless signal quality reported on your client computers), then you may want to consider trying another channel. The process is similar to the process highlighted in the previous section titled "WEP or WPA?" except that the channel selection is generally made in the Basic Setup section of the Wireless tab.

Summary

Now that you understand the basic components of a typical home network and how Windows Home Server can place unique demands on your network, you should be better able to plan and implement a network that will enable you to use Windows Home Server to its fullest potential. By locating your equipment where it will be protected from dust, dirt, and extreme temperatures, you will ensure reliable operations.

You can make decisions about the trade-offs between performance and convenience, and if performance problems occur, you will be able to pinpoint the bottleneck, and know your options for upgrading your network to alleviate the bottleneck.

You now have a basic understanding of how to configure home networking equipment, what options are important to focus on, and what features need to be disabled to ensure a simplified home networking experience.

You also know the basic steps required to enable security on a wireless connection, so that you can secure your Internet connection from unauthorized use, and protect your home network from malicious eavesdropping or network compromise.

Chapter 5

Getting Started with Windows Home Server

Now that you have selected a Windows Home Server system, created a plan for keeping your data organized, and have a home network that is ready for the demands of a server, it's time to dig in and get Windows Home Server set up and running.

Finding Your Home Server a Home

As mentioned in the previous chapter, finding a location for your Windows Home Server is not a trivial undertaking. Many factors can influence where you want to put your home server, and they must be balanced with the environmental factors that will let your Windows Home Server be useful and reliable.

Technical Requirements

In order to function, your home server needs two primary connections. The first is power; the other is a wired Ethernet connection to your home network. If you are building your own home server, or if you are purchasing a Windows Home Server through the System Builder channel (as opposed to the retail channel; see Chapter 2 for explanations of these options), you may also need the ability to connect standard input/output devices from time to time.

POWER

Almost all Windows Home Server machines operate from a single grounded three-prong electrical outlet. Some OEM devices may use a power brick, or wall wart type power supply; others use a standard computer power cord to connect to an internal power supply.

In addition to the single power outlet for Windows Home Server, you should think about the other devices that may need power in this location. If you are collocating your home network's Ethernet switch with your home server, it will need a second power outlet. Likewise for DSL or cable modems, wireless access points, or other devices.

If you build your own server, or if you purchase a manufactured System Builder model, you should also plan for the likelihood that you will have to hook a monitor to your Windows Home Server box at some point. System installation or restores will require a local monitor, so having an outlet free will save some difficulty later.

If any of your devices, laptops, or desktops rely on a wireless interface for their connection back to the server, you should also consider reserving a spot for them near the networking gear. If you ever have to do a full restore of a PC, this functionality will only work over a wired Ethernet connection. Keeping one or two outlets available near the networking gear will be very helpful for this scenario.

If your home frequently experiences brownouts or power failures, you may also want to consider getting an uninterruptible power supply (UPS) to protect your home server. Many people don't realize that the power fluctuations that cause brownouts, and the surges on the power line that follow power failures, are very hard on computer components. Although they rarely cause outright failure, they may shorten the reliable life of a given component, and component failure is the last thing you want for a home server that you are going to rely on to keep your digital life safe.

If you are relying on extension cords or power strips to get power to your home server or other network equipment, there are some safety concerns that you should remember. Unless the labeling indicates otherwise, you should only use one extension cord or power strip between the wall and your equipment. Plugging power strips into other power strips, or chaining extension cords together can lead to overloaded circuits, or even fire. When choosing a location for your home server, make sure that you select a spot where you can make enough power outlets available in a safe manner. Chapter 4 talks about planning your home server and network in more detail.

NETWORK

The other critical connection that your Windows Home Server needs is a wired Ethernet connection. This connection must reach back to your network switch, or your router or broadband modem if it has an integrated switch.

Ethernet cabling can be a bit complicated, but if you stick with manufactured cables and brand-name networking equipment, you should be able to build a reliable network just by plugging in the cables where they fit, and providing power to all the equipment. Most Ethernet devices, switches, and network interface cards in computers have two lights. One is called the *link* light, and the other is the *activity* light. When you have powered on your switch and any device, like your server, and you have connected an Ethernet cable properly between them, you should see one of the lights come on steadily. The other light will blink to indicate when the computer or device is transmitting or receiving data.

OTHER CONSIDERATIONS

In addition to the two connections that your home server needs when functioning normally, you should make sure to plan for other situations that might arise. If you are setting up Windows Home Server on a standard PC, then you need to be able to connect a keyboard, mouse, and monitor to the server for installation. My server lives on top of a wardrobe in our guest room, and for the times that I have needed a display and input devices I have room next to the server to place a monitor, and a desk next to the wardrobe for the keyboard. I have a wireless mouse and a keyboard with a long cord, which give me the functionality that I need, although not in the most ergonomic setup. The times when you need to actually work directly at a home server will be few and far between, so don't go out of your way to make a workstation-like setup around your server. If you are building your own server or purchasing a server from a system builder that includes monitor, keyboard, and mouse capability, you may want a functional way to set up a monitor and input devices. Other maintenance actions such as cleaning or adding storage will also require the server to be easily accessible.

Environmental Concerns

Although it's a great cause to try to conserve natural resources and save the earth, it is not the type of environmental concerns being discussed in this section. The server's environment simply refers to the features of the surrounding area that can affect how the server will perform. A more appropriate term might be *habitat*, but technical people will be more apt to understand what you're talking about if you use the term *environmental concerns*, as it is frequently referenced in documentation for business servers.

HEAT

Excessive heat is a major concern for your Windows Home Server. Heat can be a problem for virtually all parts of your server, including the CPU(s), RAM, and most importantly, the hard drive. Hard drives, when overheated, will start to slowly fail. At first they might just have trouble reading a file or two, but eventually, the heat will have affected the moving parts so much that the drive will just cease to work. Because the major purpose of a Windows Home Server machine relies on its hard drives, you need to be extra careful to not do anything that will compromise the reliability of those hard drives.

The source of heat in a computer is inherent to the way that computers work. The energy that comes into a computer via its electrical power supply must eventually leave the computer. The energy is used temporarily to process information, but all of that energy eventually leaks out. There are very few ways for this energy to leave. They are sound, light, and heat. The acoustic energy, or sound, and the light are a very small part of this equation. You can virtually assume that all energy that goes into your server will eventually end up as heat. If the heat is not effectively removed, then the server will get hotter and hotter until something breaks down.

Most computers, and most home servers, have one or more fans that move air over the internal components in order to cool the parts and to move the heat out of the chassis. All this is well and good, but if the heat has nowhere to go, eventually the system will accumulate heat. I was reminded of this last year when we got a new hutch for my wife's computer. The hutch had a nice little cubby for the tower computer to sit in, but unfortunately it was built with only two small holes in the back to run wires through. A week or so later, the computer started having random crashes, and we realized that the cubby where the computer sat was getting uncomfortably hot. We ended up attaching some fans to some holes in the hutch in order to forcibly remove the hot air and bring in cool air. This made things a little better, but the hutch would still get a bit warm. The computer worked OK for almost a year, but eventually the hard drive failed. Before replacing the hard drive, we cut a large hole in the back of the hutch, basically removing the entire back of the area where the computer sits, to allow for more exchange of air.

It may be tempting to tuck your home server out of sight and out of mind, but if you do so, be extra certain that it will not be in a place where it will accumulate heat.

DUST

Dust is another enemy of a reliable server. Dust can directly impact the performance of optical drives such as DVD and CD-ROM drives, but it also can cause secondary problems by restricting the airflow that is necessary to remove heat. Hard drives are sealed so that dust cannot directly interfere with their moving parts. Fans on the other hand are exposed, and I have seen many fans fail because of excessive dust buildup. Dust adhering to the blades of a fan adds weight that can cause the motor to wear out early, and uneven dust buildup can misbalance the fan causing the bearings to fail.

In all homes where people live, dust happens. If you have pets, then you will have even more dust. There are three measures you can take to protect your home server from dust.

The first is to keep the server up off the floor. Dust likes to settle to the floor, and will often get disturbed and resettle to the floor throughout the day. By keeping your home server at least two feet off the ground, you will keep if from ingesting dust from the surrounding air.

The second preventative measure that you can take is to keep the server away from any central air returns in your home. Air coming out of the vents from a central air conditioner is relatively clean having just gone through a filter, but the volume of air that gets sucked back into the returns has had an opportunity to pick up dust from the living area. To get an idea of how much dust comes into the returns, just look at the filter on your central air conditioner. Every speck of dust that is trapped in the filter had to come through one of those air returns on its way to the filter!

The third and perhaps most surprising step that you can take is to follow the manufacturer's recommended schedules for replacing your home's central air filter(s). This will protect your server, any other computers, and your family from excessive dust. The schedule that you should follow is the one that is on the packaging for the filters that you use. If no recommendations are on the filter packaging, then you are probably looking at a one-month inspection and replacement schedule. More expensive filters can sometimes go two to four months, and cartridge style filters (they are about 5 times as thick as regular filters) can last six months to a year, depending on the level of dust in your home. By keeping the levels of dust in your home low, you will limit the amount of dust that gets pulled through your server. As a side benefit, your air conditioner and heater will work better, and cost less to operate with this simple maintenance.

NOISE

The previous sections discussed environmental factors that could affect the server. This section is about an environmental factor that can affect you and your family. The amount of noise produced by your server will vary greatly. Some servers will be almost silent. Others have loud fans. My Dell E521 based home server is very quiet most of the time, but if it gets too hot, or is performing a large number of CPU-intensive operations, the fans speed up, and it can be fairly noisy. In addition to fans, computer hard drives can be noisy when they are reading and writing information, and a Windows Home Server machine can end up having quite a few internal and external hard drives.

In order for your server to be a welcome addition to your home, you should be sure that whatever level of noise it produces will not interfere with other activities in the house. A noisy server can interfere with television watching, sleeping, listening to music, or a nice quiet dinner. I've found that while the variable speed fans on my home server keep things quiet most of the time, it is actually more disruptive to have a server that changes sound levels. A steady noise will tend to fade into the background, whereas a noise that comes and goes will be noticed every time it changes.

You need to evaluate the trade-offs involved between keeping your server accessible for maintenance, and keeping it from bothering the members of your household. A location near other computers that are kept on 24 hours a day will just add to the current noise level, and will probably not be noticed. Other possible locations include a home office, sewing room, or a seldom-used guest bedroom.

The Newest Member of Your Household

As you weigh the options for where your Windows Home Server should take up permanent residence, you should keep in mind a simple qualifying test: "Would you be comfortable where you are placing the server?" Granted a typical home server takes up much less space than a person, but do the environmental factors line up with what you would want for yourself? If you would feel comfortable with the temperature and cleanliness of a location, than it is probably a good home for your new Windows Home Server.

Setting Up Your Home Server

If you have purchased a retail/OEM Windows Home Server, your setup process will be very simple. The process of setting up Windows Home Server on regular PC-class hardware is a little more time consuming, but is no more complicated than setting up Windows Vista on similar hardware, perhaps even a little simpler.

Setting Up Windows Home Server on PC Hardware

Like the process of setting up a client Windows operating system such as Windows Vista, setting up Windows Home Server is a straightforward process. Because of the manner in which Windows Home Server handles storage, there are some additional considerations if you are using drives that already contain data.

CONNECTING A MONITOR, KEYBOARD, AND MOUSE

You must have a monitor, keyboard, and mouse attached to your home server for the duration of the setup, so if you don't already have them hooked up, this is the first step.

BOOTING FROM THE SETUP DVD

The next step is to get the machine to boot from the Server Installation DVD. Many computers will boot from DVD automatically, but on some computers you must make some changes to the BIOS settings in order to boot from the DVD. The simplest way to discover if your machine is set up to boot from the DVD is to try it. Put the DVD into your system's drive and power it on. Your computer may automatically boot from the DVD, or it may display a brief message to "Press a key to boot from CD or DVD." If you watched the rebooting process closely and didn't see any opportunity to boot from DVD, you'll need the next few steps to configure your BIOS. If you booted successfully, skip ahead to the "Running the Setup Program" section. There are many different BIOS manufacturers, and they all handle this a little differently. The first step is to enter the BIOS configuration utility. This is usually accomplished by pressing a key during the initial boot up time, usually F2, Del, or Insert. Just watch your computer screen when you first power on the server, and it will generally indicate which key you need to press to get into the BIOS setup. Figure 5-1 shows an example of the Del key needing to be pressed to run setup.

Once you're in the BIOS setup utility, look for a section labeled "Boot Order" or "Boot Priority." Make sure that the CD-ROM or DVD drive is listed before the Hard Drive (as shown in Figure 5-2). Sometimes the DVD drive may actually have any number of labels depending on the manufacturer of the BIOS. I have seen them labeled CD-ROM, DVD/CD-ROM, and ATAPI/CD-ROM. If you look through the available options, there is usually only one option that looks like it should be the DVD drive.

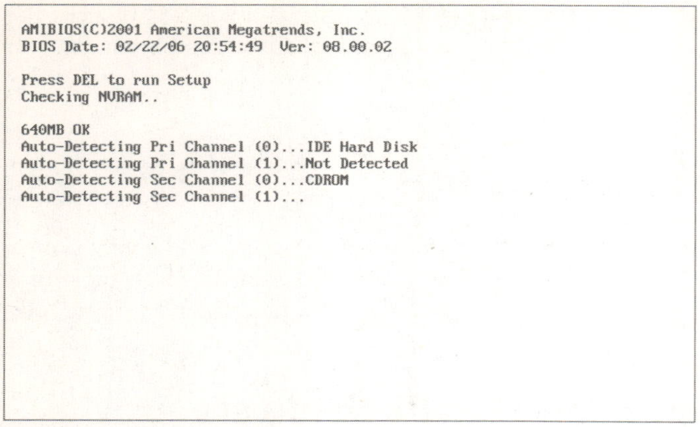

```
AMIBIOS(C)2001 American Megatrends, Inc.
BIOS Date: 02/22/06 20:54:49 Ver: 08.00.02

Press DEL to run Setup
Checking NVRAM..

640MB OK
Auto-Detecting Pri Channel (0)...IDE Hard Disk
Auto-Detecting Pri Channel (1)...Not Detected
Auto-Detecting Sec Channel (0)...CDROM
Auto-Detecting Sec Channel (1)...
```

Figure 5-1

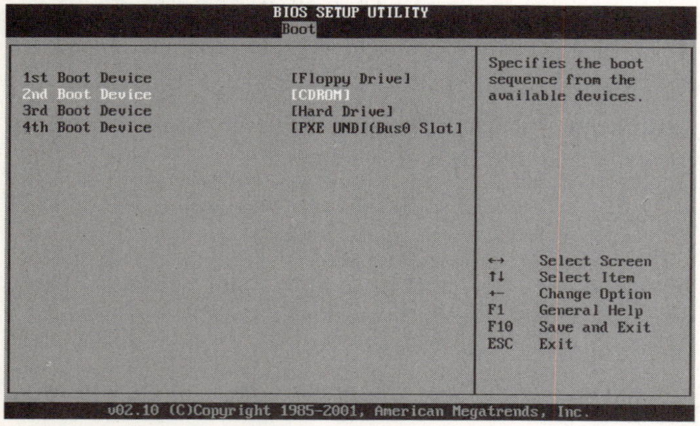

```
                    BIOS SETUP UTILITY
                    Boot

1st Boot Device          [Floppy Drive]      Specifies the boot
2nd Boot Device          [CDROM]             sequence from the
3rd Boot Device          [Hard Drive]        available devices.
4th Boot Device          [PXE UNDI(Bus0 Slot)]




                                             ↔    Select Screen
                                             ↑↓   Select Item
                                             ←    Change Option
                                             F1   General Help
                                             F10  Save and Exit
                                             ESC  Exit

         v02.10 (C)Copyright 1985-2001, American Megatrends, Inc.
```

Figure 5-2

After you set the DVD drive to be first in the boot order, you need to save the settings. Again, how you do this will vary, but on most computers this will be labeled "Save and Exit," "Exit Saving Changes," or something similar (see Figure 5-3).

After you configure your server to boot from DVD, place the Server Installation DVD in the drive, and power on the machine. If you are prompted to "Press Any Key to Boot from CD-ROM," press a key on the keyboard to initiate booting from the DVD.

RUNNING THE SETUP PROGRAM

The setup program starts automatically and first loads some files from the DVD into memory. This process can take a few minutes. You will first see a screen indicating that Windows is loading files. Next you will see a Microsoft copyright screen, and then you will see a Vista-like background with a message indicating that the setup program is initializing. After this process completes, you are presented with a GUI (graphical user interface) installation screen, as shown in Figure 5-4.

Chapter 5: Getting Started with Windows Home Server   **63**

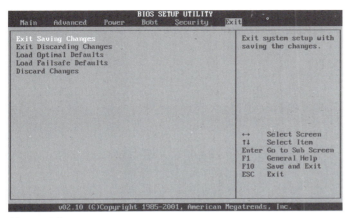

Figure 5-3

Figure 5-4

At this initial prompt there is nothing to do but click Next. The following screen shows the hard drives that Windows Home Server has detected (see Figure 5-5). You will hopefully see all of the internal hard drives you have hooked up to your Windows Home Server machine.

If the drive where you want to install Windows Home Server is not displayed, you will need to locate drivers from the manufacturer of your hard drive interface in order to use the hard drive. Certain drives or drive controllers, especially hardware RAID devices, will not be recognized automatically. (You do not need to worry if drives that you plan to use to expand your storage pool are missing. Drivers for these may be automatically loaded after Windows Home Server is installed, or you can add them after Windows Home Server is set up.) Your hardware may have come with a driver diskette that is compatible with Windows Server 2003. (This is the operating system that Windows Home Server is based on, so those will be the drivers that you will need.) Otherwise you may have to go to an Internet-connected computer and download the drivers from the manufacturer's website. After you have the drivers on floppy, CD-ROM, or USB memory stick, click the Load Drivers button and follow the instructions to select the correct driver.

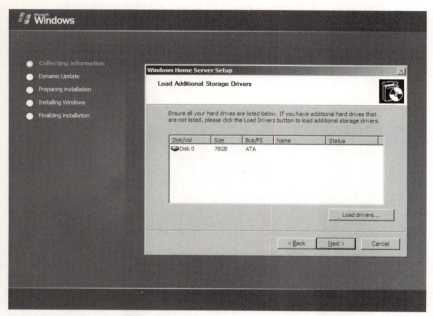

Figure 5-5

After you load any necessary drivers, click Next to continue. The next screen shows a drop-down list with only one option (see Figure 5-6). This is the screen that would have an option to do a restoration install if you already had secondary drives with Windows Home Server files on them.

Caution

If you are installing on your own custom-built server or repurposing an existing computer, take a moment to double-check that you have backed up any data from the hard drives in your server that you want to keep. The Windows Home Server installation process will overwrite all existing data, even on secondary drives. If you want to keep the data on secondary drives, you should have them disconnected while you run the installation program.

Chapter 5: Getting Started with Windows Home Server

Because this is a new installation, just leave the default option selected and click Next. Figure 5-7 shows localization options.

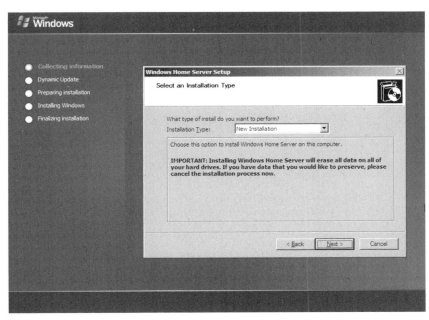

Figure 5-6

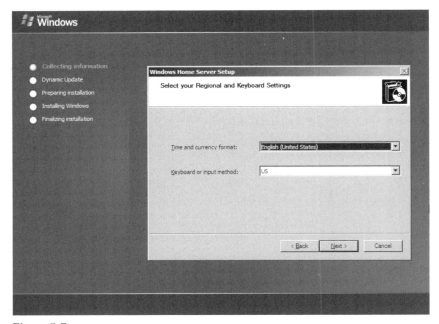

Figure 5-7

Select the language and keyboard layout that you prefer and click Next. The next screen is the End-User License Agreement (EULA), as shown in Figure 5-8. The important thing about the EULA is that it outlines the license that you have purchased. Software is not like traditional goods where you actually take ownership when you make a purchase. Instead what you have bought is the right to use the software, or a *license*. It is a good idea to read the EULA so that you understand the terms under which you are allowed to use this Microsoft software product.

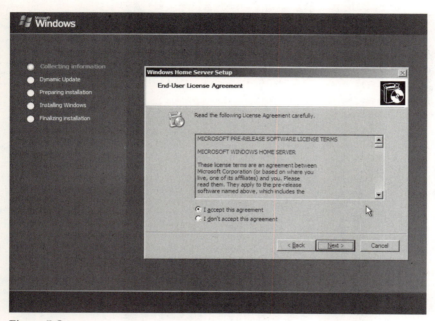

Figure 5-8

After you are comfortable with the EULA, click Next. You are now asked to enter the 25-digit product key that came with your Windows Home Server license (see Figure 5-9). This is usually printed on a sticker that is attached to either the case or the paper sleeve that the DVD was packaged in.

After entering the 25-digit product key and clicking Next, you are given the opportunity to change the name of your server (see Figure 5-10). The default name for a home server is SERVER. Accepting the default name is fine if you only plan on having one Windows Home Server machine on your local network. If you have another device that is using the network name SERVER, if you want to provide a name that is more descriptive of the function of the server, or if you just want to give your server a more creative name, you can enter it here. For example, if you plan to have two Windows Home Server machines on your network, one for family files and another to be used by home business computers, you could name the first one FAMILY and the other BUSINESS.

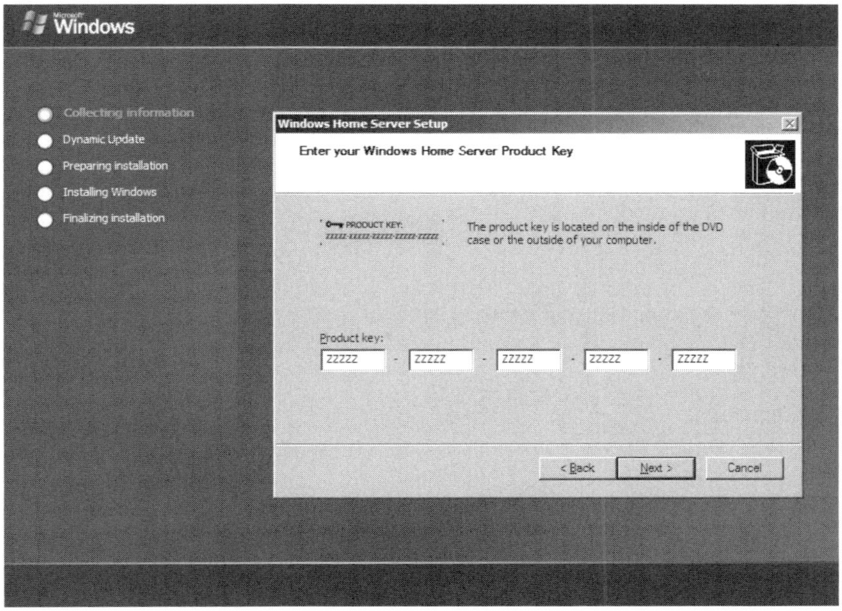

Chapter 5: Getting Started with Windows Home Server

Figure 5-9

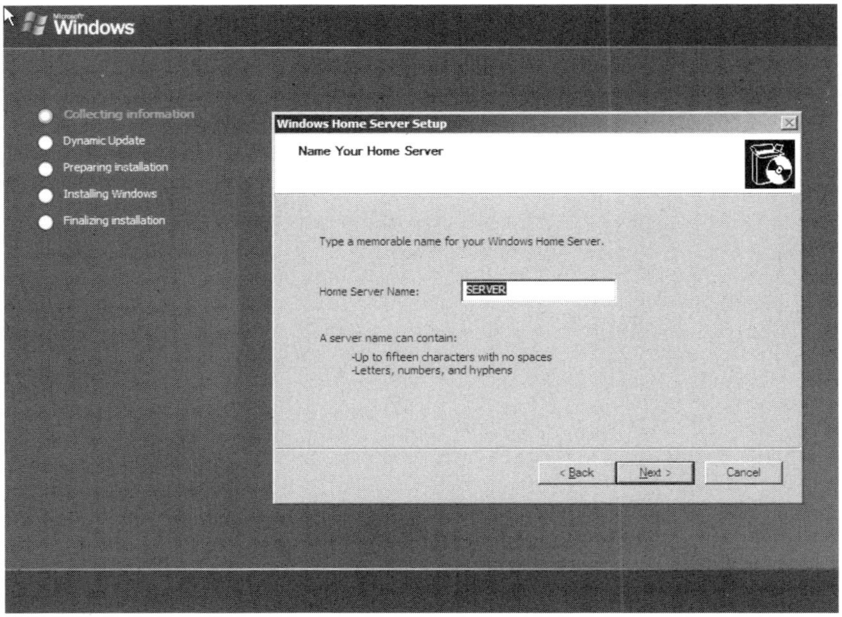

Figure 5-10

Chapter 5: Getting Started with Windows Home Server

The next screen is a very critical step to understand. You will have another chance to review the hard drives that the Windows Home Server setup has detected. Before continuing, you have to select a checkbox to confirm the fact that *all existing data will be erased* (see Figure 5-11). In a typical consumer operating system installation, like for Windows Vista, you will have the option of whether or not to erase the primary hard drive, and secondary drives are not even touched by the installation. Windows Home Server uses a technology called *Drive Extender* to enable file duplication, and this technology requires low-level control of all hard drives. Before continuing, you should review the listed drives, and double-check that you have backed up any data that was previously on the drives.

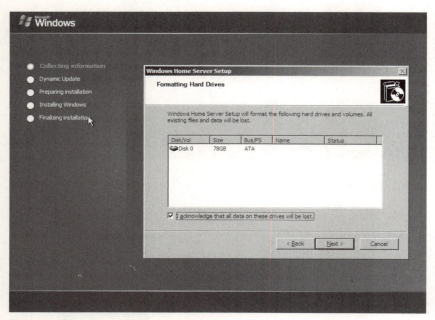

Figure 5-11

You have now made all of the necessary decisions for your Windows Home Server installation. All that is left is to click the Start button, as shown in Figure 5-12.

The Windows Home Server installation is now entering the most time-consuming stage. While the hard drives are formatted, files are copied, drivers are installed, and the system is configured, the installation will cycle through a sequence of screens showing the benefits of your new Windows Home Server. During the installation, the system may have to reboot several times. At the conclusion of this process, you are presented with a Welcome screen, as shown in Figure 5-13.

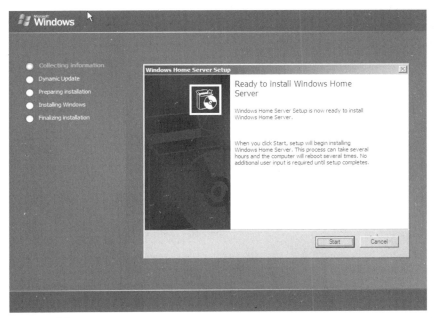

Figure 5-12

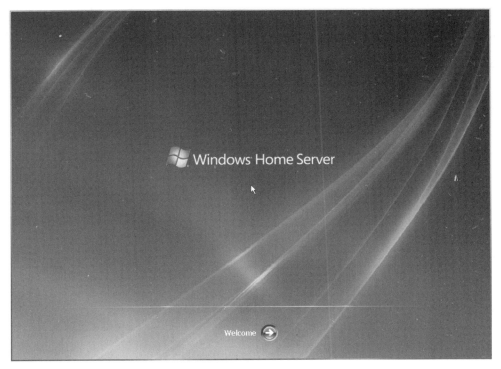

Figure 5-13

After you click the Welcome button, select a password for your home server (see Figure 5-14). Selecting a strong password that you can remember is very important. Remembering complex passwords can be a challenge. A good method is to use a sentence or phrase to create a password. For example, if you use the phrase "Sally makes lots of money in the summer!" you can create the password "Smlo$its!" by taking the first letter of most of the words, and replacing the word *money* with a dollar sign.

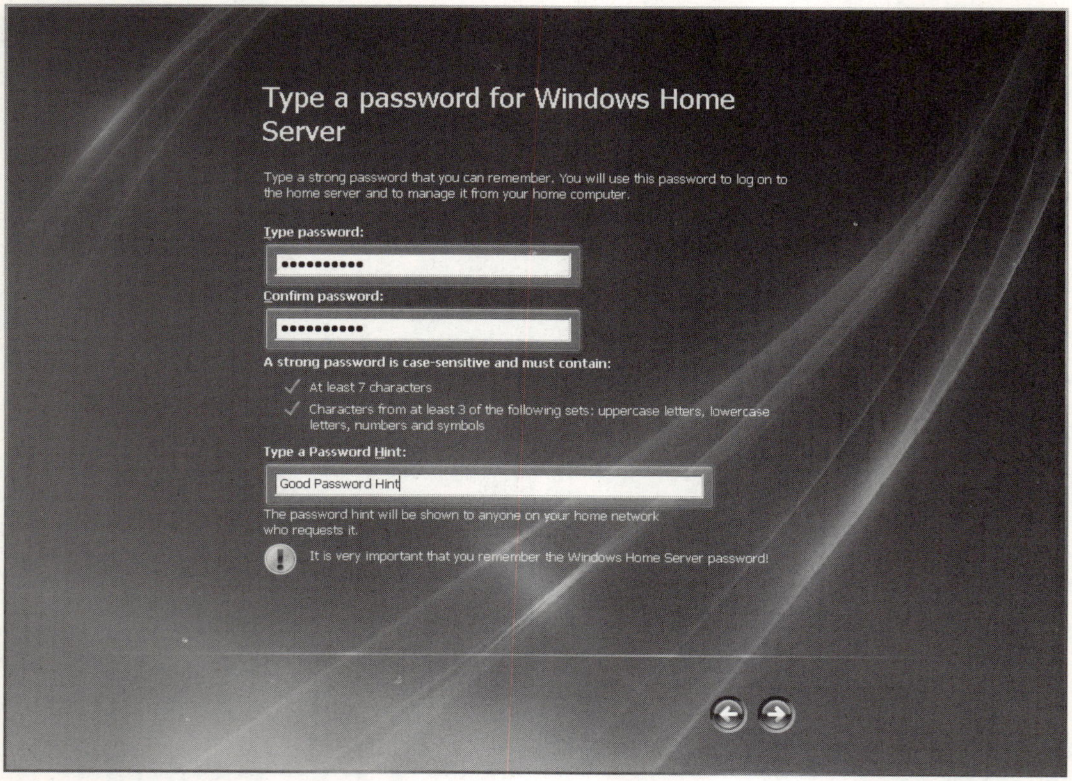

Figure 5-14

You must enter the password twice, and you can enter a hint that will help you recall the password if you forget. Although writing down passwords is generally not a good practice, you should consider writing down your Windows Home Server password and storing it in a safe location. You may not use this password very often, and passwords that are not used are forgotten very easily. Once you have set up your server, the Connector software, and your user accounts, you may go weeks or even months without needing to use your home server password, and because it is required for administration of the server, you will want to be able to find it!

After the password screen, you are prompted to configure Automatic Updates for your server, as shown in Figure 5-15. It is best to leave this option on, but if you want to be responsible for manually checking and installing updates on your server, you may choose to turn it off.

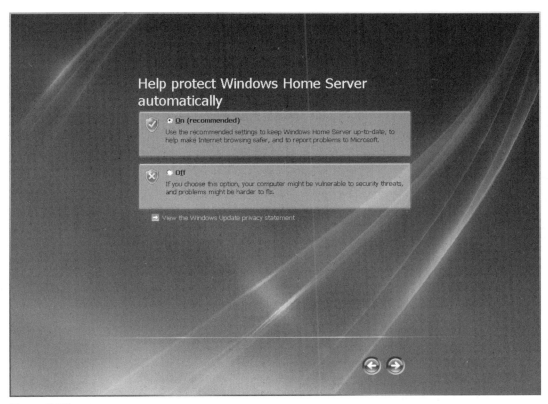

Figure 5-15

Next you are prompted to select whether you are willing to participate in Windows Home Server's Customer Experience Improvement Program as shown in Figure 5-16. This program allows the Windows Home Server software to share anonymous data about how your server is utilized with Microsoft. Microsoft uses this data to help the product team understand what features are used and how the system performs so that they can make better decisions about developing updates and future versions of Windows Home Server. You need to decide whether you are comfortable sharing this information with Microsoft. The information that is shared is very benign, but it is still a personal choice.

The next screen prompts you to turn on or off Windows Error Reporting, as shown in Figure 5-17. Windows Error Reporting automatically sends data to Microsoft whenever the Windows Home Server experiences a crash. This information is used by Microsoft to help them locate bugs so that they can be fixed via updates or in future versions of Windows Home Server. While this information is very useful to Microsoft, there is a slight chance that personal information can be included in the error report. Some crash reports may include references to files or even personal information that was present in memory at the time of the crash. Microsoft works hard to protect this information, and they promise to use it only for the purpose of fixing the software, but you must decide whether you are comfortable automatically sharing problem reports in this way.

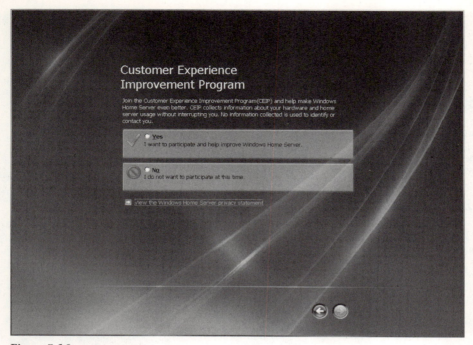

Figure 5-16

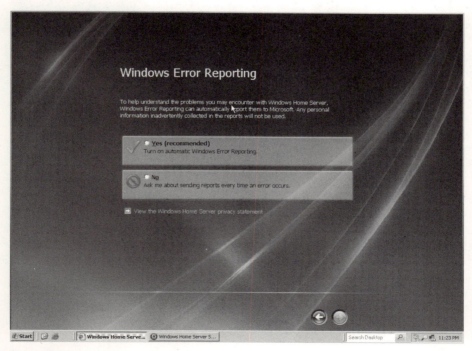

Figure 5-17

Chapter 5: Getting Started with Windows Home Server   **73**

Figure 5-18 shows the final screen of the setup program, including a few notes on how to proceed.

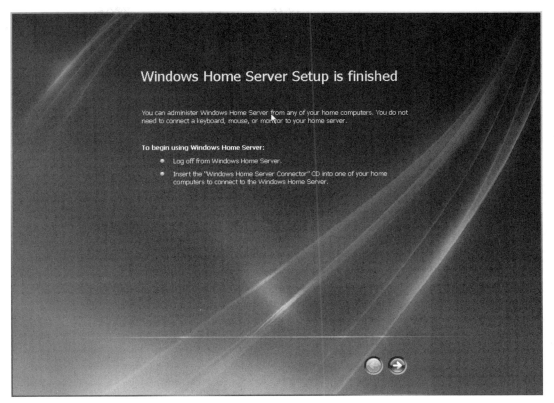

Figure 5-18

After you click the forward arrow one last time, you are presented with a fairly standard Windows desktop, as shown in Figure 5-19. Internet Explorer will open to display a warning message about interacting directly with your Windows Home Server desktop.

You may notice an alert on the desktop indicating that you need to activate Windows. Windows Home Server activation can be handled from a client computer through the Windows Home Server Console, so there is no need to act on the alert now. If you don't plan to leave a monitor and input devices attached, you can shut down your server from the Start button, disconnect the unneeded peripherals, and then power your server back on. Otherwise you can just log off, also via the Start button.

74 Chapter 5: Getting Started with Windows Home Server

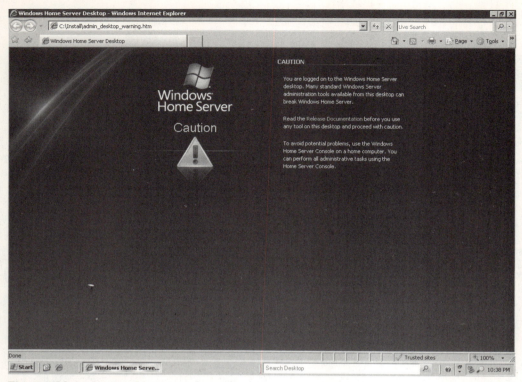

Figure 5-19

Setting Up a Retail/OEM Windows Home Server

If your server came with a quick-start guide, that is a better guide for setting up your specific server. The following guidelines highlight the general process.

After you have found a location for your server, and supplied it with power and an Ethernet connection, it is time to power it on. Find your server's power button and press it. The system should come to life, and you will see lights indicating that power is on, and that the hard drive is doing work, loading the Windows Home Server operating system.

Now is a good time to double-check that your Ethernet connection is working properly. If the switch and cabling are working, you will see one solid light on the Ethernet port where the home server is plugged into your home network's switch, router, or modem. If your home server's network port has indicator lights, you will see a solid light there as well. The other light on these interfaces might blink occasionally as the server starts up.

Some Windows Home Server machines come with a special setup program that can be run from a client computer. Others just have a default password that can be used when you first need to connect to the home server.

If your server has a setup program, the choices will likely include the server name and password. Some manufacturers may also include steps to set up user accounts, add data to the server, or configure the special features that the manufacturer has included.

Connecting Your Home Network

Now that your Windows Home Server is operational, it is time to connect your home computers so that they can be protected by, and make use of the resources available on your server. The Connector software can be installed on any computer in your home network (other than your Windows Home Server machine). This software installation is run from within Windows. To get started, place the Windows Home Server Connector CD into your computer's CD-ROM or DVD-ROM drive. The setup program should start immediately, but if not, browse and launch the Setup.exe program from the root of the CD.

Note
It is possible to load the software from Windows Home Server's shared folders. Open \\Server\Software\Home Server Connector Software\ from Windows Explorer and double-click the setup executable. If you are prompted for a username and password, use "Administrator" for the username, and your Windows Home Server's administration password. The remainder of the process is identical to installing from CD.

The Setup program begins with an introduction screen that highlights the functionality provided by the Windows Home Server Connector software (see Figure 5-20).

Figure 5-20

The next screen contains the End-User License Agreement (see Figure 5-21). Be sure that you are comfortable with the terms of the agreement before you click Next.

After the setup program searches the network and locates your Windows Home Server, you must enter your Windows Home Server administration password (see Figure 5-22). This is the password that you selected during the installation of your Windows Home Server, and is different from any user accounts that may have been set up. If you provided a password hint when you created your password, that hint can be shown by clicking the Password Hint button.

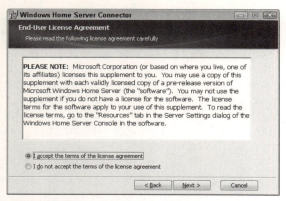

Figure 5-21

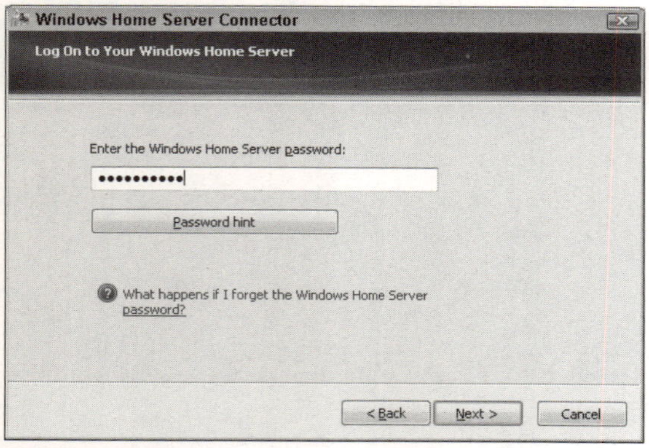

Figure 5-22

The setup program joins your computer to the Windows Home Server and sets up the Connector software for default backup settings, as shown in Figure 5-23.

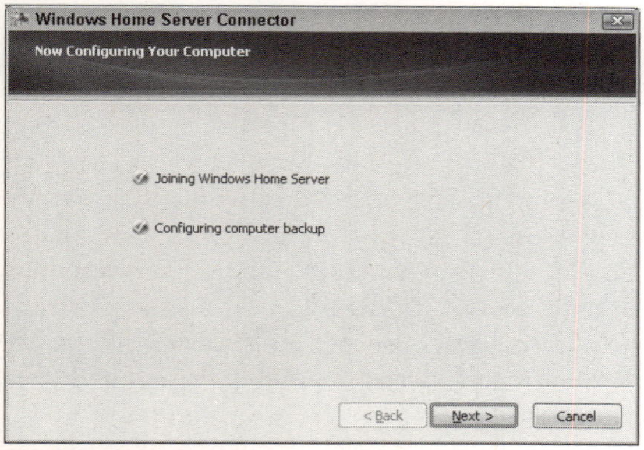

Figure 5-23

A confirmation screen is displayed (see Figure 5-24), indicating that your computer is now configured for Windows Home Server. The default backup schedule is displayed as well.

Figure 5-24

If your current username and password do not match an account on the server, you will receive an alert that indicates that your account is not recognized by Windows Home Server. It will present an option to correct this. User accounts are covered in more detail in Chapter 6.

Note

If any of your client computer's hard drives are formatted with FAT instead of NTFS, the confirmation screen will include a warning that the FAT volume will not be backed up. Windows Home Server's backup technology relies on some unique features available in NTFS, so if you want these volumes backed up, you should convert them to NTFS. The warning includes a link to more information about how to convert drives.

You should repeat the connector setup process for every computer that you want to be protected by Windows Home Server's backup functionality.

Summary

Your Windows Home Server machine is now located somewhere in your home that will balance its usefulness and reliability. The Windows Home Server software is setup, configured, and ready to serve your home network. With the addition of the Connector software, all of your home computers will be backed up on a regular daily schedule, protecting you from data loss and giving you access to previous versions of files to protect against accidental deletions or modifications.

This basic level of functionality will tend to fade into the background, but you will be able to rest easier knowing that your data is protected. The next time you accidentally delete a file, or overwrite an important document, you will be able to quickly and painlessly recover the file with just a few mouse clicks. That is the beauty of how Windows Home Server can protect your digital life.

Chapter 6

Creating and Using Accounts

User accounts are how Windows Home Server identifies who you are and what files and resources you can access. You will probably want to create a user account on the server for each individual who uses computers in your home. You may also want to make use of Windows Home Server's Guest account. Setting up accounts will give you and the members of your home network access to your computers, and your server and will give you control over who has access to specific files and resources.

Windows Home Server does not require user accounts to run its backup services. User accounts are utilized primarily to provide access control for shared folders and remote access. It is recommended that you create matching user accounts on your home computers as well, so that you can access resources on the server without having to enter an additional password.

Basics of User Accounts

User accounts are familiar to everyone who uses computers. We use them to log in to our email services, computers at work, and a variety of websites. The pairing of a username and a password is one of the most basic security mechanisms that computers use in order to identify who we are. The two tenets of security that user accounts help system designers address are authentication and authorization.

Authentication

Authentication provides the local computer and the server with a method for determining who you are. Password authentication is one of the more basic modes. It is used by most home computers, and it is the method that is utilized by Windows Home Server. Password authentication requires you to make a claim as to who you are (which is the username), and then you have to provide a piece of information that only you should know (which is your password). Assuming that you don't share your password with other people or write it down and post it by your computer, this is a reasonable and low-cost way of verifying a user's identity.

Some other kinds of authentication include biometrics like fingerprints, iris scans, and facial recognition. Smartcards are an implementation of another type of authentication known as cryptographic authentication. Cryptographic authentication is a special type of authentication that allows you to verify your identity by proving that you are in possession of a special kind of data known as a certificate, which is often stored on a chip contained in a Smartcard.

When two or more of these options are used together, it is known as multifactor authentication. The most secure systems will often combine biometrics, cryptographic authentication, and a password or PIN. By layering multiple types of authentication together, it is much less likely that someone can impersonate an authorized individual.

Windows Home Server simply utilizes a username and password pair as its method for authentication. Just knowing who you are is not extremely useful by itself, which leads to the concept of *authorization*.

Authorization

Once the computer knows who you are, it can make decisions about what you are allowed to do. In Windows we typically think of this concept in terms of file permissions. We can configure files and shares to allow or disallow access to individuals based on their identity. Windows then takes this information and makes decisions when the user attempts to access a resource.

Creating Accounts

One of the frequently requested features that didn't make it into version one of Windows Home Server was the capability of the server to function as a centralized user directory. Most people who use computers at work are familiar with the idea that a user account can be created on a server and then used to log in to any machine on the network. For both technical and product planning reasons, this functionality was left off the list for the initial release of Windows Home Server.

What does this mean for users? A bit of extra work to make things run smoothly. Whenever users attempt to access a shared resource on the server from the local network, the server is going to want to know who they are (authentication) so that it can determine whether they are allowed to access that particular file or resource (authorization). If you are logged in to the local machine with a user account that has the same username and password as an account on the Windows Home Server machine, this will happen seamlessly without requiring any additional action from the user. If the local username or password does not match, the user will be prompted to enter a new username and password before they can access the resource.

In a sense, creating matching user accounts on your local computers and on Windows Home Server is optional, but as a matter of convenience it can be very helpful. Also, Windows Home Server's Connector software will generate alerts warning you repeatedly if you don't have matching accounts set up, which can become a nuisance.

Unfortunately, creating these matching accounts requires several steps. First, you need to decide on a username and password to use. If you are running Windows XP or Windows Vista, you already have at least one account defined, and you may choose to continue to use that account's username and password. If that is the case, you just need to create the account on Windows Home Server as described later in this chapter.

The ideal mode for which Windows Home Server is designed is for each computer user to have their own unique user account, and for these accounts to be created on both the server and on all of the client machines. This model allows access to files and folders to be controlled per user, and it automatically creates a shared folder on the server where each user can keep his or her own personal files. Unless you already have implemented this one-account-per-person model, this will entail a great deal of work, especially if you have several computers. A reasonable compromise is to create accounts for everyone on the server and then only create matching accounts on the client machines that each individual actually uses.

Creating an Account on Windows Home Server

In order to create accounts and have them work properly with Windows Home Server, you have to create the same account through both the Windows Home Server Console and through your computer's Control Panel. For anyone who is familiar with how Windows domains work in a business environment, this is a bit of a disappointment, but centralized user management was something that Microsoft decided not to address in version one of Windows Home Server. It is important that you make sure that your username and passwords match between Windows Home Server and your computers. Otherwise you will be prompted whenever you try to access shared resources on your server.

The first step toward creating a usable account is to create the account on your home server. This task is accomplished through the Windows Home Server Console. The Windows Home Server Console is an application that is run from one of your client machines in order to interact with your Windows Home Server machine. Almost all configuration of Windows Home Server can be performed through this console. You can start the console by selecting Windows Home Server Console from the Start menu on a client computer, or you can right-click the Windows Home Server status icon in the system tray and select Windows Home Server Console from the context menu that pops up. To enter the Windows Home Server Console, you will be prompted to enter the administrative password for your home server. Many people get confused at this point, especially after they have created a *user* account for themselves on the server. The Windows Home Server Console always needs the *administrative* password; your *user account* password simply will not work. Because adding users to Windows Home Server requires the administrative password, it should only be performed by someone who is trusted and understands the operations of Windows Home Server. The console gives access to a multitude of settings and options, so you don't want to give this password out to everyone.

After you have opened the administrative console, click the User Accounts button at the top. This opens the User Accounts page as shown in Figure 6-1.

Figure 6-1

Chapter 6: Creating and Using Accounts

Click the Add button to display the window shown in Figure 6-2. In this window you can enter the user's first and last name, and there is a separate input for username. The username is the most important piece of information. For Windows Home Server to recognize the accounts that you use on your local computers, both the usernames and the passwords must match.

Figure 6-2

You have an option to enable remote access for the user account when you create it. This will determine if this user account can be used to access files and computers remotely through Windows Home Server's web interface. You can always change this later if you need to. The one immediate effect that selecting the Remote Access checkbox will have is that it will require you to use a stronger password for the account.

After you enter the username and other details, click Next. The next dialog box, shown in Figure 6-3, prompts you to enter a password. If you enabled remote access in the previous dialog box, Windows Home Server will require a password that is at least seven characters long and meets particular complexity requirements (which will be discussed later in this chapter in the section "Enabling and Disabling Remote Access"). Otherwise, the default password requirement simply requires that passwords be at least five characters long. You must confirm the password, and then click Next. As you enter the password the first time, the interface will display an icon next to the Length and if required the Complexity labels below the password boxes. The icon is a small circle initially, and it will change to a green check once each requirement has been met.

Chapter 6: Creating and Using Accounts

Figure 6-3

The next dialog box will give you an opportunity to configure share permissions for all existing shares on your server. If you have created any custom shared folders (discussed more in Chapter 8), or if there are other User shares on your Windows Home Server (User shares are created automatically when you create a user), this dialog box, shown in Figure 6-4, will let you set permissions for each folder to Full, Read, or None. Full allows the user to read and write files under the share. Read allows the user to open files but not change or delete them. None disallows any read access, and the user will not even be able to see a listing of the files in the folder, nor will they be able to change or delete files. These permissions options are discussed in more detail later in the chapter in the section "Changing Folder Permissions," and related permissions considerations are discussed in the sidebar "Using Passwords in the Home."

Note
Users of Windows Home Server should remember that anyone with the administrative password can give themselves access to any of the shares existing on the server, including the personal shares that are created with each user account. There is no way to prevent the administrator from accessing files, so users should be mindful of the data they store on the server, and the administrative password should be kept safe and not shared.

Chapter 6: Creating and Using Accounts

Figure 6-4

After you click Next one last time, Windows Home Server will create your account, and then show a dialog box confirming that it has created the account and set up access to shares appropriately. Click Finish to exit the confirmation dialog box.

You have now completed the first step in creating a usable account for Windows Home Server. Unless you were creating an account to match an existing account on a client computer, the next step is to create a matching account on your client computer.

User Account Control Makes Your Computer More Secure

Windows Vista will sometimes prompt and request permission to perform a task. Some people find this to be an annoyance, but it is really just one element of Windows Vista that makes it more difficult for hackers or viruses to take control of your machine. Operations and programs that require extra permissions are often marked with a shield overlaid on the program icon.

Actions such as installing software, adding user accounts, or even changing firewall settings will trigger the User Account Control (UAC) dialog box. When this happens, the remainder of your desktop is grayed out to make sure that you address the User Account Control dialog box, as shown in the following figure.

Chapter 6: Creating and Using Accounts

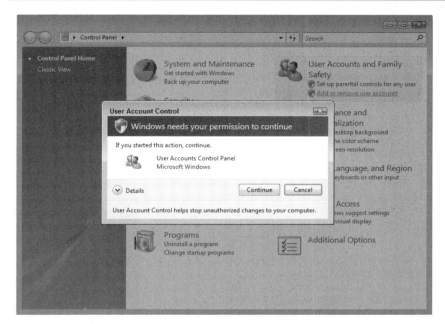

User Account Control is only useful if you train yourself to make good decisions when you are presented with a choice. If you are not currently doing something that seems like it might require elevated privileges, then you should click Cancel. For example, if you are presented with a UAC dialog box while you are surfing the Internet, reading email, or instant messaging with a friend, it may be a sign that a virus is attempting to load new software onto your PC. Carefully read the dialog, and decide if it is the result of something that you really want to do, and if not click Cancel.

One other aspect of this is that you need to train the other members of your household to always click Cancel as a first instinct and only click Continue if they know why the dialog box has appeared. My kindergartner saw me working on the computer the other day and surprised me by telling me that I should always click Cancel when those boxes pop up. Many people who have been using computers for many years have a gut instinct that tells us to click OK, because many features of software have trained us that clicking OK is just part of using a computer. "Are you sure you want to Exit the Program?" "Are you sure you want to delete this file?" You must try to retrain yourself and the other computer users in your house to always click the Cancel button unless they have a good reason to select continue.

One other interesting feature of User Account Control is that it will give you the option to enter different credentials if the currently logged in account does not have the appropriate permissions to perform the action that is being initiated. This means that you can set up your family to use Standard (non-administrator) user accounts, and if they need to do something that requires administrative rights, they will be presented with a dialog box that requests different credentials. This means that you or another person with an Administrator account can just enter their username and password without requiring the first person to log out. This feature makes it very reasonable to have just one or two members of the household that have administrative accounts.

Creating an Account on Your PC

If you need to create additional accounts on your computers, or if you have decided to create a new account to match your Windows Home Server user accounts, this section will walk you through the process. If you are only going to use your client computer's existing accounts, you don't need to create additional accounts.

Depending on your operating system version, the steps to create an account on your PC might vary slightly. The process for Windows Vista follows, but it should be similar for other versions of Windows. You need to be logged in with an account that is in the Administrators group. If you are using the first account that you set up when you installed Windows or when you set up a new PC, your account should be in the Administrators group.

The first step is to open the Control Panel. If you click the Start orb in the lower left corner of your desktop, you can select Control Panel from the menu that appears.

The default view for the Control Panel is shown in Figure 6-5. To add a user account, click Add or remove user accounts under the User Accounts and Family Safety heading. If your Control Panel doesn't look like Figure 6-5, you may have enabled Classic View. To return to the default view, just click Control Panel Home in the upper left corner of the Control Panel window.

Figure 6-5

Vista's User Account Control will ask permission to continue, because adding accounts requires elevated privileges. Click Continue and Vista's Manage Accounts screen appears, as shown in Figure 6-6.

Chapter 6: Creating and Using Accounts

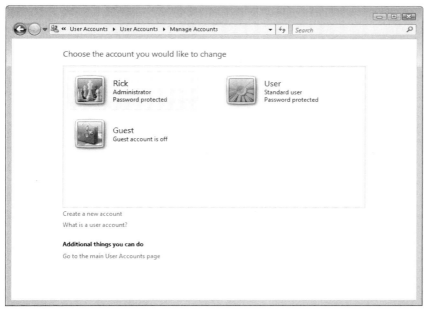

Figure 6-6

Click Create a new account from the task list at the bottom to display the Create New Account screen, as shown in Figure 6-7. There is a text box in which to enter the username. This username needs to match exactly the username that you created through the Windows Home Server Console in the "Creating an Account on Windows Home Server" section. There is also a selection for designating the new account as a Standard user or as an Administrator. For almost every situation, new accounts should be created as standard user to help protect the security of your PC. If a certain member of your family installs or uninstalls software frequently, or if they develop software, they may need to be designated as an administrator. This can always be changed later, so it's best to err on the side of security and start accounts off as standard users, and change it later if you decide you need to. Also, you should remember that you can designate an account as an administrator on a certain PC, and leave that account as a standard user on other PCs.

Next click Create Account and Windows will complete the creation of your account. Next you need to add a password to the account. After you create the account, you are returned to the Manage Accounts screen. From this screen, click your new account, and it will open the account maintenance screen for that user, as shown in Figure 6-8. From this screen you can manage the details of the account, including changing the display picture, changing the account type from standard to administrator, or like you want to do now, setting the password for a user.

Click the Create a Password task to display the Create Password dialog box shown in Figure 6-9. In this dialog box, you must type the new password into the New Password and Confirm New Password text boxes. You have the option to include a password hint as well. If you choose to use a password hint, make sure that it is something that will help you remember your password without giving any hints to someone else who is trying to gain access to your account. Also remember that this password needs to match the password that you used when you created the account on Windows Home Server.

Chapter 6: Creating and Using Accounts

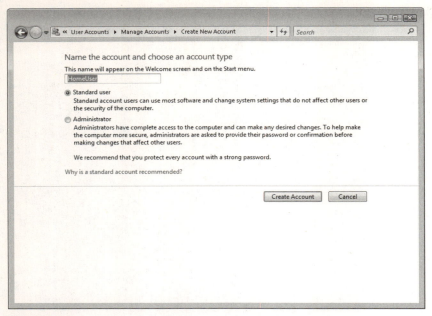

Figure 6-7

Figure 6-8

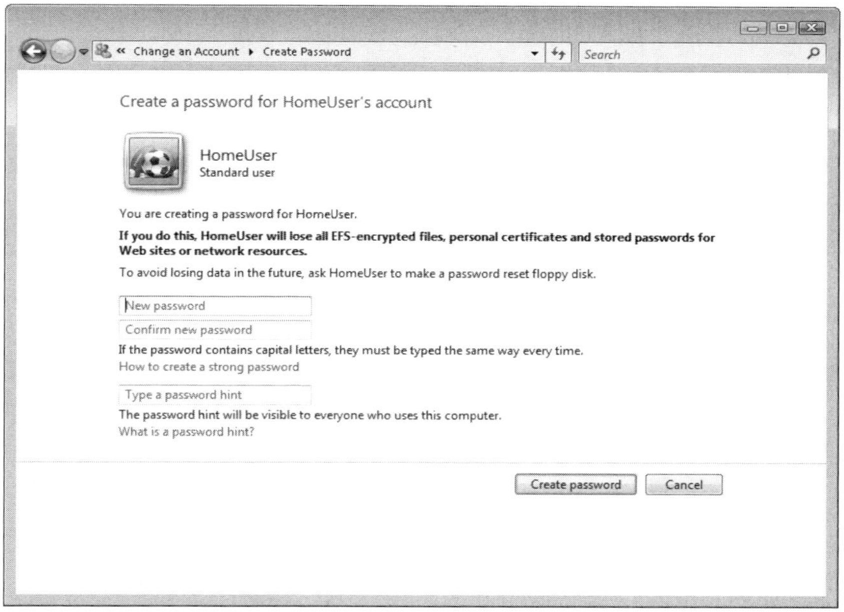

Figure 6-9

The Warnings on the screen about EFS-encrypted files, personal certificates, and stored passwords do not apply for brand-new accounts. If you use this tool to change a password after the account has been used, there is a risk of losing encrypted files or saved credentials. If you need to change a password for an account that has been used, you should first log in to that account and then open the Change your password task from the User Accounts Control Panel. That will preserve all saved credentials and encrypted files.

After you enter and confirm the password, click the Create Password button. You've now set up your new account with a password. You will need to repeat this process for every account that you wish to use with Windows Home Server, and you will also have to repeat it on each computer where the account user will want to log in. This can be a daunting task if you have a large number of computer users and a large number of PCs. You only have to do this one time, though, and it will make your home network more manageable and usable. Remember that if a particular user never uses a certain PC, then you don't need to create a matching account for them on that particular PC. Also, if an individual only occasionally uses a computer, he or she can utilize Windows Home Server's remote access website (described in detail in Chapter 11), even from within the home network, to access his or her files while working under a different user's account.

Using Passwords in the Home

Many home users do not enable passwords on home computers, and this may be a difficult transition for some people. If you only have one PC or if each PC has only one non-password protected account, and everyone runs under the same user account with no password, adding user accounts for each of your family members may seem like a hassle. In actuality, there is no requirement to use multiple user accounts with Windows Home Server, so feel free to continue operating under one account until you decide that the benefits of giving everyone their own account are worth the extra effort.

Giving everyone their own account allows you to set up *granular control* for access to resources. Granular control means that you can make different decisions for different pieces of information and different individuals. For example, you may want to give Mom and Dad access to all the files that the kids store on the server (which relates to the *Full* access level), but restrict the kids from viewing your financial files (which relates to the *None* access level). You could give a younger child access to view pictures and music stored on the server, but not give him or her the ability to overwrite or modify the pictures (which relates to the *Read* access level).

Another benefit to each individual having their own account applies to the computers where they log in. If users have separate accounts, then they can set up their profile and settings differently according to their own needs and tastes. This way using a computer can be a more personalized experience.

If members of your family are resistant to using passwords to access their computers, one option is to set passwords and then set up each computer to log in to the primary user's account. This enables the user to access resources on the Windows Home Server machine without leaving those resources unprotected. To set up auto-login on Windows Vista, use the following process: Press ⊞+R to open a Run dialog box. In the Run box, type **netplwiz** and press Enter. Windows Vista's User Account Control will ask for permission to continue, because you are modifying the security settings of the machine. Click Continue. The user accounts tool appears as shown in the following figure.

Click the box next to the Users must enter a username and password to use this computer option to deselect it. Click OK. A dialog box pops up, as shown in the following figure. In this dialog box, you can enter the username and password for the account that you want to automatically log in to the computer.

Once you enter this information, your computer will automatically log in to the specified user account when you boot up. You can still access other user accounts by choosing to log out from the first account or by using Fast User Switching. Use ⊞+L to quickly lock one account and return to the Welcome screen.

Using the Update Password Tool

One tool that Windows Home Server provides to assist with passwords is the Update Password tool. You can access it by right-clicking the Windows Home Server icon in the system tray and selecting Update Password. If your current password already matches the password for your user account on Windows Home Server, the Update Password option will be grayed out and will not be available.

Changing a Password

If you need to change the password for one of your accounts, first change it on your PC. A quick shortcut to do this is to press Ctrl+Alt+Del, and then select Change a Password on the resulting screen, as shown in Figure 6-10.

After you change your password on the PC, the Update Password tool may not be immediately available. To make it available, log off and then log back into Windows. Now you should be able to select Update Password by right-clicking the Windows Home Server icon in the system tray. The resulting screen is shown in Figure 6-11. On this screen you should select Keep my password on this computer, and then enter your new password in the Password on this computer text box, and enter your old password in the Password on the home server text box. Click OK and your passwords will be synchronized.

Updating the Rest of Your PCs

You must repeat a similar process on any other computers that you use this account for. On the other computers, select Keep my password on the home server, enter your old password in the Password on this computer text box, and enter your new password in the Password on the home server text box.

92 Chapter 6: Creating and Using Accounts

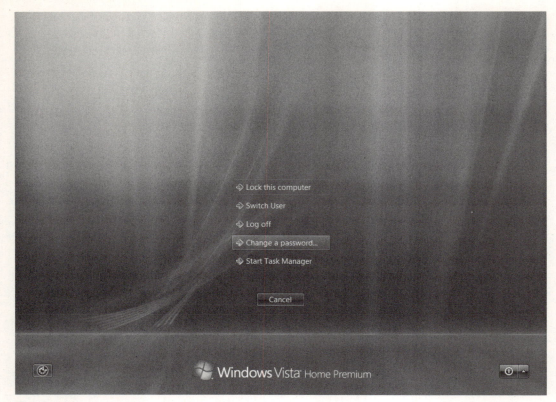

Figure 6-10

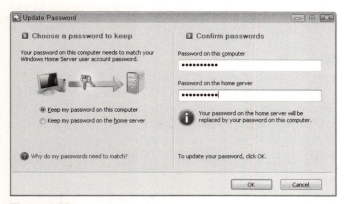

Figure 6-11

Why Is This So Complicated?

Anyone who uses computers in a corporate environment may be wondering why managing users for Windows Home Server has to be so complicated. Microsoft's business servers use a feature called an Active Directory domain to house a centralized user database. User accounts are centrally managed, and if you update a password on one computer, it applies everywhere. The desire for this functionality to be in Windows Home Server is a frequent request, and it would seem that the Windows Home Server team could have borrowed the technology to make it happen.

Unfortunately several technical and business hurdles made it so that version 1 of Windows Home Server does not have centralized user management. One of the major stumbling blocks was that the Home editions of Windows Vista and Windows XP do not support the functionality required to join the computer to a domain, and for Active Directory to work you have to be able to join the PCs to the server's domain. This is both a technological and a business hurdle. Microsoft does not include this functionality on the Home versions partly because they do not want businesses to use the less expensive Home editions on computers that are part of a business network.

It is technologically feasible that Microsoft could make it so that the Home editions could join *only* a domain that is hosted on Windows Home Server, but doing so would not be a trivial undertaking, so the Windows Home Server team left it off the list for round one. Hopefully we'll see centralized user management in version 2. In the meantime, we can hope that some enterprising developer develops an add-on that will simplify user management.

Should You Enable the Guest Account?

Windows Home Server includes the ability to have a Guest account, but it is turned off by default. Turning on the Guest account makes sense for some networks, but doing so should be considered carefully because it can impact the security of your network.

What Is the Guest Account Used For?

The Guest account is used to give permission to read, change, or create files on the Windows Home Server to individuals who do not have accounts on the server. If you have family or friends who bring computers to your home network and who you would like to have access to some of your files, then the Guest account is the right tool for the job. You can set up the Guest account to only have read access to certain shares, or you can even give write access if you want your guests to be able to change or add files to the server. If your visitors are going to use your computer, remember that if they are logged in under your account, they will have the same access to data on the server that you do. If you want to eliminate this as a risk, you can enable Windows' Guest account through the same screen shown earlier in Figure 6-6.

If you have an unsecured wireless network or a wired network that has jacks that are available to strangers, you need to be aware that enabling the Guest account may allow unauthorized individuals to access your files. If you give the Guest account read-only access, this is a problem of disclosure, but if you give the Guest account write access to any shares, a malicious individual might choose to delete or modify your data. For that matter, even a well-intentioned friend or relative might inadvertently alter or destroy files that are important to you.

If you have a good reason for using the Guest account, you should carefully consider the security that the rest of your network provides so that you make sure that you don't inadvertently leave your data vulnerable. The Guest account is not required to have a password, but if you are uncertain about the security of your network or if you just want to be careful, you can set a password for the Guest account and then simply provide that password to any guests who need it.

Enabling the Guest Account

To enable the Guest account, you first have to open the Windows Home Server Console. You do this by right-clicking the Windows Home Server icon in the system tray and selecting Windows Home Server Console. You must enter your server's Administrator password. Once the console is open, select the User Accounts object at the top. This screen was shown earlier in Figure 6-1. Click the Guest account to highlight it, and then click the Properties button on the menu bar. The Properties dialog box is shown in Figure 6-12.

Figure 6-12

In the Properties dialog box, click the Enable Account button. This starts a wizard that will assist you with configuring your Guest account. The first page of the wizard introduces the concept of the Guest account. Click Next. The second page of the wizard, shown in Figure 6-13, allows you to set a password for the Guest account. If you want to set a password, select the radio button next to Create a Guest Password, and then enter and confirm a password in the two text boxes. Click Next again.

The following page, shown in Figure 6-14, lets you set permissions for the Guest account. For every share on your server, you have the option of giving the Guest account Full access, Read access, or None. Full access allows the Guest account to read, write, delete, add, or change any file on the

Chapter 6: Creating and Using Accounts

share. Read access only allows the Guest account to open and view, but not change files on the share. None means that the Guest account will not even be able to see what files are on the share, and they will not be able to view or change the files.

Figure 6-13

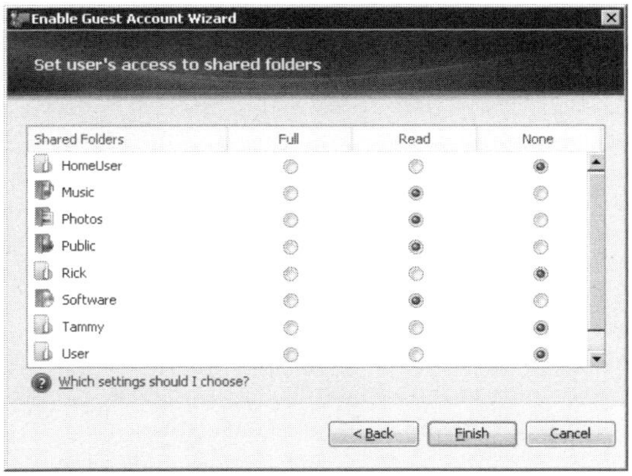

Figure 6-14

After you select the permissions you want the Guest account to have, click the Finish button to complete the wizard. Windows Home Server displays a confirmation that the Guest account is enabled. Click Done to exit the wizard.

Your Guest account is now usable. When your guests are hooked into your network and they want to access your server, just tell them to use the username Guest and if you set a password, provide them with the password. The first time they attempt to access the server, they will be prompted for a username and password.

If you ever wish to disable the Guest account or change the password associated with it, just return to the Properties dialog box and select the appropriate button.

Managing Permissions

User accounts by default have access only to their personal folder, found in the Users share, and to all of the default shares that Windows Home Server creates. If you need to give users access to different shares, or if you need to add or remove individuals who can remotely access files and computers on your network, you must use the Windows Home Server console to make these changes.

Changing Folder Permissions

Start the Windows Home Server Console by right-clicking the Windows Home Server icon in the system tray and selecting Windows Home Server Console from the context menu. Select the User Accounts object at the top to open the User Accounts page, as was shown previously in Figure 6-1. Click on the user for whom you want to change permissions, and click the Properties button on the menu bar. The Properties dialog box opens for the user. Select the Shared Folder Access tab from the top, as shown in Figure 6-15.

Figure 6-15

All of the shares available on your server will be listed, and the circles, also called radio buttons, let you select the appropriate level of access that the user needs for each share. Full access lets the user add, delete, change, and read any file in that share. Read access lets the user open and view, but not change the files in a share. None denies access to any files, and will not let the user see, add, or change any files in the share. Once you select the appropriate access for each share, click OK to apply the changes. When selecting access options, remember that you must give full access to any individuals who might need to modify the contents of a share folder, or add data to it. For example, if one of your kids likes to rip music CDs and you want them to store the music on your Windows Home Server, you must give them Full access to the music folder. Another family member may just be interested in listening to music, so you could provide them Read access so that they don't run the risk of accidentally deleting or damaging files. You should also remember to protect sensitive files such as financial documents and tax returns from younger children. In addition to personal privacy concerns, they may accidentally disclose information, or be coerced into exposing it if they have access to it, and because there is no real need for them to have access, it is better to set their permission for these kinds of files to None.

If a user is currently logged in to a machine and accessing files on the server when you make these changes, they may not take effect immediately. If a user is having trouble accessing a share that you just provided permission to, have them log out and log in again in order to refresh the permissions list with the server.

Enabling and Disabling Remote Access

Start the Windows Home Server Console by right-clicking the Windows Home Server icon in the system tray and selecting Windows Home Server Console from the context menu. Select the User Accounts object at the top to open the User Accounts page, as shown previously in Figure 6-1. Click the user for whom you want to change remote access permissions, and click the Properties button on the menu bar. A Properties dialog box opens for the user, as shown in Figure 6-16.

Figure 6-16

To enable remote access, select the Enable remote access for this user checkbox on the property page. When you enable remote access for an account, Windows Home Server checks to see if the password is strong enough, because Windows Home Server requires strong passwords to be used for remote access. If the password is not strong enough, you will be prompted to change the password in order to continue. For Windows Home Server, a strong password must have at least seven characters, and it must have at least three of the following character types:

- Uppercase letters
- Lowercase letters

- Numbers
- Symbols (such as $, @, !, %, and so on)

After you have selected the checkbox and if necessary changed the password, click OK to save the changes and exit the dialog box.

If you had to change the password for this account, remember that you will have to change the passwords for the matching accounts on your PCs. You can use Update Password tool, referenced earlier in this chapter. Just follow the instructions in the "Updating the Rest of Your PCs" subsection, and be sure to visit every computer where the password is used, including the computer you used to log in to the Windows Home Server Console.

To disable remote access, you follow these same steps and deselect the Enable remote access for this user checkbox. Remote Access is discussed in greater detail in Chapter 11.

Summary

User accounts are the method that you use to identify individuals so that your Windows Home Server can provide appropriate access to files and resources. By setting up user accounts for all computer users on your home network, everyone will have their own personal space on the server, and you can better control who has access to view or modify data on the server. An additional benefit is that individuals will have more freedom to set up their PCs in a way that suits them, because their settings will be saved separately under their unique user account.

You learned that setting up user accounts to work with Windows Home Server is a multistep process, requiring you to first set up the account on the server, and then set up an identical account on each PC where the account will be used. You also learned how to change your password, and the steps you need to take to keep your password synchronized between your PC and your server.

You also learned about situations where you may want to enable the Guest account, and you now know how to go about setting it up.

Finally, you learned how to change the access that an account has to the shares on your Windows Home Server, and how to enable or disable remote access.

Chapter 7

Creating and Managing Backups

One of the most useful things that Windows Home Server can do for your home network is to keep your files and computers backed up. With a default installation of the Windows Home Server Connector software on your PCs, Windows Home Server will automatically back up each PC every night. You can configure the times that this happens, and you can designate which drives are included and which folders are excluded. If a computer is going to be unavailable for a long period of time, you can disable backups for that machine so that it does not generate network health warnings. If you have mobile PCs, or if you turn off your PCs at night, you need to understand how this will affect Windows Home Server's ability to backup your computers and how to change the backup schedule to a more convenient time.

This chapter will teach you what the default settings are, provide you with an understanding of when the defaults may need to be changed, and show you how to make the changes if necessary.

Backup Defaults

You should understand the basics of how Windows Home Server configures backups so that you can make sure that the settings work well for your situation. For many folks the standard settings will work just fine, but there are situations where they will not be optimal or may not work at all. This section will let you know what the defaults are, and the following sections will outline the circumstances that may lead you to select different options for your Windows Home Server setup.

By default, Windows Home Server will initiate backups sometime between 12:00 A.M. and 6:00 A.M., based on the local time set on your server. Only one PC will be backed up at a given time, and this six hour window provides plenty of time to complete backups during a time when many people are not going to be using their PCs.

Windows Home Server will keep backups according to a retention schedule. The default schedule will keep three daily backups, three weekly backups, and three monthly backups.

Windows Home Server will include any hard drive volumes that were present when the Connector software was installed. If you add a disk drive or if you create an additional volume on an existing drive, or if you remove a drive or partition that was previously backed up, you must run the Backup Configuration Wizard in order to add the drive to the backup configuration, as shown later in this chapter.

Windows Home Server excludes certain folders and files that Windows uses as temporary storage, because backing these up would waste space on the server and would not be useful when restoring data. A default backup configuration excludes the system page file, user temporary files, client-side cache folders, and if present, the hibernation file. The system page file is used by Windows to supplement the physical memory in your computer. User temporary files are used by Windows and other programs to temporarily save data to disk while they are running. Client-side cache files are used to temporarily store files that make up the web pages that you view in your Internet browser. The hibernation file is usually only found on mobile computers such as laptops, and it is used to store the contents of your computer's memory so that it can be powered down and turned back on without losing any of your work. All of these various files are of little use for restoring your computer or files, so they are excluded.

Note

Hibernation is often enabled by default on laptops and other computers that run off batteries, but it can be useful on desktop machines as well. It can be enabled through the Control Panel's Power Options section. Hibernation allows you to save all of your work, all open files, web pages, and all running programs, and resume working at exactly the same point where you stopped. The hibernation file, if it exists, saves the contents of RAM when the system has been set to Hibernate. When the computer is powered back on, the contents of the hibernation file are loaded back in to RAM, and your computer will be back in the state it was in before it was put to sleep. Hibernation also goes by the name Suspend to Disk or sometimes just Sleep.

Managing Your Backup Schedule

Windows Home Server maintains a backup schedule that applies to all of the computers that it manages. Only one computer will be backed up at a time, so the backups will occur sequentially. Although initial backups can take a good amount of time, daily backups are much quicker because they only backup the files and portions of files that have changed since the last backup.

Constraints

You do not have the option of setting a different backup schedule for each computer, so you must choose settings that will allow all of your computers to complete their backups regularly. Also, the backup window must be contiguous, that is it cannot be split up to include two or more different chunks of time throughout the day. It must be a solid block of time. Lastly, the backup window must begin and end on whole-hour times, so you can't select 7:30 A.M. as a start time, you must choose either 7:00 A.M. or 8:00 A.M.

Considerations for Your Backup Schedule

For a computer to be backed up, it must either be powered on during the backup window, or it can be in Sleep or Hibernate mode. If a PC is in Sleep or Hibernate mode, Windows Home Server will power it on in order to complete the backup. As a precaution against draining the battery, mobile PCs must be plugged in; otherwise Windows Home Server will not power them on to perform a backup.

> **Note**
> Some computers and laptops will not automatically turn off after a backup is completed. For most machines this is not too big of an issue, especially because they won't be woken up if they are not plugged in. Some laptops cannot cool properly with the screen closed, so consider leaving the screen open if you know that the laptop will be woken up for a backup.

The default 6-hour time window from 12:00 A.M. to 6:00 A.M. that Windows Home Server provides is sufficient if all of your computers are desktop PCs, or laptops that are always plugged in, and if you never use the Hibernate option (also called Suspend to Disk by some manufacturers) in Windows, and if you never power down your PCs using the Shutdown option in Windows. Most multi-computer households will violate at least one of these constraints, so you will probably want to adjust the default schedule.

The defaults are provided to try to make sure that computers will be backed up during a time when they are not in use. While this is a decent goal, many PCs are used in ways such that they are not available to be backed up during times when they are not being used. I have run many backups on my home computers, and for a reasonably modern PC (Pentium 4 or newer) I've never run into any significant slowdowns because a backup was running in the background. The initial backup for each machine takes considerably longer, but the PC does not get significantly bogged down during the process.

The one consideration that you should keep in mind is that the network may get congested while your computers are being backed up. This is one of the reasons that multiple PCs do not attempt to perform backups in parallel. The main constraint on Windows Home Server's backup speed is the bandwidth available on the network connection between the PC and the server, so any extra traffic, such as browsing the Internet or accessing files on the home server, will have to compete with the backup traffic.

Deciding on a Schedule

To decide on a backup schedule, you should determine a time window that will overlap the times that your computers are available for backups, but give consideration for when the heaviest network demands are placed on your system. For example, if you always download a large amount of e-mail each morning when you power on your laptop, you probably don't want to have your computer trying to perform a backup at the same time. If your kids like to download music from Urge or iTunes after dinner, then that might be a bad time as well. Another activity that might cause conflicts is computer games that use a lot of CPU, hard drive, or network resources.

> **Tip**
> The amount of time that is needed for backups will vary greatly with your computer usage and with the speed of your network. The guideline that I have developed is to include at least 30 minutes for each computer that has at least a 100 Mbps Ethernet connection to the server, and at least one hour for every computer that will be backing up over a wireless connection or older 10 Mbps Ethernet. In addition, there is no harm in allowing a greater backup window, as long as it doesn't conflict with a time that you normally use your computers or network heavily.

Setting the Schedule

Once you have decided on the schedule for your backups, you need to tell Windows Home Server what times to use. This is accomplished through the Windows Home Server Console. Right-click the Windows Home Server icon in the system tray, and select Windows Home Server Console from the context menu. You must enter your Windows Home Server administrative password. Remember that this is different from your user password. This is the password that you entered when you first configured your Windows Home Server.

After you enter your password, the Windows Home Server Console appears similar to Figure 7-1. Select the Settings action in the upper-right corner of the console window.

Figure 7-1

The Settings dialog box is used to configure many options that apply to Windows Homes Server, and to all of the computers that it manages. The Settings dialog box defaults to the General options page. Select Backup from the task list on the left, to display the page shown in Figure 7-2. The other options shown in Figure 7-2, Automatic Backup Management and Backup Cleanup, are discussed later in this chapter.

Figure 7-2

The first section of this page, labeled Backup Time, allows you to set the backup schedule to match the needs of your home network. Use the controls in the Settings dialog box to change the hour and A.M. or P.M. designation for the start and end times. Remember that the start and end times must be whole-hour times. Also, if you have a relatively short backup window, it may be possible that a backup will continue to run past the end time. Once the end time comes, no new backup tasks will begin, but if a backup is already in progress, it will run until it completes or is manually canceled by a user. There are also some additional tasks that Windows Home Server performs during the backup window, such as the backup cleanup process that is run once a week. If this process consumes a very short backup window (for example, if it was set to 1 hour), then no computers would be backed up that night.

Note
Almost all Windows Home Server configuration dialog boxes contain hyperlinks that will open detailed information about all of the options presented on that particular dialog box.

After you have made the necessary changes to the schedule, click OK to save the settings and close the Settings dialog box. Your Windows Home Server and computers will begin using the new schedule immediately. If there was already a backup in progress when you made the change, that backup will continue to run, but all new backup tasks will follow the new schedule.

> **Note**
> Because the Windows Home Server client backup service runs as a Windows Service, the computer does not need to be logged in for a backup to run.

Managing Backup Retention

Backup Retention is just a fancy way of talking about how long Windows Home Server will keep backups before they are deleted to make room for new backups and files. Windows Home Server stores backups on the same volume as shared files, so in order to keep hard drive usage from growing unchecked, it has to periodically delete backups that are no longer needed.

> **Note**
> A volume can usually be thought of as being the same as a drive in a computer, but Windows Home Server's Drive Extender technology actually allows all of the disks that have been added to the storage pool to be used as a single volume. What this means for users is that with the exception of the system volume, which is reserved for the Windows Home Server operating software, all data is effectively stored on a single logical drive, or volume.

Considerations

For most home users, there are no hard fast rules for how long you should keep backups. In the business world there are often laws, regulations, or business rules that cover this topic, but for home users it is more a matter of the available hard drive space, and developing a level of comfort for how long you wish to keep data available.

Instead of putting a time limit on backup files, Windows Home Server requires you to specify how many backups you wish to keep. As part of this configuration, you can specify how many daily backups, weekly backups, and monthly backups to keep. Daily backups are pretty self explanatory, as they occur every day. Weekly backups are the first backup that occurs on any given calendar week, starting with Sunday. The weekly backup will usually be the backup that occurs on Sunday, but if the Sunday backup does not succeed, the first successful backup of the week will be tagged as the weekly backup. (You will be alerted about the failed backups and provided with a reason that they failed, so you should not have too many consecutive failures.) A monthly backup is the first backup that occurs in a calendar month. This will usually be the backup that occurs on the first of the month, but if that backup is not successful, the next successful backup will be tagged as the monthly backup.

Backups that do not succeed are kept in the backup list until the next cleanup cycle. They are identified with a red icon, just in case they contain data that you end up needing, but they are not counted for the purpose of the backup cleanup process. Also, if a backup is counted as a monthly backup, it will not be counted as a weekly or daily backup. Likewise, if a backup is counted as a weekly backup, it will not be counted as a daily backup. Backups are not "tagged" as daily, weekly, or monthly when they occur. They are only categorized this way during the cleanup process. Windows Home Server starts at the most recent successful backup and works its way backward. First it identifies the Monthly backups to save, then the Weekly, then the Daily, and then any other backups that have not been set manually to be retained are removed.

Keeping Important Backups

Individual backups can be marked to be saved regardless of the backup retention settings. This feature lets you tag important backups, such as the backup performed before you install a new piece of software, so that they are saved indefinitely. The last time I reformatted my laptop, I reinstalled all the software that I use, and then I created a backup and marked it to be retained. Because I keep all of my documents, pictures, and other important files on my home server, I can restore to this *clean* backup anytime my installation develops problems. I tend to install a lot of beta software on this machine, so this ability to quickly restore it to functionality to a known good configuration is a great timesaver for me.

Any time you initiate a manual backup, Windows Home Server automatically marks it to be saved. You can change this setting for individual backups through the Windows Home Server Console. To open the console right-click the Windows Home Server icon in the system tray, and select Windows Home Server Console from the context menu. Enter your Windows Home Server administrative password. The Windows Home Server Console appears, as shown previously in Figure 7-1. If it is not already selected, click the Computers & Backups tab at the top of the console window. Right-click the computer for which you wish to manage backups, and select View Backups, as shown in the following figure.

Continued

Keeping Important Backups *(Continued)*

The resulting dialog box, shown in the next figure, will display any backups that have been performed for this computer, whether they completed successfully or not. From this dialog box, you can select backups, and change whether they are included in the automatic backup cleanup process. (Note: Two of the manual backups in this figure have been changed to Manage automatically.)

If a backup is marked as Keep this backup, it will have a lock icon in the leftmost column of the backup list. If the leftmost column shows a gear icon, then it is set to Manage automatically and it is part of the pool of backups that will be counted during backup cleanup. You can change an individual backup's setting by clicking on the backup and then making a selection in the middle pane of the dialog box. There is also a Details button here that will let you change the description that is associated with a backup.

If a backup is marked to be retained, it does not factor into the count for backup retention. So if you have set Windows Home Server to keep three daily backups, and then you mark the most recent two to be kept, it will also keep the previous three days backups for a total of five.

Another thing to remember is that the backup cleanup process is only run once a week, during the scheduled backup window on Sunday. The automatic backup cleanup process is run prior to any backups, so you will usually have more backups saved than the retention settings indicate. Windows Home

Server's backup technology saves a great deal of space by only storing each file once, and only storing the changes that occur as files are changed rather than saving entire copies of the altered files.

Windows Home Server creates backups using a technology called Volume Shadow Copy, and computers are actually backed up at the *cluster* level. A cluster can just be thought of as a uniformly sized chunk of data that is stored on a hard drive, and it is actually these clusters that Windows Home Server works with when it is backing up your machine. When WHS is performing a backup, it looks at each cluster. If the cluster has been previously backed up, WHS simply adds a reference to the original cluster on your Windows Home Server machine. This saves both hard drive space and network bandwidth. The database of clusters is shared between all of the computers that are backed up on Windows Home Server, so an identical file that is on two different computers will only be backed up once, and the second backup will simply reference the first.

A side effect of this space-saving method is that removing old backups involves analyzing the files that the backup contained, and only removing the files or portions of files that are not still needed by other backups. This can be time and resource intensive, which is why it only runs automatically once a week during the scheduled backup window. One other effect of this once-weekly cleanup schedule is that the daily backup history is only enforced once a week. This means that even if you set the daily backup retention to only keep one daily backup, on Saturday you will find all the daily backups from the week are still on your server, unless you manually initiate the backup cleanup process.

A situation that may influence your backup retention needs could include travel schedules that cause you to be away from home for extended periods of time. If you frequently are away from your home for weeks on end and your computers are left on, or if they are used by other members of your household while you are gone, you may want to increase your retention window so that any changes that are made in your absence, or even accidental changes that you made before leaving, are not unrecoverable because Windows Home Server has cleaned out the relevant backups. Increasing your retention window to include daily backups for several days longer than your typical trip will provide additional security for your data. For example, if you frequently take 10 day trips for business, you may want to set Windows Home Server to retain 15 daily backups.

Another consideration would be the various users of computers on your home network. We all know that some individuals have more of a tendency to lose files, download viruses, and in general break computers. If you happen to have any of these individuals in your home, consider keeping more daily or weekly backups, so that you are less likely to lose important data if a problem is discovered some time after it occurs.

Deciding on Backup Retention

Deciding on a reasonable backup schedule may take some experimentation. Using the default settings, my home server is able to backup two computers with a variety of files and programs installed, using about 16GB of storage. My server has about 430GB available using just the internal hard drives, and our network shared folders use up about 28GB. What this means is that I can keep many more backups than the default settings prescribe, and I won't have to worry about storage space.

Another point to remember is that because of Windows Home Server's unique backup technology, each new backup only requires enough space to save the portions of the files that have changed. There is some overhead associated with each backup, but just remember that unless you change or add a large amount of files, each additional backup will use a very small amount of space.

The point of all this discussion is that with most Windows Home Server setups, the backup retention settings will be driven mostly by convenience and bookkeeping ease, and not as much by the available storage.

The setup that I decided on is to keep 14 daily backups, 4 weekly backups, and 14 monthly backups. This ensures that I can restore to any day in the last 2 weeks, which is important to me because I frequently install and uninstall test software that might break my system, and I may not know for a week or two that a piece of software has destabilized my system. The 4 weekly backups give a little bit more near-term history so that I can restore to any Sunday in the past month. The 14 monthly backups are more of a protection against deleting important files, like tax returns and other financial documents. I figure that these types of files are generally accessed at least once a year, give or take a couple of months. If a file or folder was accidentally deleted, I would likely notice it within a year, so a 14-month window should cover my needs. Additionally, any backups can be marked to be retained, so I can mark a single backup each year to be retained indefinitely as an added precaution.

The trade-off to an extended backup retention scheme like this one is that I end up keeping a large number of backups. When I restore files or systems, I like this level of control, but in all honesty, I rarely use anything other than the most recent 7 backups. The remaining 23 are there just in case, and that's what keeping backups is all about.

You will have to decide what your comfort level is, and set your backup retention accordingly. The default settings are very reasonable, so many people just choose to live with them. If you have any specific needs such as the ones covered in this section, you may want to take a first guess at what you feel will be a manageable number of backups while still meeting your needs. You can always revisit your settings after your server has been running for a few months and make adjustments. You should make sure that the backup lists maintained by Windows Home Server are not too overwhelming and that the storage space used by your backups is reasonable.

Setting Backup Retention

The previous section discussed several considerations for when you will want to alter the default retention schedule. Now you'll learn how to actually change the retention settings.

You set your home server's backup retention through the Windows Home Server Console. Right-click the Windows Home Server icon in the system tray, and select Windows Home Server Console from the context menu. Enter your Windows Home Server administrative password. Remember that this is different from your user password. This is the password that you entered when you first configured your Windows Home Server.

After you enter your password, the Windows Home Server Console appears, as shown earlier in Figure 7-1. Select the Settings action in the upper right corner of the console window.

The Settings dialog box is used to configure many options that apply to Windows Homes Server, and to all of the computers that it manages. The Settings dialog box defaults to the General options page. Select Backup from the page list on the left to display the page shown earlier in Figure 7-2.

The second section of this page, labeled Automatic Backup Management, allows you to set the backup retention for your Windows Home Server. The labels used for the different settings can be a bit confusing. The number shown is actually the number of backups of each type that will be kept. It does not indicate any particular time period for how long a backup will be kept. If you select that you want to keep five daily backups, and your computer only manages to backup successfully once a week (if you have a laptop that you do not leave plugged in, for example), it will still keep five backups, and the oldest may be 5 weeks old.

Use the controls to set your desired number of backups for each type, and your screen should look similar to Figure 7-3. Click OK to save your settings and close the dialog box.

Figure 7-3

Disabling Backups for a Computer

There are some situations where it will make sense to disable backups for a computer. Disabling backups takes a computer out of the backup schedule, and keeps the existing backups. During the backup cleanup process, the number of backups will be pared down to match your retention settings, but the most recent backups will be kept, as well as any backups that are set to be excluded from automatic backup management. This can be useful for a number of reasons.

When to Turn Off Backups

There are two main situations where you will want to disable backups for a computer. The first involves taking the computer away from the Windows Home Server network for an extended period of time. The second is for when you are removing or rebuilding a computer, but you want to maintain access to the backed up files.

If a computer is away from the home server network for more than five days, Windows Home Server will generate a warning that the health of your network is degraded. If this extends to 15 days, Windows Home Server will indicate that there is a critical problem with your network because the subject computer has not been backed up. Although this is generally a good reminder to make sure that your computers have an opportunity to back up their files, this reminder can be an annoyance if a computer is not available. In addition, the presence of this alert may cause you to ignore some other important notice about the health of your network. If a computer is going to be away from the network for longer than 15 days, it is a good idea to disable backups until the computer returns to the network. If the backup warnings that pop up after five days are too much of an annoyance, you can disable backups for shorter absences as well.

If you are going to be removing a computer from your home network, or reformatting a hard drive, it may also be a good idea to turn off backups for the computer. By turning off backups, you avoid having your network's health marked as degraded, but you can retain access to the backed up files for this machine. If you actually remove a computer from the listing in the Windows Home Server Console, the backups are deleted as well. Just turning off backups is a good alternative that will give you the option of recovering files if you later discover that you need a file that used to be on the decommissioned computer.

Remember that a disabled computer will still count against the 10-computer limit for Windows Home Server for as long as it is included in the backup list. If you reinstall Windows on one of your computers and use a different computer name, Windows Home Server will consider it an entirely different computer. If you use the same name, Windows Home Server will recognize that it is the same.

How to Turn Off Backups for a Computer

To disable backups for a computer, you must first log in to the Windows Home Server Console. Right-click the Windows Home Server icon in the system tray, and select Windows Home Server Console from the context menu. Enter your Windows Home Server administrative password. Remember that this is different from your user password. The Windows Home Server Console looks similar to the screen shown earlier in Figure 7-1. On the Windows Home Server Console screen, select Computers & Backups at the top. This tab may already be showing.

Locate the computer that you wish to temporarily disable backups for. Right-click the name of the computer, and select Turn Off Backups from the context menu. Figure 7-4 shows this action being performed for the computer named TABLET.

After you turn off backups for a computer, the Status column for that machine will change to grey, and the status description will say Off.

Turning Backups Back On

Returning your computer's backup setting to normal is similar to the process for turning backups off. Start the Windows Home Server Console just as before, and select the Computers & Backups tab. When you right-click the desired computer in the list, the last option on the menu will be Turn On Backups, as shown in Figure 7-5. Select this option to start backing up your computer again.

Chapter 7: Creating and Managing Backups   **111**

Figure 7-4

Figure 7-5

The status light will return to green, yellow, or red depending on when the last backup occurred, and the status text will change to indicate the current backup state of the machine. If the computer is behind in its backups, a backup will be scheduled and will run as soon as the Windows Home Server backup service becomes available. If you are concerned about getting the computer backed up as soon as possible (for example, if you have done a great deal of work on the computer while it was not being backed up), then you may want to start a manual backup. Otherwise you can just make sure that it stays plugged in and it will catch up during the next backup window.

Managing Volumes and Exclusions

Volumes are just another name for hard drive partitions. On most home computers, each physical hard drive has only one partition, so *volume* and *drive* are mostly interchangeable. Another way to think of this is that each volume usually has a drive letter associated with it. Your C: drive is a volume, and if you have an additional hard drive, it might be referenced as your D: drive.

Windows Home Server automatically adds any volumes that are present when you install the Windows Home Server Connector software on a computer. If you add or remove volumes later, you will have to reconfigure your backup using the Backup Configuration Wizard as described later in this chapter.

Windows Home Server also excludes certain files from the backup configuration by default. A default backup configuration excludes the system page file, user temporary files, client-side cache folders, and if present, the hibernation file. These files are not useful when restoring a PC, so their exclusion saves hard drive space without losing any real functionality. While Windows Home Server is set up to exclude some specific files, user-configured exclusions are only possible at the *folder* level. If you have other folders that you wish to exclude, you will have to run the Backup Configuration Wizard as described later.

Considerations for Volumes

Each volume on your computer is backed up separate from the other volumes. Windows Home Server's backup configuration must include each volume, otherwise it will be ignored during the backup process. Anytime you add or remove a volume, either by adding or removing a physical hard drive or by creating or deleting a partition from a drive in your system, you should run the Backup Configuration Wizard to set up your backup properly.

In some instances, you may want to leave a volume out of the backup configuration. If you have a USB drive that is not always connected to your PC, you may want to exclude it because Windows Home Server will produce warning messages if it cannot access the drive. If you have a volume that only contains transient or unimportant data, it might be a candidate for exclusion as well. The key to deciding if you want to include or exclude a backup lies in the importance of the data. Make the decision using the assumption that the hard drive is going to crash tomorrow. Do you want it backed up?

Overcoming Old Backup Habits

Some people are in the habit of splitting their main hard drive in two, and they are diligent about keeping all of their user data on one volume, while system and program files are on another. This is an old trick for making backups easier, but it might lead some folks to think that they should exclude their system volume. When you have to manually backup files, having this separation can save you a great deal of space by making it easier to back up just the files that change frequently and are most important, your data. This method assumes that you will reinstall the operating system and programs from the installation CDs should you suffer a hard drive failure. Although this method has advantages for manual backups, excluding the system volume from your Windows Home Server backup configuration will cripple one of Windows Home Server's best features. Be certain to include your system volume so that you can use Windows Home Server's System Restore functionality should you suffer a hard drive failure or data loss. Instead of having to reinstall Windows and all of your programs, your system can be returned to exactly the state it was at during your last backup, including all of you programs, settings, and files, with everything set up exactly the way you remember.

Considerations for Folders and Files

Windows Home Server also allows you to exclude certain files or folders from being backed up. The default excludes the system page file, user temporary files, client-side cache folders, and if present, the hibernation file. None of these files are useful in restoring data from a damaged hard drive and they can use a fair amount of hard drive space, so they are excluded. You should use this same concept to decide if you want to exclude additional files or folders. If a file or a folder consumes a great deal of space, and it would not be useful when you restore a computer after data loss or a drive failure, then it is a good candidate for exclusion.

Other Thoughts on Volumes and Exclusions

Keep in mind that Windows Home Server is very efficient in its use of hard drive space. When Windows Home Server backs up a volume, it only saves one copy of any file. If you have the same file located in several different folders on your hard drive, it will essentially save one copy, and make a note that the file existed in multiple locations. Likewise, for each backup that Windows Home Server performs, it does not save additional copies of files that haven't changed. It just notes that the file that it already has saved exists in the new backup as well. For this reason, you shouldn't worry about excluding volumes, files or folders unless they truly would be a waste of space.

Running the Backup Configuration Wizard

The way that you go about including or excluding volumes or setting folder exclusions is through the Backup Configuration Wizard. The Backup Configuration Wizard can run separately for each computer that Windows Home Server backs up. You can run the wizard from any computer; you

Chapter 7: Creating and Managing Backups

don't have to be at the computer that you want to configure backups for. However, you should make sure that the computer you are configuring is powered on, because Windows Home Server will communicate with it during the configuration process to get lists of drives, folders, and files.

The Backup Configuration Wizard is initiated from the Windows Home Server Console. Right-click the Windows Home Server icon in the system tray, and select Windows Home Server Console from the context menu. Enter your Windows Home Server administrative password. Remember that this is different from your user password. The Windows Home Server Console looks similar to the screen shown earlier in Figure 7-1. On the Windows Home Server Console screen, select Computers & Backups at the top. This tab may already be showing.

Right-click the computer name for which you wish to run the Backup Configuration Wizard. Select Configure Backup as shown in Figure 7-6. The Backup Configuration Wizard will start with a welcome screen describing the purpose of the wizard. Click Next to begin the wizard.

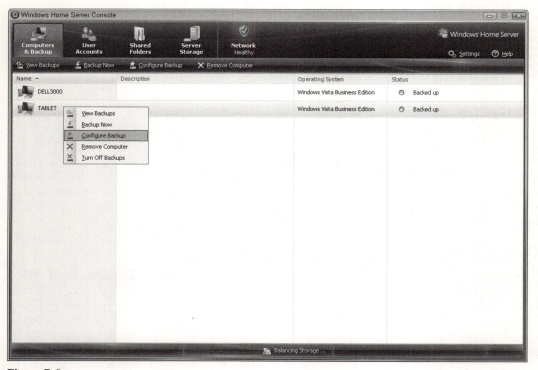

Figure 7-6

The following screen, shown in Figure 7-7, lists all of the volumes on your computer, and gives you the option to include or exclude them by selecting or deselecting the checkbox next to each one. A checked box indicates that the volume will be *included* in the backup. Select the volumes that you wish to be backed up, and then click Next.

Chapter 7: Creating and Managing Backups   **115**

Note
Remember that only volumes formatted with the NT file system (NTFS) can be backed up by Windows Home Server. Volume Shadow Copy is only available on NTFS drives, and because the backup engine relies on Volume Shadow Copy, it will only work for NTFS drives.

Figure 7-7

The next screen of the wizard lists the exclusions that are currently part of the backup configuration for this computer. Figure 7-8 shows this step of the wizard for a computer with the default exclusions.

If you wish to add to the exclusion list, click the Add button. A dialog box will pop up with a listing of your drives. You can drill down into the folders on the drive by clicking on the + next to the drive letter, as shown in Figure 7-9. Once you select the folder that you wish to exclude from being backed up, click the Exclude button. You will be returned to the previous screen and the folder you selected will be in the list of exclusions that is shown. (If you select Add again, you may notice that the folders you have excluded are still in the listing. The Add function lists all folders on the drive, so you have to rely on the exclusion list to determine if a folder has been excluded.)

Chapter 7: Creating and Managing Backups

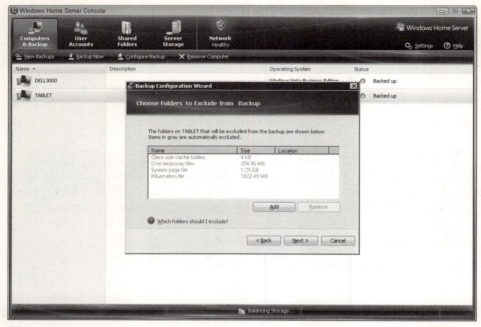

Figure 7-8

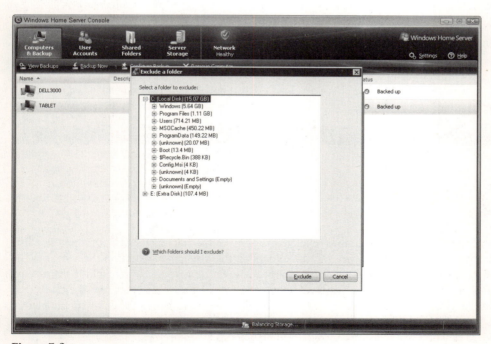

Figure 7-9

Repeat this process for any other folders that you wish to exclude. (You can only pick one folder at a time from the Add dialog box, but you can continue adding folders until all of the necessary folders are listed.) When you are done, click the Next button. A confirmation page will be shown, including a summary of the number of volumes that you have included and number of folders that you have excluded. Review the information and then select Done. If you need to make changes later, you can rerun the Backup Configuration Wizard at any time.

Special Considerations for Mobile PCs

Mobile PCs present unique challenges for your backup planning. Windows Home Server's default configuration is targeted at computers that will always be connected to the network, and which will be left powered on overnight. Laptops are often taken away from their home network, are frequently left unplugged, and are powered down overnight. If you have one or more laptops, TabletPCs, or UMPCs, then you will need to adjust your backup plan to accommodate these devices.

As was described earlier in the chapter, in order for a computer to be backed up, it must be connected to the network, either by a wired Ethernet connection or by a properly configured Wireless Network connection. It also must either be powered on, or it must be in Hibernate or Sleep mode. If a computer is powered off using Windows' Shutdown command, or if it is running on battery, Windows Home Server's connector software will not initiate a backup.

There are two different tactics for accommodating your mobile computers. The first is to adjust your backup schedule to include times that your mobile computers will be in use and connected to the network. While initial backups can be quite time-consuming, especially over slower wireless links, subsequent backups do not take nearly as long. My TabletPC typically finishes its daily backup in less than 5 minutes, so it is not too much of a bother to have it back up while I am using it.

Although it does not take long, you should be mindful of the fact that your computer will be using additional resources while it is performing a backup. There is an increase in CPU utilization and hard disk activity, and when it is transferring data to the server it will utilize your network connection to its fullest. Windows Home Server's Backup software does a good job of balancing network traffic, so it won't disrupt anything, but it may cause software or music downloads to slow down, and it may make Internet browsing a bit slower for the duration of the backup. You can choose to either extend the backup window into the morning, or make it cover part of the late afternoon or evening, depending on when your mobile computers are most likely to be running. In fact, you can extend the backup schedule to include the entire day if you think it might be necessary to be sure your machines have an opportunity to be backed up. If you need to adjust your backup schedule, see the "Setting the Schedule" section earlier in this chapter.

The other tactic that you can try is to adjust your family's behavior related to mobile PCs so that they can be backed up during the normal nightly backup window. To do this you must be sure that they meet the requirements for being backed up. You need to either plug them into a wired Ethernet connection, or make sure that their wireless network connection is operational. You can either leave them running overnight, or you can configure them so that they go into Sleep mode overnight. Most modern laptop machines are configured to go into Sleep mode when you close the screen on the

Continued

Special Considerations for Mobile PCs *(Continued)*

computer, but if you are relying on this in order for the machines to be backed up, you should double-check. In Windows Vista, you can verify or adjust this setting through your computer's Control Panel. Click the Start orb in the lower left of your screen, and select Control Panel from the right-hand column of the Start menu. Select the Mobile PC task. (If you do not see Mobile PC listed as an option, your Control Panel may be in Classic View. If this is the case, return to the normal view by clicking Control Panel Home in the upper left of the screen.) Under the Power Options heading, select the Choose what closing the lid does task. The resulting screen is shown in the following figure.

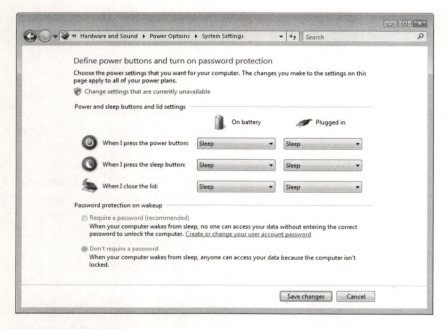

Check to make sure that the selection for the When I close the lid option is listed as Sleep both for the On Battery column and the Plugged In column. You should make this selection for both columns because you may be unplugged when you close the lid of your computer, even if you plan to plug it in later. This leads to the other thing you need to do to allow your mobile computer to be backed up. You must remember to plug in the computer before you leave it for the night.

It may be a good idea to employ both of these tactics in order to give your mobile computers the best opportunity to be backed up. If you try to schedule the computers to be backed up at night, they will be backed up along with the other computers, but you can also extend the backup schedule into the day so that they will still be backed up if they were not available overnight.

Turning Off Computers

There is a wide variety of opinions about whether you should power down your computers overnight. Much of this is because of the fact that many of the earliest hard drives would suffer additional wear by being shut down and started up again. Modern hard drives do not share this same attribute, but the suggestions live on. For any computer purchased in the last ten years, the decision of whether to power it off when it is not being used is strictly one of convenience, with consideration for the power that it uses when left on.

If you turn off your computers, you should remember that they will not be backed up. Windows Home Server's default schedule only works when computers are available to be backed up overnight. If you like to power down your machines overnight, you should make a slight adjustment to your routine so that the machines can be backed up. Instead of selecting Windows' Shutdown option from the Start menu, you can make a habit of selecting the Sleep option. If your computer has a Sleep button (usually these buttons have a picture of a crescent moon), then you can just use this button to put your computer to sleep.

With Windows Vista you can also set your computer to go to sleep if you press the power button. To do this, you need to change a setting through your computer's Control Panel.

1. To change this setting, click the Start orb in the lower left of your screen, and select Control Panel from the right-hand column of the Start menu.

2. Select the Hardware and Sound task. (If you do not see Hardware and Sound listed as an option, your Control Panel may be in Classic View. If this is the case, return to the normal view by clicking Control Panel Home in the upper left of the screen.)

3. Under the Power Options heading, select the Change what the power buttons do task. The resulting screen is shown in "The Special Considerations for Mobile PCs" sidebar. If you are working on a desktop computer, the screen will not include separate columns for On Battery and Plugged In.

4. From this screen, change the selection for the When I press the power button: to Sleep.

5. Next click the Save Changes button.

Now you can put your computer into sleep mode just by hitting the power button. Sleep mode allows your computer to be powered back on very quickly, and it will let Windows Home Server keep your machine backed up without wasting electricity when your computer is not being used.

Summary

In this chapter you learned how to configure all of the different options related to backing up your computers. You learned what the default configurations for backup are. You now understand the rationale for these defaults, and you also know what considerations might make you want to change these defaults. You learned about Windows Home Server's backup schedule, and how to change it.

Chapter 7: Creating and Managing Backups

You now understand how Windows Home Server decides what backups it will retain, and how to change these settings to meet the specific needs of your home network. You learned how to disable backups for a computer, and the situations where it makes sense to do so. Next you learned how Windows Home Server deals with disk volumes and folder exclusions, and how you go about changing these settings by using the Backup Configuration Wizard. Lastly, you learned how shutting down your computers can affect Windows Home Server's ability to back up your data, and you now know how to configure your computers so that the Windows Home Server software can wake the machine to complete a backup.

Chapter 8

Digital Spring-Cleaning

In Chapter 2 you developed your strategy for how you want to organize and make your data accessible using Windows Home Server. The next step in this process is locating and reorganizing data from the various computers on your home network, and moving them to the appropriate locations on your Windows Home Server. The hardest part will be changing your behaviors and the behaviors of others in your household so that they can help implement the new strategy.

This chapter discusses some methods and tools for finding, gathering, and sorting your important data according to your strategy. It also goes over techniques you can use to make it easier for yourself and others to stick to the plan.

It is important to remember that any efforts to keep data organized will be met with resistance. Creating order from disorder takes effort, and the more people that are involved, the harder it will become. As covered in Chapter 2, keeping your strategy simple and easy is the best tactic for getting everyone, including yourself, on-board with keeping order in your digital life.

When you have setbacks, personal or otherwise, in your efforts to get and stay organized, remember that you are already ahead of the game. You have a strategy for organizing your digital life, and any data that falls outside of the strategy can simply be staged, sorted, and brought in-line.

If you find situations that repeatedly cause difficulties with your strategy, remember that your strategy is a living concept. Adapt your strategy to fit new facets of your digital life whenever you see a need. Remember to be flexible, without falling into the trap of creating unnecessary complexity.

As the title of this chapter suggests, keeping your family's digital life organized is a cyclical process. Similar to keeping a house in order, you have to develop habits to keep your data in order most of the time as well. Some people manage to maintain their houses in total order, and spring-cleaning just involves throwing out a few older items. For other folks, spring-cleaning involves emptying half the house out onto the lawn, and renting a truck to haul away the excess junk. Try to understand what type of digital life you lead, and plan your efforts accordingly.

Revisiting Your Strategy

You should review the strategy that you developed in Chapter 2 prior to actually making any changes. Even after a short break, you may find categories of data that you have overlooked, or you may notice unnecessary complexities in your plan. Take a few minutes to decide if your strategy is ready to be put into place.

As you prepare to dive into the process of reorganizing your data, you should revisit your commitment to keeping your data in a centralized location. Remember the benefits that are highlighted in Chapter 2. By keeping your data in a central location, you make it easier to keep your data safe by utilizing Windows Home Server's shared folder duplication technology. This will make sure that even if you suffer the loss of a hard drive, your data will be safe. In addition, keeping your data on Windows Home Server's shares makes it easier to access files from any computer in your home. Also, when you are away from home you can retrieve files through Windows Home Server's remote access features, or you can upload files to the proper location from any computer via the Internet.

Note

If you do not have multiple hard drives in your Windows Home Server machine, you cannot enable folder duplication. Without folder duplication, your data may actually be less safe if you only have it stored on the server. The best long-term plan is to add an additional internal or external hard drive to your Windows Home Server, as described in Chapter 12. If you aren't ready to add more storage to your home server in order to allow folder duplication, then you should consider keeping a copy of your data on one of your desktops, or using one of the online backup services that are highlighted in Chapter 14. An online backup service is a good idea even if your home server supports folder duplication, because it will allow you to recover your data even if you have a catastrophic failure on your server, such as a lightning strike, fire, or theft.

As part of this review, you should also consider if there are files that you shouldn't move to your Windows Home Server. The following situations might warrant keeping certain files on the client computer where they already reside:

- If accessibility of the files from other computers on your network is not desired
- If the files are large and are edited or changed often
- If the files require a special application in order to be opened, and you only have that application on a specific computer

Remember that your files will still be protected even if you don't move them to your Windows Home Server. Nightly backups will keep them safe from loss, even if you experience a total hard drive failure on the computer where they are stored. There are good reasons for moving files to the server, but there are exceptions where the benefits of keeping them on a computer are more important.

Before You Begin

Before you begin the spring-cleaning process, you should make sure that all of your data is backed up. This is a fairly typical warning that many people tend to ignore, but this is a great opportunity to use your new Windows Home Server to do the right thing and make sure your data stays safe. It's also extremely easy to do! For each computer that you plan to *clean*, run a manual backup and give it a meaningful label like "January 2008, Pre-Cleanup." To perform a manual backup on a computer, follow these steps:

1. Right-click the Windows Home Server icon in the system tray, and select Backup Now from the context menu, as shown in Figure 8-1.

Chapter 8: Digital Spring-Cleaning **123**

Figure 8-1

2. In the dialog box that pops up, enter an appropriate description in the text box as shown in Figure 8-2, and click the Backup Now button.

Figure 8-2

3. Your computer will be scheduled for a backup, and if no other backups are currently running, a backup will begin in a few seconds. If the backup service is busy, you will receive a notification indicating this is the case, and the backup will begin as soon as it is free. When the backup completes, you will receive a notification as shown in Figure 8-3, indicating that the backup has completed successfully.

Figure 8-3

4. Complete this backup process for all of the computers that you will include in your spring-cleaning, and you can rest assured that all of your files are safe.

When you move a lot of data around, it is easy to accidentally delete or misplace files. If you happen to accidentally delete a file that you later decide you need, you can always come back to these backups and retrieve it. The recovery process is covered later in Chapter 10.

Also, in the future when you see warnings that advise you to "back up all of your data" before proceeding, you can actually follow the advice with this simple process!

UNC Paths

Using shared folders on your Windows Home Server will be easier once you understand a little bit about how shared folders are referenced. The most common format for referring to files and folders that are stored on Windows Home Server is called a UNC path. UNC stands for Universal Naming Convention, and it defines a very generic format for referencing files and folders in a networked environment.

Most computer users are familiar with the way that Windows (and every Microsoft operating system since DOS) references local files. These are typically in the format `DRIVE:\Folder\File`. For example, a document might be saved as `C:\Documents\MyDocument.doc`. *C:* tells you what volume it is saved on, `Documents` is the name of the folder where it is saved, and `MyDocument.doc` is the filename.

UNC paths are very similar to this, except that they replace the notion of the file being saved to a particular volume with the idea that the file is saved on a particular computer. The generic format for a UNC path is `\\COMPUTERNAME\Folder\File`. It is generally assumed that if you are referring to a UNC path, then you are accessing files via the network share interface on the computer or server.

As you do with locally saved files, you can nest folders inside of other folders, so you can end up with long filenames like:

`\\hpserver\Software\Add-Ins\photoSyncBeta2.msi`

As you can see, this file, named `photoSyncBeta2.msi`, is saved on a computer named *hpserver*, located in the `Add-Ins` folder that is found in the `Software` shared folder.

Most user interface elements use this normal UNC format to refer to network accessible files and folders, but you may run into one more format, especially if you run into errors. Internally, there is a slightly longer format known as *Long UNC*. The same example file previously mentioned would be referenced as:

`\\?\UNC\hpserver\Software\Add-Ins\photoSyncBeta2.msi`

This longer format is used within windows, so it might show up in system logs or error messages, but users should generally not have to worry about it.

Setting Up

The first step toward implementing your strategy is to create any shares or folders that will be part of your organizational strategy. You can use the ideas that you developed in Chapter 2 and create locations on your Windows Home Server for your important data.

Creating User-Defined Shares

If you need to create user-defined shares as top-level categories for your data, you use the Windows Home Server Console. Right-click the Windows Home Server icon in the system tray on one of your computers, and select Windows Home Server Console from the context menu. You must enter your server's administrative password to continue. Once the console appears, select the Shared Folders tab from the top of the window. Select the Add action from the menu bar, as shown in Figure 8-4.

Figure 8-4

In the resulting dialog box, give the folder a name and provide a description that will act as a reminder to you and others what the purpose of this share is. If you have more than one hard drive in your Windows Home Server, folder duplication will be on by default, and unless the data you intend to keep in this share is unimportant, you should leave this checked. Once you have given the share a name and description, as shown in Figure 8-5, click Next.

In the following screen, shown in Figure 8-6, you can adjust the security settings for your new share. Select the appropriate radio buttons to give users Full or Read access, or set to None to deny access, and then click the Finish button. Remember, that Full access allows the user to read, write, modify, or delete any files in the share. Read allows the user to open, view, or copy files, but they cannot modify or delete the file on the server. None denies all access. The user will not even be able to see a listing of the files, although Windows Home Server will allow them to see that the share exists. After you click Finish, you receive a confirmation that the share has been set up successfully.

126 **Chapter 8:** Digital Spring-Cleaning

Figure 8-5

Figure 8-6

Note

You may notice in Figure 8-6 that no users are assigned Full access. When you create a new shared folder, Windows Home Server gives all non-guest users Read access by default, but nobody is given the ability to actually move or save files to the share! Unless you give at least one user Full access, you will not be able to actually use your new share. The guest account is defaulted to the None level of access, and you should leave it this way unless you specifically want to provide access to this share to people who are visiting your network and who don't have usernames and passwords for your home server. If guests need access to a folder, you should use Read access. You should almost never give Full access to the guest account, because it might allow someone to accidentally damage or delete files from that share.

Creating Subfolders

As you get ready to move files onto your server, you will likely want to create additional organization within the shared folders. You accomplish this by creating subfolders underneath the shared folder. Just as you need Full access in order to copy files to the share, you need Full access to create these subfolders. Although the process of opening a window to view the shared folder is different, from that point forward the process is exactly the same as the process for creating subfolders on a local hard drive on your client computer.

Note

If you already have some of your files organized like you want on a client computer, you may not need to create all of the subfolders for those files. If you copy or move entire folders to Window Home Server's shares, the organization (that is, the subfolders) will stay intact. Also, if you plan to store files directly in the top-level shared folder, you will not need to create subfolders for that share.

To create a new subfolder on your home server, first open the Shared Folders on your server. You can do this by double-clicking the Shared Folders on Server icon on your desktop. (If this shortcut is missing, you can open the same window by pressing ⊞+R and typing \\SERVER into the Run dialog box.) From the window that opens, select the top-level share that will contain your folder by double-clicking its name. From here, you should right-click the empty space in the folder display window, select New from the context menu, and then select Folder from the top of the New submenu. Figure 8-7 shows the creation of a new folder under Windows Home Server's Music share.

After you create a new folder, Windows highlights the folder's name, which defaults to New Folder, as shown in Figure 8-8, and you can provide a more useful name simply by typing the new name and pressing the Enter key.

Continue this process for the other folders that are part of your overall strategy. You don't need to create all of the bottom-tier folders at this point. For example, in the chronological picture organization scheme, you shouldn't create all of the monthly folders; those folders will be created later when you first find a picture that belongs in a given month. If a folder is part of your core strategy, such as a Finance folder under a newly created Documents share, then it should be created now.

128　Chapter 8: Digital Spring-Cleaning

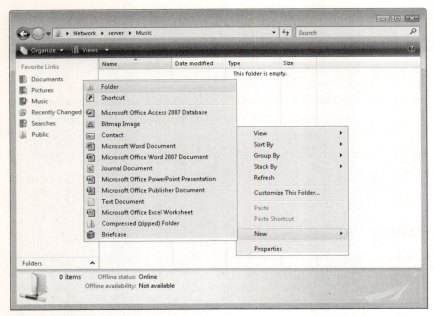

Figure 8-7

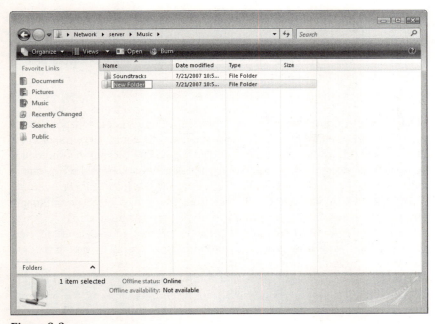

Figure 8-8

Data Collection

The process of collecting data involves finding all of the locations to where your important files have spread, and moving them to locations where they belong. Common locations for files include the Desktop, Documents, Music, Videos, Pictures and Downloads folders for any actively used account, extra hard drives (typically the D: or E:), USB flash drives, and other removable storage devices. You can also find your data by using search tools. Windows Vista's built-in search capability is a quick way to track down other locations where files may be hiding.

Once you have found your files, they can either be placed directly into their final location, or if they need closer examination prior to sorting, you can place them in a folder that I like to refer to as the Staged folder. If I know that I am going to have to examine a set of files in order to sort them into their final location, I like to create a folder named Staged at the root of any category in my folder hierarchy, and I use this location as a *temporary* holding area for files that need to be inspected and sorted.

Is the Staged Folder Just Another Name for *Unsorted*?

When you were developing your strategy in Chapter 2, I warned against the creation of an Unsorted folder because it creates a catchall location that can be abused, and which discourages good data management habits. Some folks may think that I am now advocating this same folder using a slightly different name. In practice the ideas are fairly similar, but there is a significant difference between the two, which leaves *Unsorted* on my bad list, but which allows the staging folder to be part of a healthy cleanup process.

The main difference is that creating and using an Unsorted folder would be an element of an organizational strategy, whereas the Staged folder is a tool that is used during the process of collecting and organizing your data. The Staged folder should be created when you begin your cleanup, and it should be deleted at the end of your cleanup process after you have moved all of the data out of it.

In addition, the name implies impending action. When data is Staged, it is apparent that you are about to do something with it. An Unsorted folder is more like a catchall junk drawer, and for most things, if you want to be able to find them quickly and easily, a junk drawer is the last place they should be placed.

Tip

If you name your staging folder !Staged the exclamation point will cause Windows to display it first in any listing that is sorted alphabetically; this will make it easier to find.

Finding Your Data

The first step in your reorganization is finding your data. There are several methods that you should use. The first is a manual search. I suggest using this method first because it will capture the overwhelming majority of the files that you should transition to your Windows Home Server.

Your manual search is carried out via Windows Explorer. A quick shortcut to open Windows Explorer is to press ⊞+E. From the window that opens, double-click your system drive, usually your C: drive. From here, double-click Users. (On older operating systems the folder may be named Documents and Settings instead.) In this folder, you will find one folder for each user that has logged on to that particular machine. Double-click the user account that you wish to clean up first.

Note

If you are not logged in as an administrator, you will only be able to access your own account. To perform cleanup for other accounts, you must either log in under those accounts, or log in with an account that is designated as an administrator.

For Windows Vista machines, the main folders of interest are going to be the Documents folder, the Desktop folder, and if you use them the Music, Pictures, and Videos folders. A sample user folder is shown in Figure 8-9. On older machines, you may find a folder named My Documents, and a My Pictures folder located in My Documents. Whatever the case, you should do a little bit of exploring underneath the user folder to find your files that might be hidden. Double-click a folder to open it, and look at the files that are contained. To return to a previous folder, use the Back arrow located in the upper-left corner of the window.

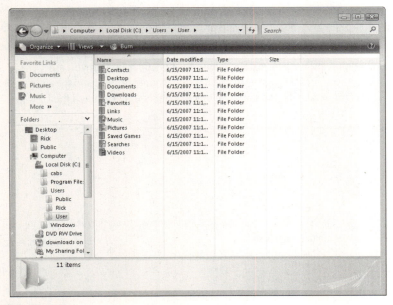

Figure 8-9

If you have a bunch of mixed files, it can be useful to sort them by different attributes. For example, you can sort them by File Type, or for pictures you can sort by Date Taken. This is easiest to do in Windows Explorer's Details view. To select Details view, click the down arrow next to the Views menu item, and then select Details from the pop-up menu, as shown in Figure 8-10. Now you can sort by any of the columns that are being displayed. To select a column for sorting, just click the heading of the column. To reverse the sort order, just click the heading again. Under Windows Vista, you also have many additional options for grouping and sorting files based on the various columns. When you place the mouse cursor over a particular column heading, a triangle will appear on the right side of the heading. Click this triangle to see options for grouping and filtering.

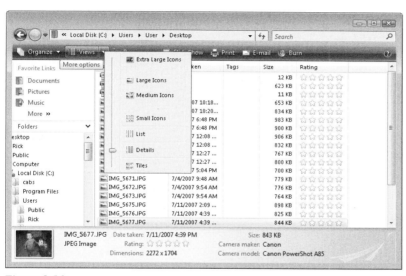

Figure 8-10

If you wish to explore other metadata options, right-click any of the column headings in the Details view, and you will be presented with the option of checking or unchecking commonly used metadata fields, as shown in Figure 8-11. Experiment with these fields, or select More from the context menu to see even more options. Different fields are useful for sorting different types of files. I like to sort photos by Date Taken because I like to store them chronologically. It might be useful to sort Word Documents by Author. Which fields are useful to you will depend on the decisions you have made concerning your organizational strategy.

There are a number of tricks that will make things easier once you have located some files and you are ready to move them. The first is multi-select. Windows Explorer supports several different kinds of multi-select. One method is to drag a box around a set of files using your mouse. This is shown in Figure 8-12.

Another method is to use Shift+Select. To use this method, select a single file in the list, and then hold down the Shift key while you select another file. Windows will select both files that you clicked and any files that are listed between the two.

Chapter 8: Digital Spring-Cleaning

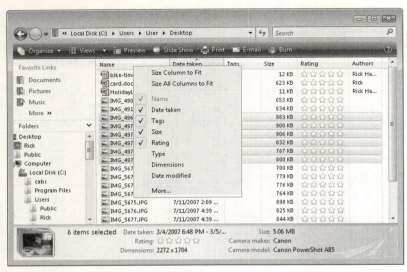

Figure 8-11

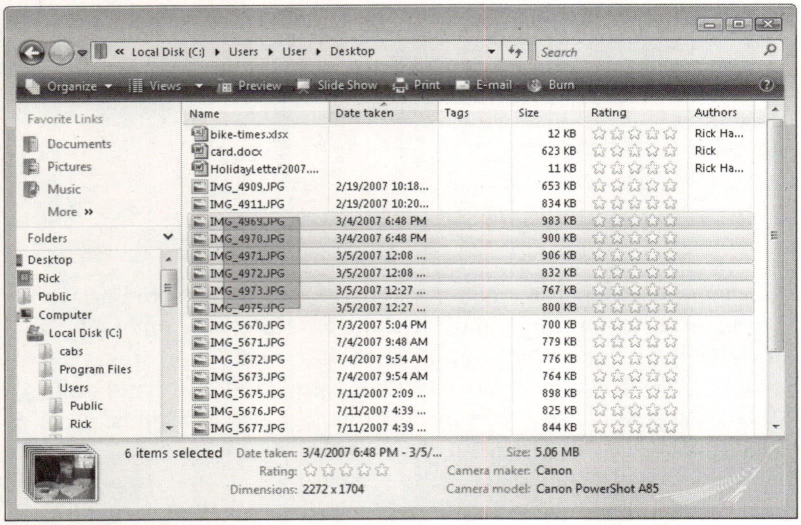

Figure 8-12

The third method can actually be used in conjunction with the first two. While holding down the Ctrl key, you can click on any file to add or remove it from the selection.

To select all files in the current folder, press Ctrl+A on your keyboard. You can then use the preceding methods to remove files from the selection if necessary.

Reminder about Wireless Networks

Remember that your wireless network is considerably slower and more susceptible to congestion than a wired Ethernet connection. When you are moving a large number of files from a computer to your server, you may want to temporarily connect any computers directly to a switch that is connected to your server. Long Ethernet cables are available from retailers like Best Buy or Amazon, and a 50- or 100-foot cable can be purchased for $15 or $25. Having a long cable handy will allow you to connect a computer via a faster link for bandwidth-heavy operations such as moving files or restoring a computer from a backup. After you are done, the Ethernet wire can be coiled up and stored in a closet until the next time you need it. A wired Ethernet connection is actually required to perform a full restore on a computer (described in detail in Chapter 10), so having a long cable handy will be appreciated if you ever need to restore one of your computers that is normally connected via wireless.

Moving Files

After you find and select a set of files, it's time to start moving them to your server! You need to open another copy of Windows Explorer to make this easier. You can either double-click the Shared Folders on Server icon on your desktop, or you can use the ⊞+R shortcut, and enter **\\SERVER** in the Run dialog box. From here, you can navigate to the folder where you wish to move the files by double-clicking folders.

If you have enough screen space, resize and position the windows side by side, as shown in Figure 8-13. This makes the file-moving process easier.

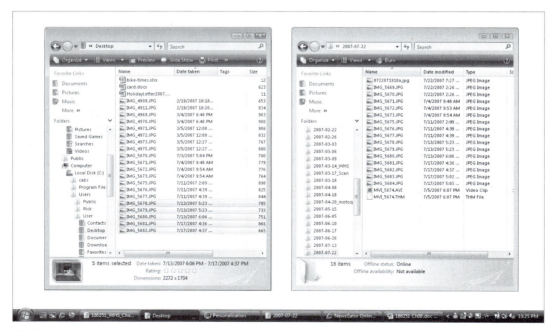

Figure 8-13

Chapter 8: Digital Spring-Cleaning

Take your mouse and instead of using the more-often used left mouse button, click and hold the right mouse button on one of the selected files. While still holding the right mouse button down, drag the mouse over to the destination folder for the files, and then release the mouse button. A menu will pop up, as shown in Figure 8-14. Select Move Here from this menu, and the files will be moved from their original location to their new home on your server. Just as you can move individual files or groups of files, you can select and move individual folders or groups of folders.

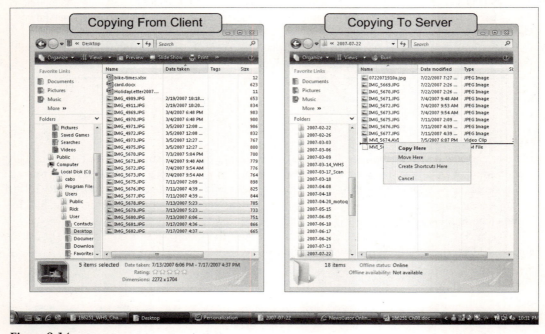

Figure 8-14

If you do not have enough screen space to line up the windows side by side, there is another trick to make things easier. While you are dragging the selected files (with the right-mouse button held down), hover the mouse over the destination window's taskbar listing at the bottom of the screen. After you have hovered over it for a short while, the destination window will pop up in front of the other windows and you will be able to continue to drag the files to their destination. Alternately, you can right-click the source files and select Cut and then right-click the destination folder and select Paste.

Some people are more inclined to copy files, thinking that they will just go back later and delete the files once they are copied, but this is a bad idea for a couple of reasons. The first is that you might accidentally delete files that really haven't actually been copied to the server. Now this isn't catastrophic, because you followed the advice to back up your computer before you began, but it is an added headache if you have to go restore files just because they were accidentally deleted. The other problem is that you might copy the same file into multiple locations on the server. During one pass, you may think that it belongs in one folder, and on another pass you might select a different destination.

Sometimes selecting a destination folder is a bit of a judgment call, so there's a good possibility of ending up with multiple copies of the same file.

The idea behind moving files is that once a file is moved, it can be considered *taken care of*. You are done with it, and no further action is needed. You want to act on each file once, and only once, and moving the files as you go will ensure that this is the case. The urge to copy files is rooted in a *just-in-case* mindset, where people like to keep their files in their original location until they know that they are safely copied to their new location. Windows does a pretty good job of not deleting the original unless the move is successful, so that it adds one layer of safety. Another layer of safety is the backups that you performed prior to moving any files. If a file accidentally goes missing, you can always retrieve it from the backup. (The process for recovering files is described in Chapter 10.)

Continue this process until you have effectively cleaned your computer of files that you would rather have stored on your Windows Home Server.

Staging

As you work your way through your computer's hard drive, you may find files that don't have a specific home. When you encounter these files, it is acceptable to create a `Staged` folder on the home server, as mentioned earlier, so that you can move them off the computer and revisit them later. For example, when I am bulk-copying photos from my computer to the server, I put them in a `Staged` folder located at the root of my Photos shared folder. From there, I can arrange them by date, and review them for specific subjects before creating folders to sort them into. A good rule of thumb to follow is that if a set of files will require you to create more than one folder in order to organize them according to your strategy, then it is acceptable to create a single staging folder instead and revisit them later.

To keep the staging folder from becoming a catchall unsorted folder, you should make a commitment to review, empty, and delete all staging folders before you move on to the next computer in your spring-cleaning effort.

Checking for More Files

After you have manually collected and transferred files to your server, you can use Windows Vista's search capability to check if you missed any pockets of files. Open the search function by clicking the Start orb and then select Search from the right-hand side of the menu. A search window will open. Now type a query in the box in the upper right-hand corner of the window. Some searches that are useful include:

- `*.jpg`: Locates photos stored as JPEG files.
- `*.doc*`: Locates Microsoft Word Documents (the trailing * makes sure that Windows locates both older style `.doc` files and newer `.docx` files).

A query for JPEG files is shown in Figure 8-15. Once you locate a file that you think should be moved, right-click it and select Open file location from the context menu, as shown in Figure 8-16. A window will open and you can inspect the folder to see if other files need to be moved to the Windows Home Server as well. Use the same methods outlined in the "Moving Files" section earlier in this chapter to relocate any outstanding files.

Chapter 8: Digital Spring-Cleaning

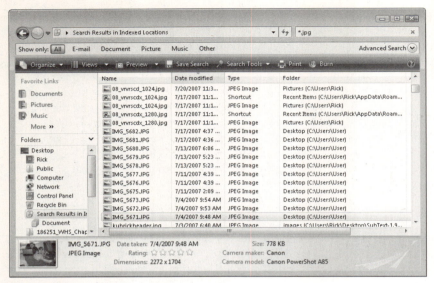

Figure 8-15

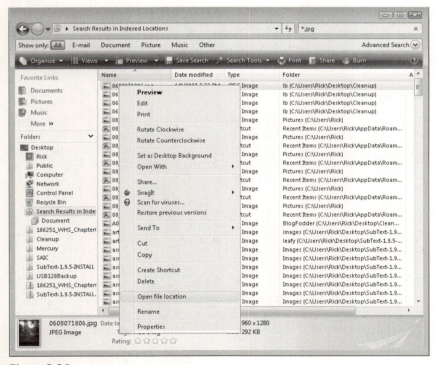

Figure 8-16

A Caution about Search

Using search tools to find files can be useful, but you should be careful about relocating files if you don't understand what their purpose is. The search function may return files that are part of Windows or part of one of your other installed programs, and moving these files may make programs stop working, or cause errors for Windows. As a general rule, you should not relocate any files that you find under `C:\Windows\` or `C:\Program Files\`. Files are really only useful to have on your home server's share folders if you understand what their purpose is and what data they contain, so it's best to leave any mystery files in their original location.

Continue the manual search process for each computer on your home network until all of your important data has found a new home on your Windows Home Server's shared folders.

Learning New Habits

Now that your data is centralized and organized, you should start thinking about developing some new habits so that you can maintain this newfound order. The philosopher George Santayana wrote "Habit is stronger than reason," and this truth will be the root for a personal challenge for those trying to organize their digital lives.

To create new habits, you must be both disciplined and creative. To encourage the other users of your home network to follow your lead, creativity will serve you better.

Setting a Good Example

This is a good lesson for any change management challenge for many reasons. First, if others notice you following the plan, you will have better luck convincing them that it is a good idea. Nothing torpedoes a well-planned change initiative like seeing the leader circumventing the new rules.

A second reason to strive to set the example is that it will force you to see the pain points in the new strategy. It will show you areas that are too hard, and give you the information that you need to make things work more smoothly.

Lastly, don't get frustrated when you or others lapse in adherence to the strategy. Remember that human nature is very strong, and old habits are hard to break. Strong rebukes won't motivate others to get on-board with your plan. Instead, strive to find out what you can do to make the plan easier to follow.

Creating Shortcuts

Windows Home Server creates two default shortcuts when you install the connector software, but you will need to create many more shortcuts if you want Windows Home Server to become the primary location that your family uses to store files and data.

Use your knowledge of where files were being stored, and create shortcuts to help direct yourself and others to the Home Server's shared folders. For example, I tend to save a lot of documents on my desktop, and in the `Documents` folder in my user directory. To help me remember to save these to the Windows Home Server, I created two shortcuts in each location. One shortcut points to the Documents custom share that I created. The other one points to a `Documents` folder that is contained in my personal share on the server. Now when I go to save a document from Word, I am presented with shortcuts that will take me to the location where I really *should* be saving my files.

Chapter 8: Digital Spring-Cleaning

To create a shortcut like this, open the Windows Home Server's shared folders either by using the Shared Folders on Server icon on your desktop, or press ⊞+R and type **\\SERVER** in the Run dialog box. From here, locate the folder that you wish to create a shortcut for. Right-click the folder and select Create Shortcut from the context menu, as shown in Figure 8-17. If you are at the top level, the shortcut will be created on your desktop. If you are working within a shared folder creating shortcuts for subfolders, then the shortcut will be created in the current directory. After a shortcut is created, you can move it using a process similar to what you did when moving files to the server. Open another Windows Explorer window, navigate to the location where you want the shortcut, right-click and drag the shortcut to the destination, and select Move.

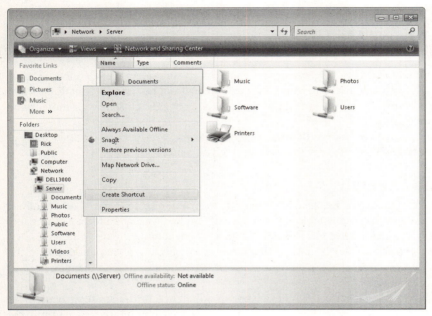

Figure 8-17

Once the shortcut is in the proper location, right-click it and select Rename. Now type a friendlier name that will make it clear to you and to others exactly where this shortcut leads. For example, for my Documents shortcuts, I named the one that points to the Documents share "Shared Documents on Home Server," and I named the one that points to the `Documents` folder under my personal user share "Personal Documents on Windows Home Server." Providing descriptive names like this makes it clear when I am saving a file that I can click the shortcut to get to a better location to save my files. I have also created shortcuts for my wife that lead her from all of the old locations where she used to save files, to the new location on the server. This serves a double purpose. It helps her to locate files so that she isn't frustrated that I have moved everything, and it gives her an easy way to start saving files to the shares on the home server.

On Windows Vista, you can also add shortcuts to folders on your Windows Home Server to the Favorite Links in the navigation pane. Just click and drag from the desired folder to the Favorite Links area in a Windows Explorer window to add that location to the list.

Reminding Others of Benefits

While I conceded earlier that habit is much stronger than reason, you should not ignore reason altogether. As part of your encouragement to yourself and your family members, you should point out the benefits of keeping data on the Windows Home Server. Remind the other members of your household that centralized storage makes it easier to keep their data safe. Show them how to access their data from other computers in the household, and after you learn how to access files remotely (this is covered in Chapter 11), share this feature with them as well.

It may be helpful to pull together a simple document that highlights both the benefits of utilizing Windows Home Server, as well as the details of your specific organizational plan. A single page that highlights the main benefits of keeping data on the server and lists the basic organizational scheme can be provided to computer users in your home and posted near client computers so that the information is readily available. An example document is shown in Figure 8-18. (This document is available from `http://whsbook.com/files`.) You should also be certain to point out successes, such as the fact that Mom's photos have all been uploaded to the server so that everyone can see them.

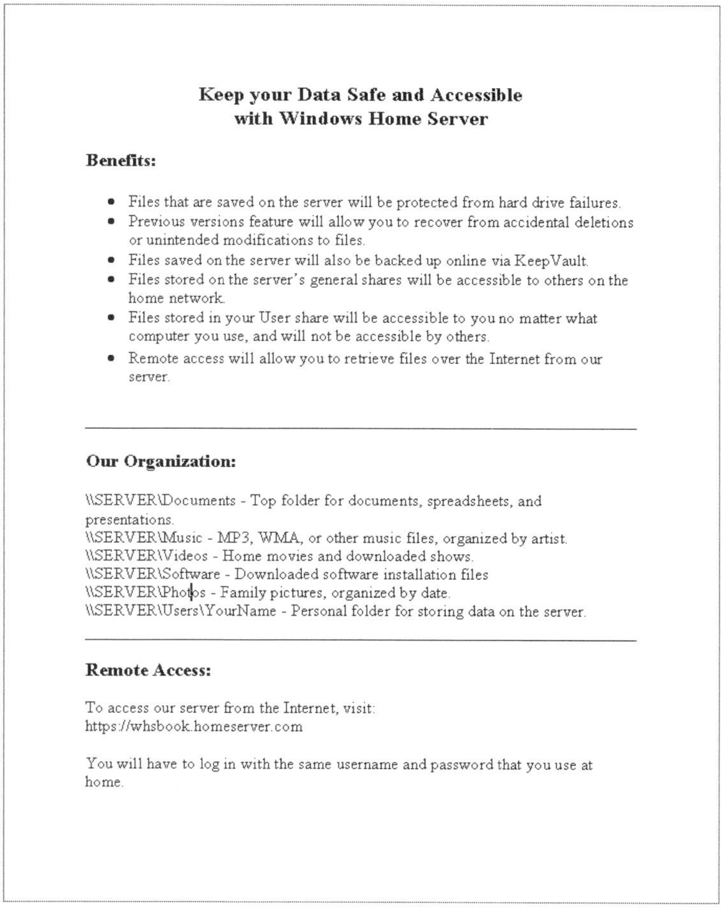

**Keep your Data Safe and Accessible
with Windows Home Server**

Benefits:

- Files that are saved on the server will be protected from hard drive failures.
- Previous versions feature will allow you to recover from accidental deletions or unintended modifications to files.
- Files saved on the server will also be backed up online via KeepVault.
- Files stored on the server's general shares will be accessible to others on the home network.
- Files stored in your User share will be accessible to you no matter what computer you use, and will not be accessible by others.
- Remote access will allow you to retrieve files over the Internet from our server.

Our Organization:

\\SERVER\Documents - Top folder for documents, spreadsheets, and presentations.
\\SERVER\Music - MP3, WMA, or other music files, organized by artist.
\\SERVER\Videos - Home movies and downloaded shows.
\\SERVER\Software - Downloaded software installation files
\\SERVER\Photos - Family pictures, organized by date.
\\SERVER\Users\YourName - Personal folder for storing data on the server.

Remote Access:

To access our server from the Internet, visit:
https://whsbook.homeserver.com

You will have to log in with the same username and password that you use at home.

Figure 8-18

Revisiting Spring-Cleaning

After some time has passed, you will have to revisit the spring-cleaning process. Even the most disciplined Windows Home Server user will occasionally slip and save a file on the local drive. Take this opportunity to review several aspects of your strategy. If a certain type of file is always getting left out of the strategy, make sure that your strategy clearly addresses this category. If a particular location ends up accumulating files, then create shortcuts there to make it easier to jump to the right location on the home server. Some programs also include options to set a default save location, so consider looking at the programs that are used to create the files, and see if they include this option. Lastly, remember that setbacks are normal. Creating order from disorder is an uphill battle. Maintain your strategy as a living plan. Modify the plan when necessary, adding and deleting categories and folders to better fit how you create and use your data.

Summary

Now that you have read about the process of digital spring-cleaning, you are ready to sweep through the computer on your home network and transition to a centralized storage strategy. You reviewed the strategy that you developed in Chapter 2, and you are now ready to charge ahead and implement your organizational plan. You understand what files should be left on the local hard drive, and you have committed to brining the benefits of centralized storage on Windows Home Server to your home network.

You understand that before you begin the spring-cleaning process, it is a good idea to back up all of your computers, and you know how to do so easily with Windows Home Server. You know how to create user-defined shares for top-level categories, and how to create subfolders for subcategories.

You learned the common locations for finding files that need to be moved to the home server, and you learned how to use Windows Vista's search function to find other locations where files may be hiding. Once you locate your files, you know how to move them to their proper destination, and you understand how and when to use a staging folder to make the transition easier.

Lastly, you learned some tips and tricks for making it easier for the users of your home network to adhere to the new organizational plan.

Chapter 9

The Center of Your Digital Home

In addition to serving as a central location for storage of your important files and keeping your home computers protected from data loss, Windows Home Server can also serve as the center of your digital home. You can connect your printer to your Windows Home Server so that it will be accessible to all of the computers on your network. You can also use Windows Home Server to serve media files to Media Connect devices like an Xbox, Xbox 360, some DVR models, or a dedicated media connector like one of D-Link's MediaLounge series of devices. With your media shared from your home server, you can view home movies and digital pictures on your TV, or listen to your digital music files through your home stereo.

Centralizing Your Printer

By moving your printer to a central location, you can make it available to all of the computers in your home. There are several benefits to making this change. Many households have multiple printers just because this is the easiest way to make sure that you can print from each computer. Unfortunately this may mean keeping stock of different types of ink, or using lower-quality printers. It's also difficult to print from laptops and mobiles because this often means connecting them to the printer directly. Other people have managed to set up printer sharing over their home networks, but sharing a printer from one client computer means that computer must always be on when you wish to print, and it's often difficult to get things working correctly with account permissions and firewall settings.

If you decide to use your Windows Home Server to centralize your printer, you will reduce the overhead required for maintaining your home's printer. You can now stock extra ink for a single model of printer. You can also keep extra paper in one location, near the single printer. Printing will also be a more uniform function across your network. The central printer will be available to each computer, including mobile devices like notebooks, TabletPCs, and UMPCs.

With a single central printer, you might also be able to justify purchasing a higher-quality printer such as a color laser printer, because it will be easy to make use of it from all of the computers on your network. Whether you are selecting a new printer or deciding which of your existing printers to use as a centralized resource, it is a good idea to consult industry references like *Consumer Reports*, *PC Magazine*, or *Consumer World* (www.consumerworld.org). These resources can help you determine what printer will give you the best output or which will offer the lower cost-per-page printing.

> **Note**
> If you consolidate your printing, you can save extra printers as backups, or if you have a college-bound student in the house, you may want to save an extra printer for them to take to school.

Limitations

It is important to note several limitations to using a printer with your Windows Home Server. The first is that your printer must have drivers available that will work under Windows Server 2003. Windows Server 2003 is the operating system at the core of Windows Home Server, and in order to install a printer, you have to be able to find drivers for it. This may seem a little counter-intuitive, because you will almost always be printing from a client system running Windows Vista or XP, but the server needs to be able to communicate with the printer, so drivers will be required. Many consumer-focused printers do not have drivers available to support Windows Server 2003, so you may want to do some research before you relocate your printer. You can find out if your printer is supported under Windows Server 2003 by searching for drivers on your printer manufacturer's website. An alternative resource that shows if devices have passed Microsoft's compatibility testing for different Microsoft operating systems is Microsoft's Windows Server Catalog, which can be found at `www.windowsservercatalog.com/`.

Another limitation is that many multifunction devices that include scanners and fax machines will only work as printers over the network. Again, check your printer documentation and the manufacturer's website to see if these functions can be accessed over a network. If the manufacturer doesn't say anything about network access for these functions, you can assume that they won't work.

Setting Up Your Printer

As the previous section highlights, the ability to act as a central location for sharing your printer is based on the fact that at its core, Windows Home Server is based on Windows Server 2003. Some printers support what is known as *silent installation* under Windows Home Server. With silent installation, you can simply plug the printer in via USB, and Windows Home Server will detect, install, and share the printer. Unfortunately, the number of printers that will install in this manner is relatively small, but it is worth trying just in case! To see if silent install is supported, just plug the printer in to your Windows Home Server via a USB cable, and then power the printer on. (Note: Your Windows Home Server does not need to be powered down in order to connect a USB printer.) After waiting at least 5 minutes, open a connection to the server from a client computer by pressing ⊞+R, then entering \\SERVER, and clicking the OK button. If your printer has been installed silently, it will show up in the listing of the top-level shares. If the printer does not show up, you may have to install and/or share it manually.

The capability to manually install printers is not enabled through the Windows Home Server Console, so it requires you to log in to your Windows Home Server via Remote Desktop. In the server world, this is also known as connecting via Terminal Services. What this means is that you start a client application on one of your computers, and you can actually log in to your server, see your server's desktop, settings, and everything else, just as if you had connected a monitor and keyboard to your server. For retail Windows Home Server machines that do not have monitor or keyboard connections, this is the only way to interact directly with the server. You must connect using Windows' Remote Desktop Connection program and then install the server just as if you were using a keyboard, mouse, and monitor connected directly to the server.

Connecting the Printer

Most modern printers connect via a USB cable. You need to find a location for your printer that is convenient for your home's computer users, but that is also close enough to your home server. USB cable lengths top out at sixteen feet (5 meters), but a longer cable should give you some flexibility to put your printer in an accessible spot.

After you connect the USB cable to your Windows Home Server machine and to the printer, plug in the printer and turn it on.

Logging in to Your Home Server

The next step is to log in to your Windows Home Server machine via remote desktop connection on a client computer. This can be accomplished from any computer with a wired or reliable wireless network connection.

You can start the Remote Desktop Connection program by clicking the Start orb, and then selecting All Programs, Accessories, and then Remote Desktop Connection. Alternately, you can use the @@ma001+R shortcut to open the Run dialog box, type **mstsc** in the Open text box, and then click OK. When you first open the Remote Desktop Connection window, it will look similar to Figure 9-1.

Figure 9-1

Type the name of your server, usually SERVER, in the box labeled Computer, and then click Connect to connect to your server. When you are prompted to select or enter a user, either choose or type **Administrator** for the username, and type your Windows Home Server administrative password into the password field. This is the same password that you use to connect to the Windows Home Server Console. The interface for entering a username and password is different under different versions of Windows. Figure 9-2 shows how the dialog box appears under Windows Vista.

Note

If you have difficulties connecting to your server via Remote Desktop, try logging in to the Windows Home Server Console, and then leaving the console window open while you open the Remote Desktop Connection. This is a quick way to resolve an issue where a firewall on one of your machines is blocking Remote Desktop Protocol (RDP). Because the Windows Home Server Console utilizes RDP, opening it should also open these ports, and most firewall software will recognize the console software and configure itself accordingly.

Chapter 9: The Center of Your Digital Home

Figure 9-2

After you have successfully connected, your screen should look similar to Figure 9-3. If your Remote Desktop Connection application is configured to use full-screen mode, you will see a small tab at the top of the screen instead of the windowed frame shown in Figure 9-3. This tab is known as the connection bar, and it can be used to access the same functions as the buttons on the window frame. Both interfaces allow you to minimize or close the Remote Desktop window. If you close the window using the X on the window frame or on the connection bar, any programs that are currently running on the server will continue to run until you reconnect and close them, or until the server is rebooted.

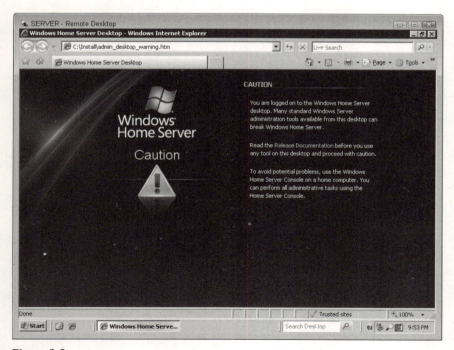

Figure 9-3

The first thing that Windows Home Server shows is a warning that using some tools directly on the server can break the functionality of the server. Simply adding a printer is a safe operation, but you should heed the warning and refrain from using most tools directly on the server.

Adding Your Printer

Adding a printer to your server is similar to adding one to a desktop computer. Click the Start menu and select Printers and Faxes, as shown in Figure 9-4.

Figure 9-4

In the window that opens, shown in Figure 9-5, you will see a listing of any printers that have previously been added, as well as a virtual printer driver called the Microsoft XPS Document Writer. You may see an additional printer listed if you have a printer configured on your client computer. The default settings for the Remote Desktop Connection program actually connect any local (client) printers to the server so that you can print from the server to the client. This can cause a bit of confusion if you don't understand what is going on. This extra printer should have a note indicating that it is actually connected from the client, with the name of the client computer in parentheses, as shown in Figure 9-5.

From here, double-click the Add Printer icon to display the Add Printer Wizard screen, as shown in Figure 9-6. Click Next to continue.

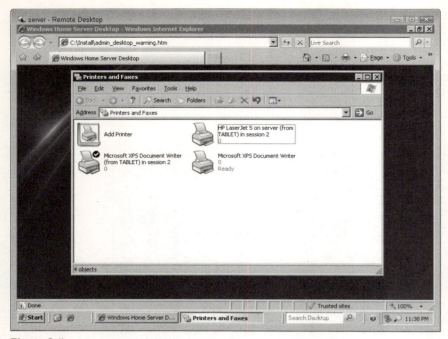

Figure 9-5

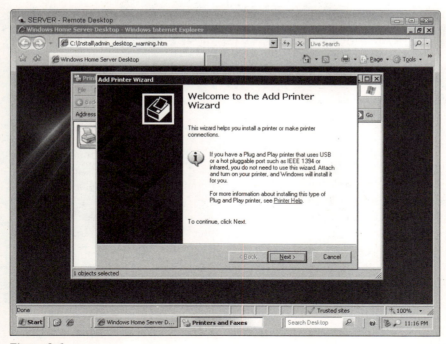

Figure 9-6

Chapter 9: The Center of Your Digital Home   **147**

On the following screen, shown in Figure 9-7, you select the type of printer that you are configuring. You can set up Windows Home Server to act as a print server for a networked printer that has a built-in network adapter, but for this example, select a local printer. Remember that when the dialog box refers to *this computer*, it is actually referring to your Windows Home Server box. Confirm that the checkbox for automatically detecting plug-and-play printers is checked, confirm that your printer is plugged in to your server and powered on, and click Next.

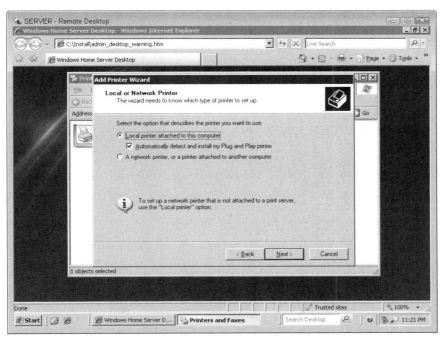

Figure 9-7

If your printer is detected automatically, the wizard will display information about your printer. If detection fails, you will see the screen shown in Figure 9-8 and you will have to manually select the manufacturer and model of your printer. If your printer was detected correctly, you can skip the next two paragraphs.

To manually select your printer, click Next. On the following screen, shown in Figure 9-9, you must select the port to which your printer is connected. For USB printers, you should select USB001 (Virtual printer port for USB). For parallel printers, select LPT1: (Recommended Printer Port). If your printer uses a different port, select the appropriate interface just as you would on a desktop computer.

If your printer drivers are included with Windows, you can just select the printer manufacturer and model from the dialog boxes, as shown in Figure 9-10 and then click Next. If you have downloaded drivers for your printer to your client computer, or if you have a CD-ROM with the drivers, you can copy the drivers to your server's software share at \\SERVER\Software, and then use the Have Disk button and Browse to locate the drivers. (In the Browse dialog box, you can type **\\SERVER\Software** into the File name text box and then press ENTER to quickly locate the software share.)

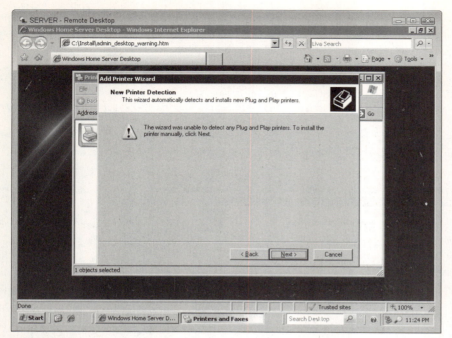

Figure 9-8

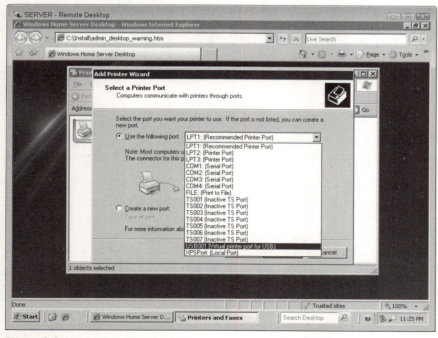

Figure 9-9

Chapter 9: The Center of Your Digital Home   149

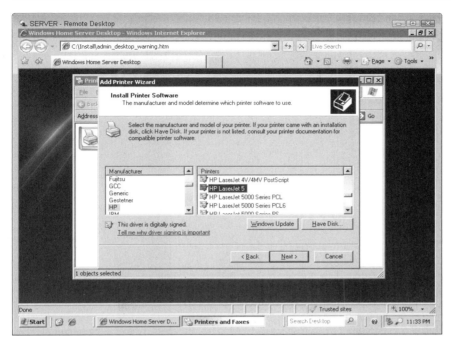

Figure 9-10

Once you locate the appropriate driver for your printer, you are presented with a screen that allows you to name the printer, as shown in Figure 9-11. You can accept the default name, or give it a more meaningful name if you want. The option to select this as a default printer for a Windows Home Server machine is fairly meaningless, because working from the Windows Home Server desktop is not recommended. This same option is important when you are setting up a printer on a client, but it can be ignored when setting up a printer on your home server.

In the next dialog box, shown in Figure 9-12, you have the option of sharing your printer and giving it a share name. Sharing the printer is the whole reason that you are doing this, so make sure that the radio button next to Share name is selected, and give the printer a more friendly name if you desire. Click Next to continue. If the share name is longer than eight characters you will receive a warning that the printer may not be accessible from MS-DOS workstations. As long as you don't have any really old computer running MS-DOS that you want to print from, it's OK to just click Next to continue through this warning.

The next dialog box, shown in Figure 9-13, gives you the option of including additional details for the printer. This is mostly a holdover from the corporate side of Windows Server, where the location might be used to differentiate among many similar printers on a large network. It isn't necessary to fill in the details, but you can do so if you want. Click Next to continue.

The next dialog box offers the opportunity to print a test page, as shown in Figure 9-14. Leave the selection set to Yes, and click Next. A single test page should be printed on the printer.

The last page of the wizard shows a confirmation of all of the selections you have made, as shown in Figure 9-15. Click Finish to exit the wizard.

Chapter 9: The Center of Your Digital Home

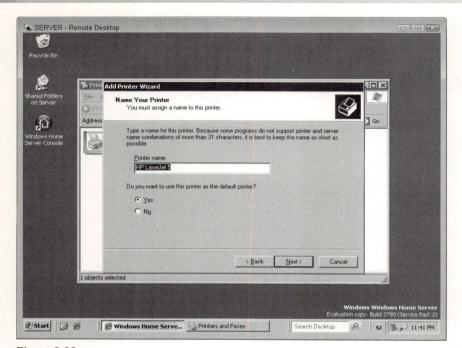

Figure 9-11

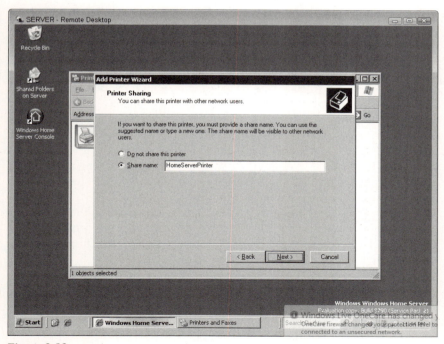

Figure 9-12

Chapter 9: The Center of Your Digital Home 151

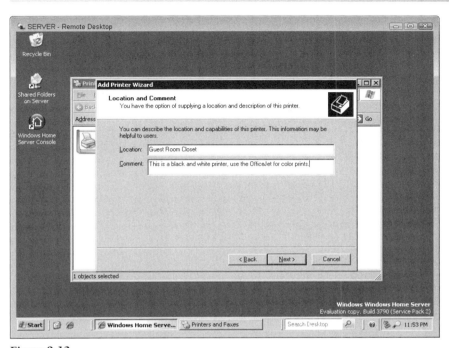

Figure 9-13

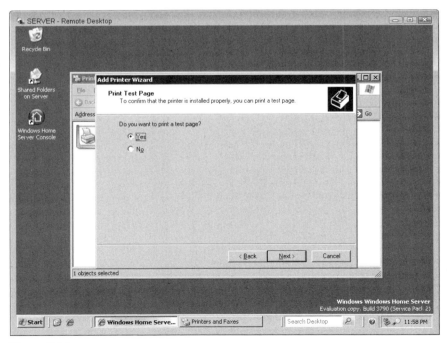

Figure 9-14

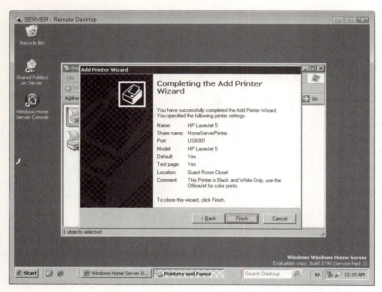

Figure 9-15

Logging Off from Your Server

To properly disconnect from your server's Remote Desktop session, click the Start button in the Remote Desktop window, and select Log Off, as shown in Figure 9-16. Click Log Off in the confirmation pop-up, and you will be disconnected from your server.

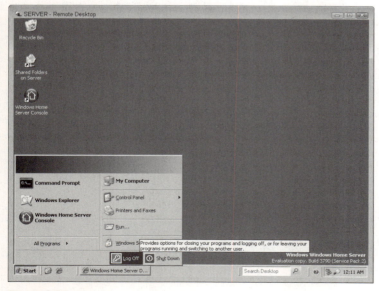

Figure 9-16

Your printer is now properly set up and shared from your Windows Home Server. The next step is to connect your client computers to the shared printer.

Use Caution when Connected Directly to Your Windows Home Server

The warning that you see when you connect to your Windows Home Server's desktop should be taken seriously. Remember that you are going to be relying on this server to protect all of your household's important files and data, your *digital life*. Even if you like to experiment with computers, you should keep in perspective the importance of this particular machine, and only make changes where you understand the consequences, not just in general terms, but in how they might affect the technology that is unique to Windows Home Server.

In particular, you should avoid running anything directly on your Windows Home Server that directly accesses hard drives, or that interacts with the server's Internet Information Server (IIS) settings. You don't want to use tools that directly access the hard drives because Windows Home Server's Drive Extender technology expects to be the only thing accessing the hard drives. Drive Extender interacts at a low level with the drives included in the storage pool, and some common tools can break that interaction. Windows Home Server's Remote Access features rely on the Internet Information Server settings being unchanged. Actions such as changing ports, or adding websites to the server could break Remote Access.

Another important warning is that you should not directly access the files on Windows Home Server's D: drive. Casual exploration will show that it appears that the D:\Shares folder holds the shared folders for Windows Home Server. Drive Extender expects all access to the shared folders to be accomplished through the shared folder interface, that is, \\SERVER\Documents, and so on. Unfortunately, if you access these files directly, you are bypassing the Drive Extender technology and you may leave your files unprotected or you could even corrupt the files.

Remember that your Windows Home Server machine is meant to be a reliable place to store data and backups, and refrain from experimentation that could put the safety of your files in question.

Connecting Clients to Your Shared Printer

Connecting to a shared printer is a quick process, and you will want to do this on all computers that you want to print to the shared printer. To start, use the @@ma001+R shortcut to open the Run dialog box, then type **\\SERVER** into the Open text box, and click OK. This opens your Server's root network share folder. Your printer's share name will probably be shown in the resulting dialog box, as you can see in Figure 9-17. If not, you can open the Printers share by double-clicking it.

In either folder, you can connect the printer to the local client computer by right-clicking the icon for the printer and selecting Connect from the context menu, as shown in Figure 9-18.

154 Chapter 9: The Center of Your Digital Home

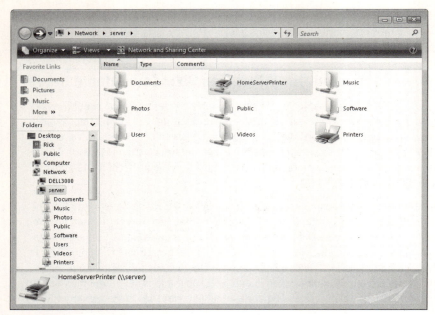

Figure 9-17

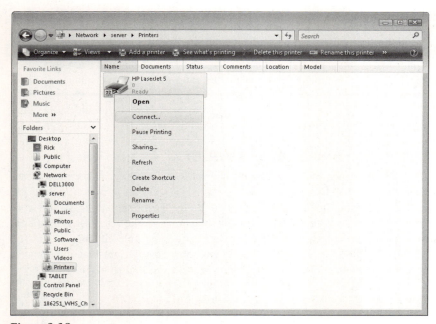

Figure 9-18

A pop-up dialog box will indicate that the printer is being connected. Under Windows Vista, you may also receive a warning about copying drivers from an untrusted machine (unless these drivers were previously loaded on the client). When installing the drivers, you may also receive a User Account Control (UAC) prompt informing you that administrative access is required to proceed. After any warnings, the printer installation progress will be displayed in a dialog box. When the dialog box disappears, the printer has been successfully added to the local client. You can double-check that it has been added by going to your computer's Control Panel and selecting Printer from the Hardware and Sound section. The Printer control panel will also allow you to change the default printer to select the shared printer as the default if you desire.

Repeat this process on each machine that you want to connect to the shared printer.

Sharing Media with Windows Home Server

Storing all of your media on your Windows Home Server is great for keeping it protected and for making it accessible to all of the computers on your network. There is another category of devices that will allow you to expand your home network to include your televisions, home audio systems, and even digital picture frames. By making your media more accessible, you can enjoy your entertainment in more convenient ways, and you can experience memories that are brought back by photos and movies.

Note
The ups and downs of centralized storage and advice for developing and executing a plan for moving your data are addressed in Chapter 2 and Chapter 7.

Setting Up Media Library Sharing

To set up Windows Home Server to make your media available across your home network, you must log in to the Windows Home Server Console. You can open the console quickly by double-clicking the Windows Home Server icon in the system tray on one of your client computers. You must enter your home server's administrative password to access the console. This is the password you selected when you initially set up Windows Home Server. Once you enter the password, the Windows Home Server Console appears, similar to Figure 9-19.

Click the Settings menu option in the upper right corner of the console window to display the Windows Home Server Settings dialog box. On the left side of the dialog box, select the Media Sharing tab, and you should see a screen similar to Figure 9-20. For each type of media that you wish to share on your network, change the selection to On.

This screen includes a note that *enabling* allows any digital media receivers on your home network to access the content that you share. Digital media receivers include many different consumer devices, but could also be other computers on the network. Media Connect, the protocol that digital media receivers use to access content on your server, does not require authentication in order to download content from a server. This means that your data is available to any device or computer on your network. For most home networks, this should not be too great of a concern, but if you are on an unprotected network, or if you have an unsecured wireless network, you should consider the fact that using the media sharing feature allows anyone on your network to view your media. If you have children in your household, you should also be mindful of the fact that anything in the Music, Photos, or Videos shares will be accessible across the network and via any media extender devices. Enabling Media Sharing effectively overrides any access permissions that you have set on these three folders. If you have content that may be inappropriate for youngsters, you should move it to a different share on your Windows Home Server. After you have made the selection, click OK to save the settings and close the dialog box. You can exit from the Windows Home Server Console using the X in the upper right corner of the console window.

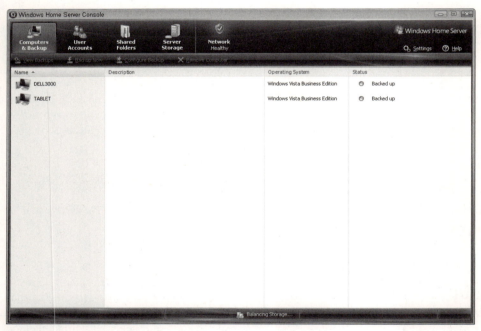

Figure 9-19

DRM and Media Files

Many media files that are purchased from online stores contain a technology called digital rights management, or DRM. DRM limits the way that you can use the media file and often restricts how many computers the file can be played on or what you can do with the file. Copying DRM protected files to Windows Home Server does not remove DRM, so you will still be subject to the same restrictions that were in place before. The media should still play properly on any computer where it is licensed, and it will not play on machines where it is restricted. The effect on the usability of the media file will be identical to what you would experience if you simply copied the file to several different machines.

Figure 9-20

Accessing Media from Your Xbox 360

Many people have an Xbox 360 game system connected to their home network for gaming, but the Xbox 360 is also a Media Connect–enabled device, which means it can be used to view media that you have stored on your home server.

All of the usual warnings about network speed apply to media sharing as well. If you are using a slower wireless connection, be aware that viewing large video files may not work well, and playing music may incur some lag as the data is transferred. A 100 Megabit or 1 Gigabit Ethernet connection is best, and because the Xbox 360 includes a Gigabit Ethernet interface, anything slower than gigabit will become the bottleneck for viewing media. With that said, most media files seem to play well over a 54 Mbps wireless link or a 100 Megabit Ethernet connection.

To view media from your Xbox 360, use your controller to access the Media Blade on the Xbox interface. Your screen should look similar to Figure 9-21.

On the following screen, shown in Figure 9-22, you should select that you want to view media from a computer. Windows Media Connect is enabled on Windows Media Center Edition, and can be enabled on computers running Windows Vista as well. Your Windows Home Server is just another device that can serve media via Windows Media Connect. The options for additional sources of media differ for Music, Pictures, and Video, but for connecting to your home server, the appropriate selection is always Computer.

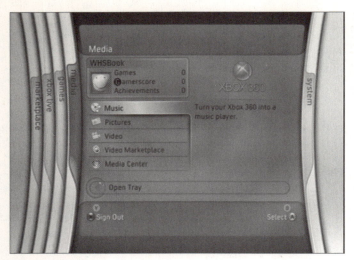

Figure 9-21

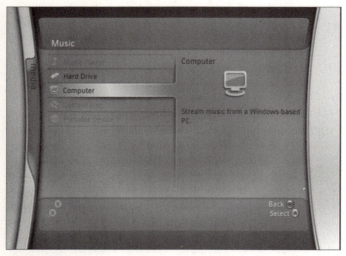

Figure 9-22

The following screen prompts you to download and install software to enable media sharing, as shown in Figure 9-23. Windows Home Server includes this software functionality by default, and as long as you have enabled it through the Windows Home Server Console, no further changes are necessary. You do not need to download any software; just select Yes, continue to move ahead.

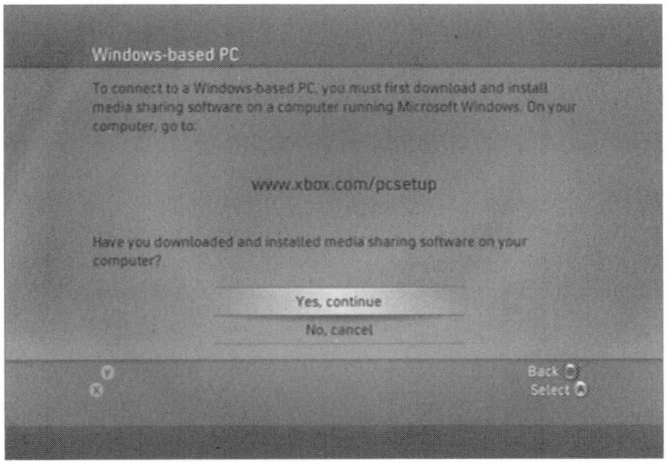

Chapter 9: The Center of Your Digital Home 159

Figure 9-23

Your Xbox 360 will now search for computers that are offering to share media files. Your Windows Home Server's name should appear in the list, as well as any other Media Connect–enabled computers on the network, as shown in Figure 9-24. Use the controller to select your computer.

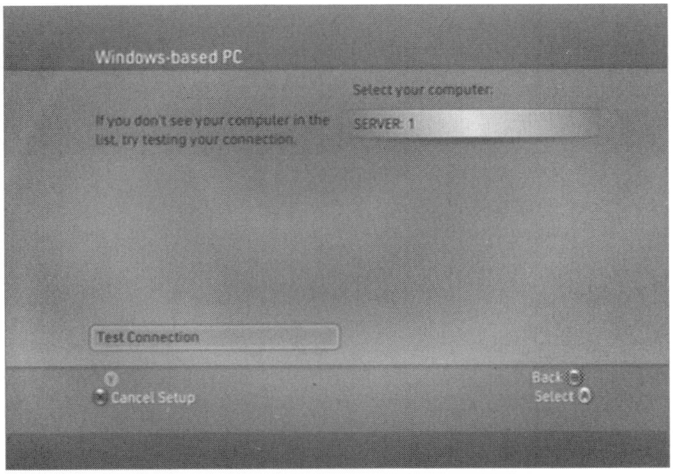

Figure 9-24

The next screen defaults to the Albums view, shown in Figure 9-25. You can use your controller and follow the on-screen prompts to browse by artist, and view song info or start playing music.

Figure 9-25

Once your server is connected, you won't have to select it again. When you select other media types and select Computer for the media source, you will automatically be brought to the browse screen for that media type. The Photos browse screen is shown in Figure 9-26, and it lets you browse by folder, and at any point it lets you start a slideshow that will show all files in the current directory and any subdirectories below.

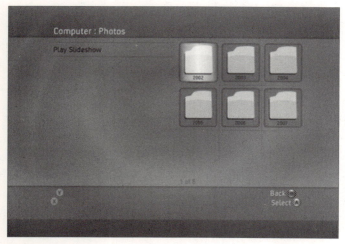

Figure 9-26

The video interface is similar, but you have to select an individual video to play from a folder, rather than having the ability to view all videos in a particular folder. The video selection interface is shown in Figure 9-27.

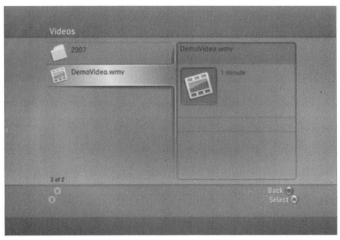

Figure 9-27

Accessing Media from Other Devices

Each device that you use to access content from your Windows Home Server will have its own unique interface. If you have a dedicated set top box, like any of the MediaLounge devices from D-Link, the interface is fairly intuitive and similar to that of the Xbox 360. Figure 9-28 shows the video selection screen from a D-Link DSM-320 MediaLounge device. Having a device like this connected to your TV enables you to view digital home movies on your TV, or to set up a slideshow of your favorite photos. I like to let the MediaLounge play a shuffled slideshow of all of the digital photos that are stored on my home server. It's a nice background to have running on the TV during family events, while you are cleaning the house, or reading a book.

Figure 9-28

Other devices that can make good use of the content on your Windows Home Server include network music players such as the Roku Soundbridge line of devices, or even wireless digital photo frames such as the MemoryFrame 8104 from DSI Solutions. The Soundbridge devices are similar to network media players like the MediaLounge line, but they are meant specifically for serving up music files to a home audio system. Network music players generally have better front-panel controls than the media players, because they cannot rely on a TV screen to provide feedback to the user, and can expand the usefulness of your digital music library. A wireless digital picture frame such as the MemoryFrame can give you a standalone device that can show pictures and movies.

Summary

In this chapter you learned about two more ways you can make Windows Home Server the center of your digital home. First you learned how centralizing your printer can allow you to make better use of your printer by sharing it with all of the computers on your network. Next you learned how to use Windows Home Server to provide access to all of your digital media, not just to computers on your network, but also to other digital media players. This enables you to enjoy your media through your television, home audio system, or through other dedicated devices throughout your home.

Chapter 10

Recovering Lost Data

Everyone loses data. It is not a question of *if* but rather *when* you will experience it. Many folks have become numb to certain occurrences of data loss, having been burned so many times by less than reliable computers that they have come to *expect* a certain amount of unrecoverable lost data.

There are many ways that data can be lost. Sometimes we accidentally delete a file or folder that we later realize we need. These files can sometimes be recovered from Windows' recycling bin, unless they were too large, or too much time has passed, or someone emptied the recycling bin.

Another more troublesome way to lose data is to accidentally save changes over an important file. This often happens when we decide to use an old document as a template for a new document. We open the older file, start adding, deleting, and modifying text, and then we accidentally click Save instead of Save As. Windows' recycling bin can't save you here, and the only hope is an up-to-date backup, which thankfully Windows Home Server provides.

Some other more serious cases of data loss occur when a hard drive suffers a total failure. There are many different ways in which a hard drive can *crash*, but whether it is a mechanical or electrical failure doesn't really matter to most people, because in either case all of the data on the hard drive is effectively gone. Some companies specialize in recovering data from crashed drives, but the prices usually make this option unreasonable for home users.

The last (and hopefully most rare) way that data can be lost is through the loss or theft of a computer. Just this week I was talking to some of our friends who recently experienced a break-in at their home. They live in a good neighborhood, and they have a dog in the house, but when they stopped by the house to drop off a few things between errands they found broken glass and missing belongings. Their PC was one of the casualties of the break-in, and it's heartbreaking to hear the laundry list of files that they will probably never see again. E-mails and digital photos are among the most irreplaceable files that can be lost.

Beyond actual theft, portable computers such as TabletPCs and laptops are frequently lost in airports, taxicabs, and other public places. Nobody plans on losing their computer, but busy schedules and distractions often cause people to lose track of their computer or computer case. If you are lucky, some kind person will be able to track you down and return your computer, but it may very well end up going home with someone else, at a pawn shop, or damaged.

Whatever the circumstance, data loss can be stressful. It can cause you to miss deadlines, lose precious memories, or even cost you money. Keeping data on your Windows Home Server, and keeping your computers backed up with Windows Home Server's Connector software means that you are protected from most of the problems that can arise. In this chapter, you will learn how to recover lost data, restore previous versions of files, and recover a computer that has suffered a hard drive failure, or that has been corrupted by bad software or virus infection.

Recovering Data from Backups

In the event that you accidentally delete a file from one of your client computers, or if you make changes to a file and wish to recover a previous version, you will need to recover the file from a backup that Windows Home Server has performed.

Your Windows Home Server's retention settings, covered in Chapter 7, will determine how many backups you have to choose from. In most instances, you will know soon after you lose data that you need to recover it, so you can simply go to the most recent backup and recover the file. If the data was removed at some point in the past, you may have to dig back through the history of backups in order to locate the file, but rest assured that you can recover data easily.

To recover data from a backup, you need two types of permissions. You need both Windows Home Server administrative permissions and administrative permissions on the specific computer from which you are trying to retrieve information.

The process of recovering data from a backup is accomplished through the Windows Home Server Console, which requires the Windows Home Server's administrative password. Unfortunately this means that other computer users in your home will either have to know the administrative password, or they will rely on you to recover data for them. This may be an occasional hassle, but at least the data is *recoverable*. Later in this chapter you'll see that data stored on Windows Home Server's shared folders is easier to recover, so that is yet another argument for keeping as much data as possible on the server's shared folders.

Another difficulty is that the process of recovering files from backups requires administrative permissions on the computer where you are performing the backups. Windows Home Server basically mounts the backup as a virtual drive, so it requires low-level privileges in order to work. Windows Vista's User Account Control feature will prompt you for permission, or if you are logged in as a non-admin user, it will prompt you to enter administrator credentials.

You do not necessarily have to be using the computer where the missing or corrupted data was originally located. The recovery process will actually be much faster if you use a client computer that is connected to the server via a fast wired Ethernet connection, either 100 Mbps or 1 Gbps. (For more information on how to design your network to make the most of Windows Home Server, refer to Chapter 4) The process of opening backups and retrieving files can be network intensive, even if the files being recovered are relatively small. The extra speed that a wired connection provides will be noticed and appreciated.

Opening Backups

You open backups through the Windows Home Server Console. To open the console, right-click the Widows Home Server icon in the system tray, and select Windows Home Server Console from the context menu. Enter your home server's administrative password. When the console opens, confirm that you are on the Computers & Backups tab by clicking the icon in the upper left corner of your screen. Your console should look similar to Figure 10-1.

Chapter 10: Recovering Lost Data **165**

Figure 10-1

Note

The Windows Home Server Console utilizes a fixed-sized window that is just under 1,000 pixels wide by 700 pixels high. If you are using an older display that runs at 800 by 600, or if you are running a newer display in portrait mode (such as a TabletPC), you may find that a portion of the screen is not viewable.

Locate the listing for the computer that used to have the data you wish to recover. Right-click the computer name, and select View Backups from the context menu, as shown in Figure 10-2.

The resulting screen shows a listing of all of the backups that have been performed for the selected computer. All attempted backups will be listed. The Status column indicates if a backup was completed without error. If it failed, it will list the word *Failed* and the icon will be a red circle with a white X. The first column shows whether a backup is set to be managed automatically, with a gear icon, or if it is set to be kept indefinitely, with a lock icon. The date and time the backup was started and a description are listed as well. The backup list appears similar to Figure 10-3.

Chapter 10: Recovering Lost Data

Figure 10-2

Figure 10-3

You should select the most recent backup that completed successfully, but which also occurred prior to the data loss from which you are trying to recover. It is possible to recover data from backups that did not complete successfully, but you cannot be certain if an incomplete backup will contain the file, so it's better to select a successful backup, and only try to recover from a failed backup if the data is not available from any of the completed backups.

Once you decide which backup to open, click it to select it and then select Open from the bottom section of the dialog box. If this is your first time opening a backup using this computer, you may be prompted to allow a driver installation. This driver installation only occurs one time, but it will include warnings like the one shown in Figure 10-4.

Figure 10-4

Note

If you are logged in directly on the Windows Home Server machine or via remote desktop, you cannot open a backup for viewing. The process of opening a backup relies on the Windows Home Server Connector software, and because the Connector software cannot run on Windows Home Server, this functionality is not supported. Similarly, if you are connected to the Windows Home Server Console remotely (explained more in Chapter 11), you cannot open backups.

After the driver installation is completed, a window opens that allows you to access any files contained in the backup. You will notice that the backup is actually mounted as drive Z: on your local computer. If you already have a Z: or if another backup is still open, Windows Home Server will search backward through the alphabet in order to find a free drive letter.

You are provided a familiar Windows Explorer interface for browsing the backup and recovering files. The mounted drive only allows you to read data from the backup. You cannot change or delete any data. This keeps you from accidentally changing or deleting important files and keeps the integrity of the backup intact. The initial screen is shown in Figure 10-5.

Chapter 10: Recovering Lost Data

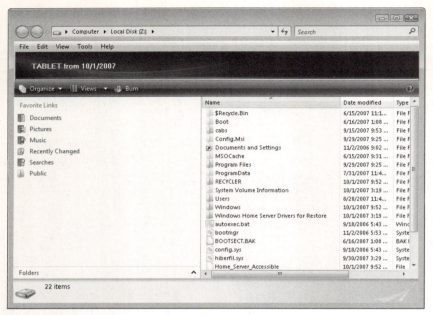

Figure 10-5

You must browse through your directory structure in order to find the missing data. On Windows Vista machines, almost all user-created files can be found under C:\Users\UserName\Desktop\ or C:\Users\UserName\Documents\, where UserName is replaced with the account name of the individual that saved the file. Under older operating systems such as Windows XP, the base user directories can be found under C:\Documents and Settings\, and the Documents folder is actually called My Documents. You can also use Windows search functionality to locate files, but because the contents of the backup are not indexed, searching will be slow and Vista's advanced search features will not be enabled.

Once you locate the files or folders that you need to recover, you simply copy them back to your regular hard drive just as if you were copying them from a CD, USB Memory Stick, or other hard drive. Remember that when you copy a file, Windows Home Server is extracting the file from the backup and copying it over the network, so you will have to be patient for larger files.

Once you have located and copied the data you need back up to your local hard drive or to a file share on your home server, you can close the backup window. The Z: drive will automatically be unmounted.

If you need to open another backup in order to locate a file, just switch back to the Windows Home Server Console, select a different backup and start the process again. Another interesting feature is that you can open multiple backups at the same time. Each one will be assigned a different drive letter, and then you can compare file modification dates, or even contents, in order to better decide which version of the data you need to restore.

Restoring Files on WHS Shares

If you keep most of your files on your Windows Home Server box, then you will rarely have to use the procedure from the previous section. If files are kept in Windows Home Server's shared folders, not only can they be protected by Drive Extender's file and folder duplication, but it is also much easier to retrieve deleted files or restore previous versions of files that are accidentally changed or damaged.

An additional benefit is that restoring files on Windows Home Server's shared folders does not require administrative privileges. If you have access to the folder, you can restore lost or damaged files.

This capability of Windows Home Server is enabled by a feature of Windows known as *Volume Shadow Copies*. Windows Home Server automatically takes a snapshot of your shared folders every twelve hours, at midnight and noon. As long as your file existed before the most recent snapshot, you can use Windows *Previous Versions* feature to bring it back. Previous Versions is also considerably faster than opening backups from the Windows Home Server Console.

Restoring a Deleted File

If you accidentally delete a file from a file share, you can recover it from a previous Volume Shadow Copy snapshot. To do this, you use Windows' Previous Versions capability.

First, you have to open the shared folder where the file was located. Open your shared folders using the Shared Folders on Server shortcut on your desktop, or press ⊞+R and type **\\SERVER** in the Run dialog box to open a window to your shared folders. Browse to the folder that used to contain the file you wish to recover. Right-click in some empty space in the window (away from any files that are listed) and select Properties, as shown in Figure 10-6.

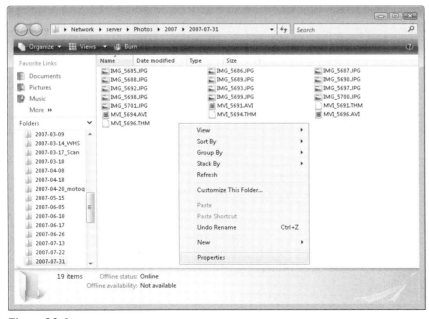

Figure 10-6

In the properties dialog box, select the Previous Versions tab, as shown in Figure 10-7. In this tab, you can select from any of the previous Volume Shadow Copy snapshots. Select the most recent snapshot that occurred before the file was deleted, and then click the Open button. For recovering individual files, it is not a good idea to use the Restore button. The restore functionality restores all files in the current directory to the state they were in when the Volume Shadow Copy snapshot was taken, and this may not be what you actually want. By using the open function, you can examine the files, and even open and view them to be certain they are the version you wish to restore.

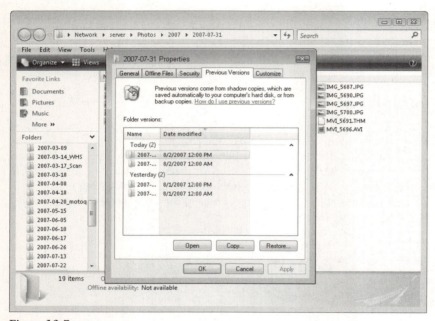

Figure 10-7

A dialog box similar to Figure 10-8 appears, and all of the files that were in the folder at the time of the snapshot will be listed. The address bar will include a note indicating when the snapshot occurred.

From the resulting window, you can view the previous version of the folder in order to locate the missing file. Once you have found it, you can simply drag it to the original folder, or to a different location. If you can arrange the windows side by side, just left-click and drag the file from the Shadow Copy window to the destination. If you don't have enough screen space to arrange the two folder windows side by side, left-click and hold on the file you need to restore, while holding the mouse button down, drag the file over the top of the button on the taskbar that represents the original folder, and the window will be brought to the front. While still holding the mouse button down, drag the file into the destination folder's window, and release the mouse button. The shadow copy folder is a read-only representation of the folder in its previous state, so you don't need to worry about damaging it. It will not allow any files to be deleted or changes to be made.

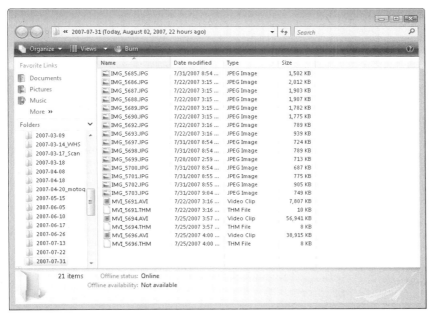

Figure 10-8

Restoring a Previous Version of a File

If you accidentally overwrite a file on a shared folder, Windows Home Server can help you restore a previous version of the file. This functionality also relies on Volume Shadow Copies, so the process is similar to the previous section.

Open the shared folder where the damaged file is located. To do this, open your shared folders using the Shared Folders on Server shortcut on your desktop, or press @@ma001+R and type \\SERVER in the Run dialog box to open a window to your shared folders. Browse to the folder that contains the file you wish to restore. Right-click the file that you are looking to restore and select the Restore previous versions option from the context menu, as shown in Figure 10-9.

If you are working on a slower network, it may take a few seconds for the resulting dialog box to appear. The dialog box will show any previous instances of the file, and will include a notation for the date that that version was last modified, as shown in Figure 10-10. Click the version of the file you wish to restore, and then click the Restore button at the bottom of the dialog box.

You will be prompted to confirm the restore action, and a note will indicate that the restoration cannot be undone. Click OK, and your file will be restored to your hard drive.

Chapter 10: Recovering Lost Data

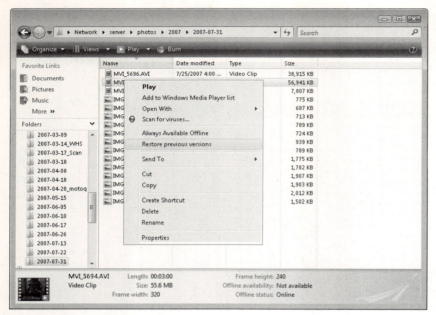

Figure 10-9

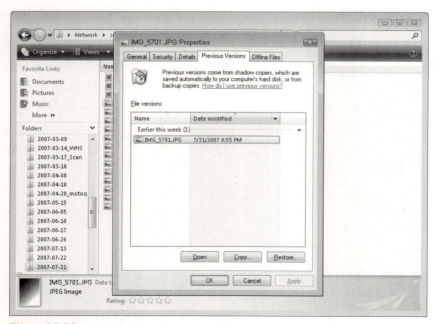

Figure 10-10

Recovering from a Hard Drive Failure

There are many different ways that a hard drive can fail. A true hard drive *crash* occurs when the physical mechanisms in your hard drive fail. Sometimes this is accompanied by a grinding noise or a futile clicking sound, or sometimes total silence. Other times a component on the controller board goes bad. Hard drive failures can occur because of power surges, accidental jarring of the computer, or sometimes the components of the drive just wear out and cease to function.

If you experience a true hard drive failure on one of your client computers, the first step to recovery is getting a new hard drive. If you are comfortable working inside your computer, a replacement hard drive can be bought from a local computer shop or online retailer. Different computers require different processes for replacing a hard drive, so we won't try to cover them all here. Some laptops are a little more challenging because they use smaller connectors and components. Your computer user's manual will sometimes contain step-by-step instructions for removing and replacing your hard drive.

Note

Recovery is only supported when you are restoring a backup to the exact same computer from which it was created. Windows Home Server will allow you to run the recovery wizard on different hardware, but the restored machine may not boot or may suffer from significant driver problems or system instability. In addition, if your original computer had an OEM Windows license (noted on the licensing sticker attached to the machine), your new installation may be considered an illegal copy, both in the eyes of the law and by Microsoft's Windows Genuine Advantage automated anti-piracy program.

If you are not comfortable replacing the drive and can't find a friend or relative who is willing to help, most local computer shops will install a new hard drive for a nominal fee. Some stores will even install it for free if you purchase the drive from them. The only special instructions that you need to provide are that you do not need any of your software reloaded. The drive can be left blank because Windows Home Server will restore all of your data.

If your old hard drive was relatively full, you should try to select a new drive that is at least as large as your old drive to avoid possible problems. Some folks have experienced problems because they assumed that the 80GB drive that they purchased was the same size as their old 80GB drive, but different drives can actually be slightly different sizes. If you can get the same exact manufacturer and model number as your old drive, you will be safe, but otherwise you should consider buying a drive that is noticeably larger (by at least one gigabyte) so that you can be sure that you can restore your backups. Windows Home Server is able to restore to a smaller drive if the data contained in the backup is small enough, but depending how the data is stored on the drive, it is difficult to figure out exactly how large a drive is required. Besides, if your old drive was close to full, it's a good time to upgrade so that you have more space.

Do Hard Drives Deserve a Second Chance?

Some folks may be tempted to give a malfunctioning hard drive a second chance. Sometimes you can reformat a bad drive, and it may function fine for a period of time. Unfortunately the technology in hard drives rarely improves once it has exhibited signs of failure. The tolerances are so delicate that once a hard drive stops working properly, the failure can cascade causing total failure, or worse: It may appear to be working while your data is quietly corrupted in the background.

Hard drives have come down in price considerably over the past decade, so replacement drives are very reasonable. It has been my experience that once a drive displays any characteristics of data loss, it is only a matter of time before the drive gives out totally. You may be able to squeeze a few weeks or even a couple of months out of a marginal drive, but you should remember that any data saved on that drive is questionable and could be lost at any time.

Keep in mind that data loss may not be evident immediately. If a portion of a drive platter develops a defect, you may not notice that the data is corrupt until you actually try to access a certain file. In general, Windows Home Server will allow you to recover data easily, but if the damage goes undetected for a long period of time, Windows Home Server may no longer be retaining backups that contain a non-corrupt copy of the file.

Once a hard drive has given you a reason not to trust it, replace it as soon as possible so that your computer will stay reliable and your data will be safe.

Other Reasons for Using System Restore

In addition to hard drive failures, there are many other reasons that you may want to restore a computer to a previous state. If your computer is infected by a virus, or if you installed a software package or device driver that causes your system to become unstable, you may decide that the best option is to restore your hard drive back to a state when it was working smoothly. If you keep all of your documents and data files on your Windows Home Server, this is a very convenient option. Even if you don't normally keep your files on your Windows Home Server shares, you can temporarily move your files to your user share so that restoring from an earlier backup will not cause any data loss.

Remember that using system restore will remove all data from the volume that you restore too, and the only data left on the drive will be the data contained in the backup. If your backup configuration includes exclusions, those folders will disappear. Make sure that you save any recently modified files, and make sure that any excluded directories do not contain important data before you proceed. If your computer is still functional, you may even want to perform a manual backup (described in more detail in Chapter 7) before you proceed. This will not address excluded files, but it will give you the option of recovering individual files from the backup if you later realize that something is missing.

Starting Recovery

After you replace the failed hard drive, you begin the recovery process by booting from the Windows Home Server Restore CD that was included with your Windows Home Server system or with the Windows Home Server System Builder software package. Place the CD in the system's DVD/CD drive, and power on the system. If you are prompted to press any key to boot from CD, just press any key on the keyboard to boot from the recovery CD. If your system does not boot from the CD, see the "Setting Your System to Boot from CD" sidebar for tips on changing your BIOS Settings.

Your system may take a while to boot, but the progress will be shown on a screen similar to Figure 10-11. During this time, the recovery CD is loading a variety of drivers and components to support your system, and then it initializes the restore wizard.

Figure 10-11

The next screen, shown in Figure 10-12, requires you to select the language and keyboard layout that you wish to use for the recovery process. Select the appropriate options for your PC and click Continue.

Figure 10-12

The next screen displays a summary of the critical devices that the recovery wizard has detected. To perform a restore, the wizard needs to detect your network adapter, and your hard drive. If you are using typical equipment, it will likely be detected. The summary screen is shown in Figure 10-13.

Chapter 10: Recovering Lost Data

Figure 10-13

If the number of devices shown in parentheses does not match what you have in your computer, you can select the Show Details button in order to review the device listing and install drivers if necessary. The resulting screen is shown in Figure 10-14. From this screen you can click the Install Drivers button and follow the prompts to load drivers for any hardware that was not detected. After you load your drivers, or if your devices were all listed in the summary screen, click Continue. The Windows Home Server Restore Computer Wizard will now launch.

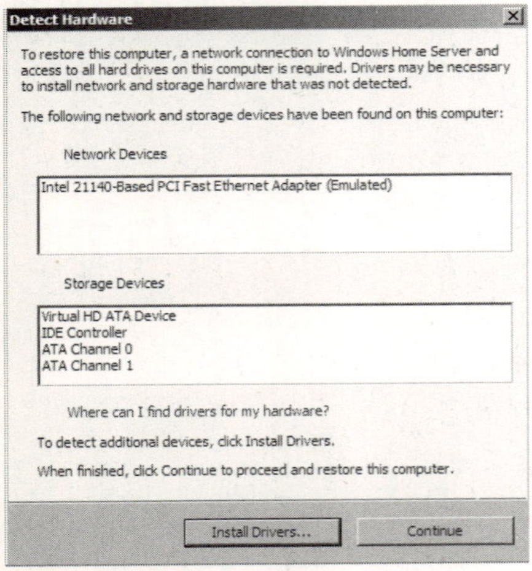

Figure 10-14

Setting Your System to Boot from CD

If your system does not boot from the CD, your BIOS setting may need to be changed to allow you to recover using the Windows Home Server Restore CD. To get into your BIOS settings, reboot your machine and look for instructions on the initial start-up screens. Different manufacturers use different

Chapter 10: Recovering Lost Data

hot keys, but almost all indicate which key needs to be pressed with instructions on the screen. Common hot keys include Del, F1, F2, and Ins. Press the appropriate hot key and you should be presented with a BIOS setup screen, similar to the following figure.

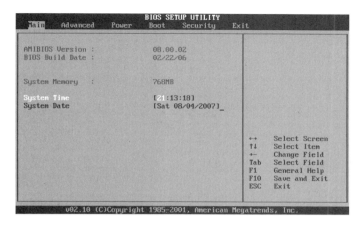

Different manufacturers use different BIOS setup programs, but there are similarities between them. To set your system to boot from a CD, you must locate a section that has a title like *Boot*, *Boot Order* or *Boot Devices*. The following figure shows that this section is found by selecting a Boot tab at the top of the screen. Note that there are instructions on the right side of the screen showing what keys can be used to navigate the interface. Most BIOS setup programs do not include mouse support, so you must use the keyboard.

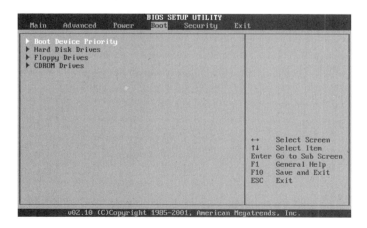

In this BIOS, you have to select the Boot Device Priority option from the Boot tab in order to make the appropriate changes. The resulting screen is shown in the following figure. Some BIOS programs will just have the priority listed right on the Boot screen.

Continued

Setting Your System to Boot from CD (Continued)

```
                    BIOS SETUP UTILITY
                    Boot

1st Boot Device        [CDROM]              Specifies the boot
2nd Boot Device        [Hard Drive]         sequence from the
3rd Boot Device        [Floppy Drive]       available devices.
4th Boot Device        [PXE UNDI(Bus0 Slot]




                                            ←→   Select Screen
                                            ↑↓   Select Item
                                            +-   Change Option
                                            F1   General Help
                                            F10  Save and Exit
                                            ESC  Exit

            v02.10 (C)Copyright 1985-2001, American Megatrends, Inc.
```

On the priority screen, use the keyboard to make sure that the CD-ROM drive has priority over any other devices. Sometimes the CD-ROM is listed as CD, CD-ROM, DVD, DVD-ROM, or DVD/CD. Find whatever device looks like it refers to your CD-ROM drive, and move it to the top of the list.

Read the on-screen instructions for how to save the changes and exit. On this BIOS you just have to press F10, and this is a fairly common hot key. If the BIOS prompts you to confirm the changes, do so. The system should not reboot, and it should boot from the recovery CD. During the boot process, you may be prompted to press a key in order to boot from CD/DVD.

The Restore Computer Wizard

The remainder of the recovery is handled by the restore wizard. There is an initial welcome screen describing what the wizard will do. Click Continue to begin the restore process. If the wizard is able to locate a single Windows Home Server machine on your network, it will proceed to a screen prompting you for the password to your Home Server. If it cannot find your home server, you will be presented with options to either Search again or Find my home server manually, as shown in Figure 10-15.

The recommended option is to simply search again. Check all of your network cables, be certain that any switches and routers are powered on, and make sure that your Windows Home Server is running as well. The only time that you should need to use the manual configuration is if your server is named something other than SERVER and you have segmented your network into multiple subnets. If this is the case, select the option to find your server manually, and provide the wizard with the name that you have assigned your server. Otherwise, troubleshoot your network until the wizard is able to locate your home server. Once the wizard has located your server, you can continue to the next step.

Chapter 10: Recovering Lost Data 179

Remember that Windows Home Server's restore function will not work over a wireless network. If you are using a machine with a wireless link, you must temporarily hook it into the switch or router with a wired Ethernet cable.

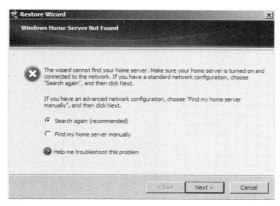

Figure 10-15

If the wizard finds multiple Windows Home Server machines on the network, you must select the server that you wish to restore a backup from, as shown in Figure 10-16.

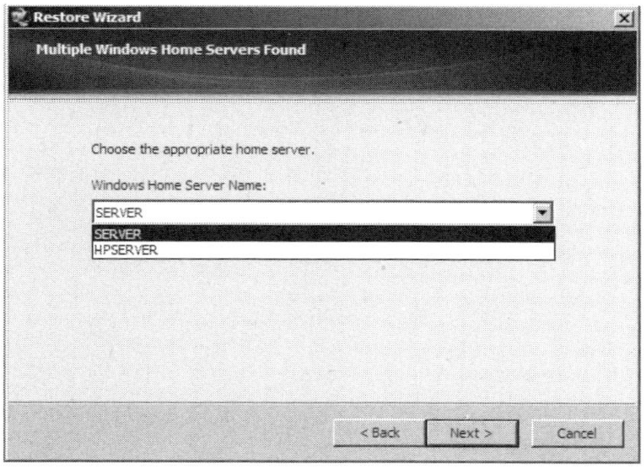

Figure 10-16

The next step requires you to enter the Windows Home Server administrative password, as shown in Figure 10-17. This is the password you created when you first set up your Windows Home Server. Enter the password and click Next.

Chapter 10: Recovering Lost Data

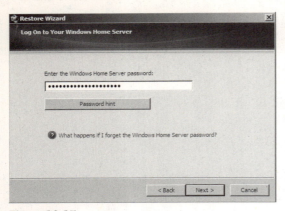

Figure 10-17

The next screen, shown in Figure 10-18, requires you to select the computer that you are going to restore. Select the name of the computer that you are restoring, and click Next.

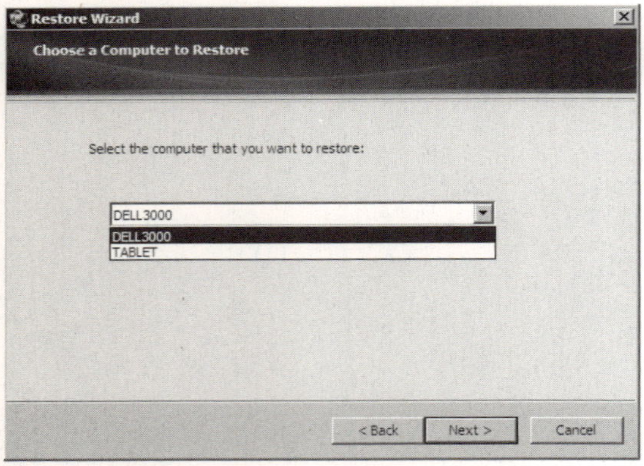

Figure 10-18

Now you must select the particular backup that you wish to restore, as shown in Figure 10-19. The date and description for all of the backups for the selected computer will be shown. You can view the details of any particular backup by selecting it and clicking the Details button. The details include a summary of the excluded files and the size of the backup. Select the backup you wish to restore to your computer and click Next.

If this is a new hard drive with no partitions, as will often be the case when you have replaced a failed drive, the Wizard will indicate that it has not found any initialized disks. Click OK to clear the warning dialog box, and then click the Run Disk Manager (advanced) button. Some new disks will have been initialized by the manufacturer, so you may not have to complete this step.

Chapter 10: Recovering Lost Data   **181**

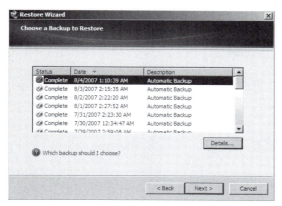

Figure 10-19

In the resulting screen, shown in Figure 10-20, you must initialize your drive. If you use any operating systems that are older than Windows Vista, such as Windows XP, then you should use the MBR style for your disk. If you only use Windows Vista, you can select the GPT option.

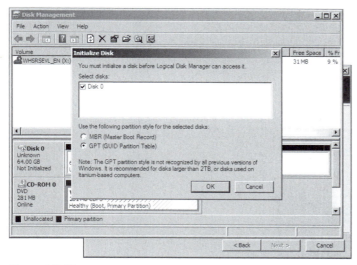

Figure 10-20

After the disk is initialized, you need to create a volume to restore your backup to. Your new hard drive should be listed, and it should have a black bar over a section listed as Unallocated. Right-click this section and select New Simple Volume from the pop-up menu, as shown in Figure 10-21.

Chapter 10: Recovering Lost Data

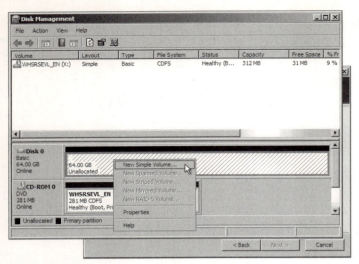

Figure 10-21

Click through the New Simple Volume Wizard; accepting all of the defaults will create a single volume that makes use of all available space on the hard drive. If you have a need for multiple volumes on a single disk, you may choose to create a smaller volume for the restore. The Disk Management tool will now format the new volume. Wait until the format is completed and the new volume is listed as Healthy, and then close the Disk Management window by clicking the X in the upper-right corner.

Now you must select the source volume that you want to restore from the backup, as shown in Figure 10-22. Most computers will only have one volume, the C: Volume 1 listed. If you have more volumes, you will have to select where each volume should be restored. For the basic case, select the C: Volume 1 as the source and it will default to be restored to the newly created C: Volume 1 on your new hard drive. Click Next to continue.

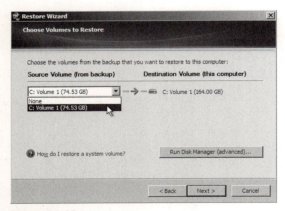

Figure 10-22

Chapter 10: Recovering Lost Data 183

In the following screen, shown in Figure 10-23, you will have one last chance to confirm your selections. The restore wizard does this to warn you that all data on the destination drive will be lost once you continue. If you were reusing an older hard drive, or if you have multiple hard drives in your computer, this is a chance to make sure that you are restoring to the correct volume. Once you check the volume selections, click Next to continue.

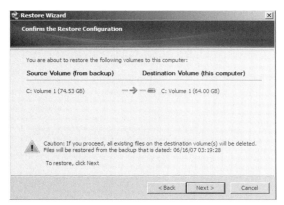

Figure 10-23

The restore process will now begin, and the recovery wizard will show an estimated time to completion. This estimate is very rough, so it's best to take a break from watching this process and go do something else. I have seen restores take anywhere from 45 minutes to 2 hours, depending on the amount of data and the speed of the network, computer, and server.

After the restore process is complete, you'll be presented with a final screen, similar to Figure 10-24. Click the Finish button and your computer will restart.

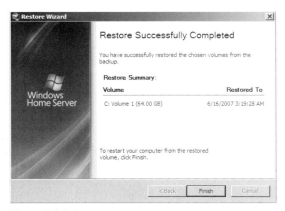

Figure 10-24

Your computer is now restored and all of your data is restored to exactly the state it was in when the backup was performed. You may be prompted to run a disk check when you reboot, or Windows may warn you that the computer was not shut down properly. This is an artifact of the way in which the backups are performed. Because Windows Home Server takes a snapshot of the hard drive while it is running, when you reboot your machine, Windows will think that you just rebooted your machine without shutting it down properly. Just select the option to start Windows normally, and your computer will start up.

Privacy, Security, Identity, and Other Things to Remember

As you see in this chapter, Windows Home Server goes to great lengths to make certain that your data is protected. While this is almost always a good thing, there is some downside to having all of this data stored on your home server.

Our computers contain an amazing amount of information that reaches into every aspect of our lives. The data on your computer can be used to deduce a great deal of information about you and your family. If you prepare your taxes on your computer, the files will include your social security numbers, income, full names, and employers' names. If you use direct deposit, the tax files will also include bank account information. Other privacy gold mines can include stored passwords, credit card numbers, and other sensitive information that you would not want to fall into the wrong hands.

Having this data on a server is not that much more dangerous than having it on a computer, but the compact nature of most Windows Home Server boxes could make them an easy target for thieves and would-be identity thieves.

The other aspect of Windows Home Server that can add some risk is the fact that it keeps a history of recoverable files. This means that if you purposefully delete something from your computer, Windows Home Server will keep a copy for as long as it keeps a backup that contained the file. If you have any manual backups that contained the file, it will be kept indefinitely! For files that you might later want to recover, this is in fact a very good thing, but for files that you actually want to disappear, this can be a problem.

How can you protect yourself? The first is to physically secure your Windows Home Server box. Some OEMs include a bracket that will accept a simple cable lock, which is available from most local computer shops or retailers. If your server does not have a bracket, there are kits available that include a bracket that can be attached to the case with epoxy. Other options include keeping the server in a locked room, or simply keeping it out of site.

Another tactic you can employ is to use a strong password for your Windows Home Server administrator password. Without this password, would-be identity thieves will not be able to gain easy access to your backups and files. Don't rely on the password as your only line of defense. For a determined hacker, passwords are only a minor nuisance, and if a thief happens to also get away with a computer that has the administrator password saved, the password will offer no protection at all.

The last tactic is to simply be aware of the data that is on your home server. If you ever purge data from your computer and you really want to make sure that it is gone, you have the option of deleting any previous backups that included the data. After you have deleted the data in question, you can perform a manual backup of the computer, just in case, and then log into the Windows Home Server Console and delete all of the older backups. This will eliminate the option of retrieving other files that have been deleted, so you have to weigh the importance of saving some files against the importance of making sure other sensitive files are deleted.

Being aware of the data also ensures that if your Windows Home Server ever goes missing, you will know what actions you need to take in order to protect yourself. If you lose tax files for example, you may want to sign up for a credit monitoring service. If you lose a document that contains passwords, you will know that you need to change those passwords.

Summary

This chapter walked you through the process of recovering from several different ways that you can lose data. You learned how to extract files from the backups that Windows Home Server performs, so that you can retrieve accidentally deleted files, or recover files that have been accidentally changed. You learned how to use Windows' Previous Versions feature to retrieve files that were accidentally deleted from your Windows Home Server's share directories, or to restore an earlier version of a file that was accidentally changed or corrupted.

You also learned how to make use of Windows Home Server's computer restore functionality. By booting from your system restore CD, and running the restore wizard, you now know how to restore a computer after a hard drive crash, virus infection, or a software installation gone wrong.

Chapter 11

Remotely Accessing Files and Computers

With more and more of our personal information and data stored on our home computers and on our home servers, it can be convenient or even necessary to have access to these files when we are away from home. Windows Home Server makes this possible through two different types of remote access: connecting to your home computers and your Windows Home Server.

Files stored on the Windows Home Server shared folders are accessible through a web-enabled interface. You can access individual files, or you can download entire directories, which will be automatically compressed into a .ZIP file for transfer to you through any Internet browser.

You can also remotely access your computer desktops, if your operating system supports this feature. This allows you to access your own programs and files just as if you were sitting at home.

To set up this functionality, you have to configure your server and networking equipment properly. Allowing remote access from the Internet is a somewhat complicated concept, but Windows Home Server has many features to make it easier and friendlier to set up and to use. You will also want to learn a bit about the security ramifications of the changes you are making to your network so that you can allow access to the right people, while keeping your data protected from others.

Enabling Remote Access on Your Server

The first step to allowing remote access is to configure your Windows Home Server to allow inbound connections. Although there are two different types of remote access that Windows Home Server supports, there is only one option to configure, and it covers both modes.

You enable remote access through the Windows Home Server Console. Start the console by double-clicking the Windows Home Server icon in the system tray on one of your client computers. Enter your home server's administrative password to open the console. When the console opens, the screen looks similar to Figure 11-1.

Click the Settings button in the upper-right corner of the console window to open the Windows Home Server Settings dialog box. Click the Remote Access item in the left pane to display the remote access settings for your Windows Home Server. The screen looks similar to Figure 11-2.

The first section of this setting page, labeled Web Site Connectivity, is where you enable remote access functionality for your server. The button in this section effectively turns remote access on and off.

Chapter 11: Remotely Accessing Files and Computers

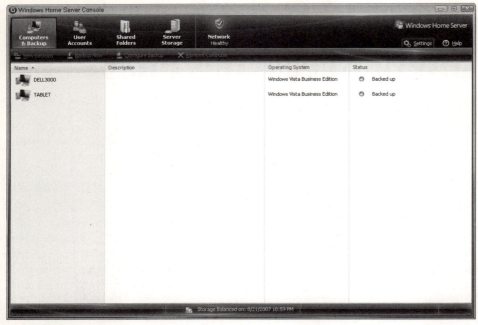

Figure 11-1

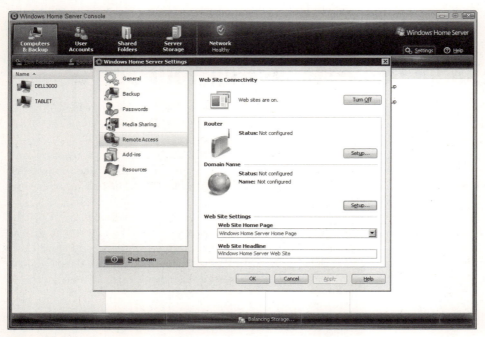

Figure 11-2

Chapter 11: Remotely Accessing Files and Computers

Caution

While there are buttons at the bottom of the dialog box to Apply or Cancel changes, you should note that the Turn On/Turn Off button takes effect and the setting is saved immediately, even if you click Cancel following a change.

You should now set up your custom homeserver.com domain. (You're skipping the Router section for now. It is covered in greater detail later in the chapter.) Click the Setup button under the Domain Name heading to initiate this process.

The first step of the wizard will require you to log in with a Windows Live ID, as shown in Figure 11-3. If you already have a Hotmail account or an account that you use with Windows Live Messenger (previously MSN Messenger), you can use it to log in here. Otherwise click the Get your Windows Live ID link to set up a new account. After you enter a valid account, click Next to continue.

Figure 11-3

The next step of the wizard, shown in Figure 11-4, provides the opportunity to review the Windows Home Server Privacy Statement and the Windows Live Custom Domains Addendum. These documents have important information about how Microsoft uses the information and data that is generated as a result of using a custom homeserver.com domain. Once you are comfortable with the terms of the policies, select I Accept and click Next to continue.

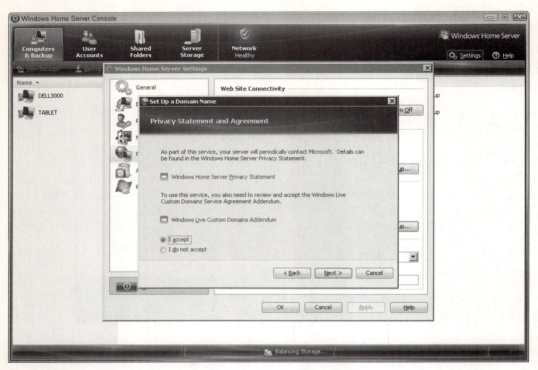

Figure 11-4

The next screen is shown in Figure 11-5. This is the page that allows you to select a domain name for your server. A good domain name is one that can be easily remembered by members of your household. After you enter a name in the first box of the domain name and select from the options in the drop-down list, click the Confirm button to see if your domain name is available. Because the purpose of this feature is to make your server available on the Internet, your server must have a unique name. (Note: The livenode.com domain shown in the screenshot was used during the beta testing of Windows Home Server. Most people will only have the option of selecting homeserver.com.) After you have a domain name that you are happy with, click the Finish button.

The last page of the wizard shows a confirmation screen, shown in Figure 11-6. This page shows the link that will be used to access your server from the Internet. Whether this link will work from inside your home network depends on both your home router and your Internet provider's configurations.

After you exit the wizard, the Remote Access settings page should look similar to Figure 11-7. The Domain Name section now includes buttons labeled Details, Change, and Unconfigure. The Details option shows you diagnostics regarding your server's connection to and accessibility from the Internet. The Change option lets you alter your domain name, and the Unconfigure option lets you disconnect your server from the homeserver.com custom domain server and remove the settings from the server. You can also change the page heading and the starting page in the Web Site Settings boxes at the bottom of the page.

Chapter 11: Remotely Accessing Files and Computers   **191**

Figure 11-5

Figure 11-6

Chapter 11: Remotely Accessing Files and Computers

Figure 11-7

Because there is some uncertainty as to whether using the full address will work from within the network, you can test your current changes by using a slightly different method. Minimize the Windows Home Server Console and open up an Internet Explorer window. Type **http://server** into the address bar. If everything is working, you should see a page similar to Figure 11-8.

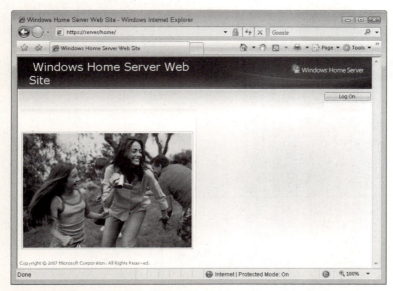

Figure 11-8

Note

Internet explorer will detect that this is a local connection to a server rather than a connection to an Internet site. You may notice an alert regarding the fact that you are connected to an intranet site. This alert is just a notice, and no action is necessary.

Your server is now set up for remote access. Next you will configure user accounts to allow remote access.

Configuring User Accounts for Remote Access

Windows Home Server limits the users that can remotely access files and computers. You have to give specific permission to each user that will want this access, and that user will have to use a strong password. For a password to be considered strong, it must contain at least three of the four categories of characters, including uppercase letters, lowercase letters, numbers, and symbols like punctuation characters. You can configure your server to allow weak passwords (any password allowed), medium-strength passwords (at least five characters), or strong passwords for regular user accounts, but if you wish to use an account for remote access, it must have a strong password, regardless of the password policy in place on the server.

Note

You might want to consider setting up a separate account for remote access to a limited subset of files on your home server. If you want to be able to give relatives read-only access to pictures or files, you can set up a separate account for this purpose. For more details on creating accounts, refer to Chapter 6.

You configure accounts to enable remote access by using the Windows Home Server Console. To open the console, double-click the Windows Home Server icon in the system tray of one of your client computers. When it opens, the console should look similar to Figure 11-9. If your console is currently displaying a tab other than the User Accounts tab, click User Accounts in the upper-left corner to switch.

Right-click the user account for which you wish to enable Remote Access and select Properties, as shown in Figure 11-10.

The properties dialog box looks similar to Figure 11-11. From here you can enable or disable remote access for this user by selecting or deselecting the checkbox labeled Enable remote access for this user.

Chapter 11: Remotely Accessing Files and Computers

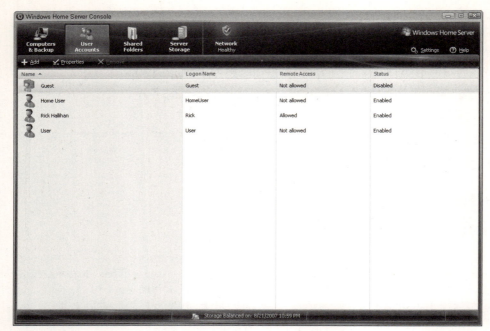

Figure 11-9

Figure 11-10

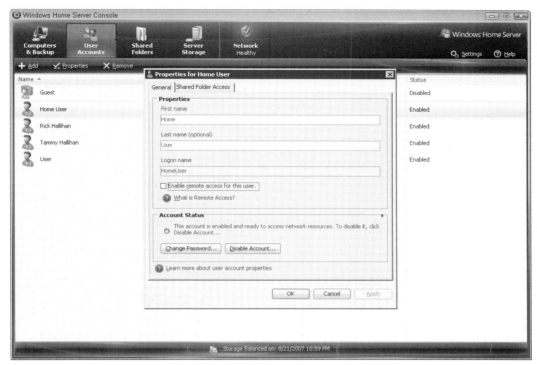

Figure 11-11

If the password for this account does not meet the complexity requirements to be considered a strong password, you will be prompted to create a stronger password, as shown in Figure 11-12.

Note

To be considered a strong password by Windows Home Server, the password must be at least seven characters long, and it must contain at least three of the following letter categories: uppercase letters, lowercase letters, numbers, and symbols (like !, $, #, and so on).

If you are prompted to change the password, click Yes to continue, and then enter and confirm a new strong password in the resulting dialog box. After you change the password, click OK to save the change in your settings.

Repeat this process for any other user accounts that you want to be able to access your home network resources remotely.

Before you can access your system from outside your network, you must configure your broadband router or modem to allow inbound connections. Before you move on to that step, you can test how the remote interface works by logging in to your Windows Home Server from one of your client computers on your home network.

Chapter 11: Remotely Accessing Files and Computers

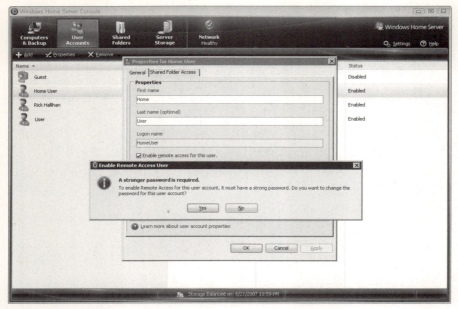

Figure 11-12

To test the connection, open an Internet Explorer window and type **http://server** in the address bar. You should see the same screen shown earlier in Figure 11-8. Click the Log On button in the upper-right corner of the window. On the next screen, you will be prompted for a username and password. Use one of the accounts for which you have enabled remote access, and click the Log On button. If you successfully log on, you should see a window similar to Figure 11-13.

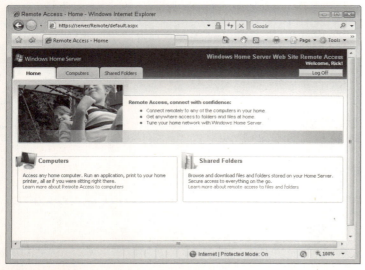

Figure 11-13

You can explore the interface from here and see how you will be able to access different files and computers. Remote access to computers requires some additional setup, which will be discussed in the next section.

Internet Explorer versus Firefox

For the purpose of working with your Windows Home Server, Microsoft's Windows Internet Explorer has a bit of an edge over Mozilla's Firefox. The ability to connect remotely to the Windows Home Server Console and to computers that support Remote Desktop relies on an ActiveX control that must run in the browser. Because ActiveX is only supported under Internet Explorer, functionality will be limited under Firefox.

Access to the file shares works very well through Firefox, and the interface detects which browser you are using and hides the options that are not available. Users of Opera or other browsers that do not use the Internet Explorer rendering engine will have the same problems as Firefox users.

Configuring Your Broadband Connection

Most consumer broadband connections are not set up to allow inbound traffic from the Internet, but using your Windows Home Server for remote access will require exactly that functionality. By design, most broadband modems are configured to block inbound requests in order to reduce the possibility of Internet viruses and worms being allowed into your network. Connections to your Windows Home Server will have to pass through your broadband modem, and be routed to your home server.

Basics of IP Addresses and Routing

The Internet and most computer networks use a protocol known as the Internet Protocol, or IP, as the basis for how they address traffic and move it from one computer to another. Each device on a network has an IP address, and your computer needs to know this address in order to connect to the device. The most often used standard for IP addresses currently is IPv4 (Internet Protocol Version 4), and IPv4 addresses are usually similar to 66.129.67.209. Each of the four numbers is known as an octet, and will range from 0 to 255.

Some addresses are reserved for private networks, with the most popular being the 192.168.*x.y* and the 10.*a.b.c* sets, where the letters are replaced with different numbers depending on the network. Addresses in this pattern are not routable on the Internet, and traffic addressed to or from these addresses will be dropped by Internet routers.

Home networks typically use a technology called Network Address Translation (NAT) in order to allow them to use private network addressing for the home network, but still enable connections to the Internet. Basically, NAT uses one routable Internet address (assigned to your connection by your ISP), and translates addressing from your privately addressed local network to the Internet address. From the perspective of the Internet routers, all traffic originating from your home network comes from the single Internet address. The NAT device, normally your modem or router (such as a DSL or Cable modem), keeps track of what local computers are connected to each remote server, and when data returns from the Internet servers, it is readdressed with the private address of the appropriate computer and forwarded to that computer on your local network.

One of the major benefits of NAT is that it acts like a firewall by default, disallowing any inbound connections. This is good for the security of your home network, but it creates difficulties in allowing features like Windows Home Server's remote access to work.

The way that you allow a connection to your Windows Home Server device on your home network is to set up port forwarding on your broadband router or modem. This basically tells the router that any inbound traffic on certain ports should be readdressed and forwarded to your home server.

Note

If your network includes more than one router or if it includes a modem that is separate from the router, you will configure port forwarding on the device that is considered your edge router. This is the router that receives an address from your Internet service provider (ISP). Some ISPs place their modems into bridge mode and then configure a separate home router to get an address from the ISP. Bridge mode basically means that traffic passes through the modem without being modified or changed. Other ISPs will allow the modem to serve as the router, and then in a confusing turn, they set up the home router to act as a bridge. If you have this type of setup, you will have to determine where the NAT function is being performed, and configure port forwarding at that device.

Setting Up Port Forwarding for UPnP Routers

For home routers that support the UPnP (Universal Plug ans Play) protocol, you *may* be able to have Windows Home Server automatically configure port forwarding for you. This method does not always work, but if it does it saves you the hassle of figuring out the specifics of configuring the feature on your home router.

If you're not sure if your router supports UPnP, you can try this method just the same. If it fails, it will not harm your computer or network in any way, but if it succeeds, you won't have to worry about digging into your router configuration.

This method of setting up port forwarding is done through the Windows Home Server Console. If you do not still have the console open from earlier, start the console by double-clicking the Windows Home Server icon in the system tray, and then enter your server's administrative password. The initial console window was shown earlier in Figure 11-1. Click the Settings button in the upper-right corner of the console window to open the Windows Home Server Settings dialog box. Click the Remote Access item in the left pane to display the remote access settings for your Windows Home Server. This screen was shown earlier in Figure 11-2.

From here, you click the center button labeled Setup under the Router heading. After prompting for confirmation, Windows Home Server will attempt to connect to your router and configure it using the UPnP protocol. It will then display a dialog box indicating whether it has been successful

Chapter 11: Remotely Accessing Files and Computers 199

or not. If it is successful, then your router should be configured and ready to allow remote access to your Windows Home Server from the Internet. If it is not successful, you must manually configure your router, as is outlined in the following section.

There is one more thing that is important to note here. In the Domain Name section of the Remote Access settings dialog box, you will see that Windows Home Server is automatically testing the connection from the Internet to your server. While it is running the test, you will see Status: Testing. If the test is successful, it will read Working, and different errors will be listed as Unknown, Configuration Errors or Not working. If you experience an error, click the Details button. This screen will show additional information similar to Figure 11-14. If any errors are listed, you can click the Learn more about your domain name status link for details on specific errors. Unless the status is listed as Working, you will have to manually configure your router to enable remote access.

A single red X on the Verifying your Web site is accessible from the Internet option with passes on the remaining elements may indicate that your ISP is blocking inbound connections to your machine from port 80. This is a fairly common practice. If this is the case, you may still be able to access your home server by using https://yourdomain.homeserver.com (note the s that was added to http).

Figure 11-14

Manually Setting Up Port Forwarding

Different models and manufacturers of modems will have unique interfaces for setting up port forwarding. The following example procedures are for a Westell model 327W DSL Modem and Wireless Router unit. The interface on your home router may be different, but the procedure should be similar.

The first step is to determine the IP address of your home router. If you don't already know the address, you can usually find it in your router's documentation. Many routers default to 192.168.0.1. You can check whether this is the case by opening an Internet browser like Internet Explorer and typing **http://192.168.0.1** into the address bar. If you are presented with a configuration screen for your router, then you have the correct address. If the address has been changed from the default, or if you can't locate the documentation, the following procedure can be used to determine the address.

Open a command prompt. To do this, you can click the Start orb in Windows Vista (Start menu in Windows XP), and then select All Programs, Accessories, then Command Prompt. A window with a black background should appear, similar to Figure 11-15.

Figure 11-15

At the prompt, type **ipconfig** and press Enter. The resulting listing is shown in Figure 11-16. In this listing, look for the section that applies to the network connection you are currently using. For wireless connections this is usually labeled Wireless LAN adapter, and for wired Ethernet it is usually labeled Ethernet adapter. In the section that applies to your network connection, look for the line that has the default gateway. That line is highlighted in Figure 11-16. The default gateway is almost always your home router, so this address can be used to access the home router. Make a note of this address.

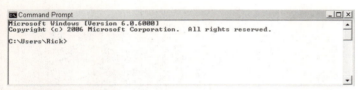

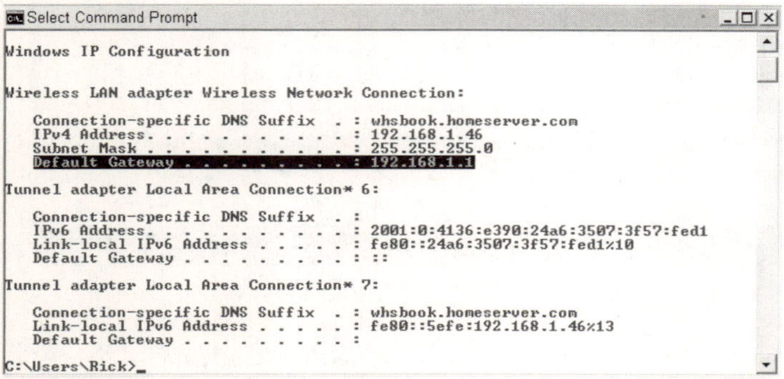

Figure 11-16

Now that you have the IP address, you can access your router's configuration interface. Open up an Internet Explorer window, type the IP address for your router into the address bar and press Enter. Some brands of router will now prompt you for a username and password. Other devices such as the Westell 327W do not require a password unless you actually want to make changes or access security sensitive settings on the router. The initial screen is shown in Figure 11-17.

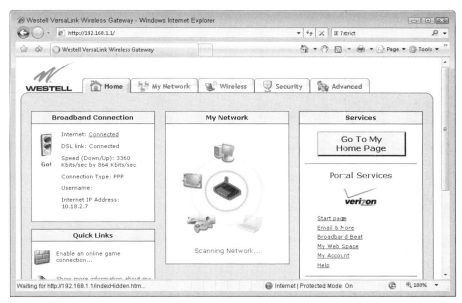

Figure 11-17

Next you have to find the section of the configuration that will allow you to set up port forwarding. On the Westell 327W, this is found on the Security tab in the Applications subsection. You may have to poke around a bit but once you find an area that refers to Ports, Port Forwarding, or NAT, you are probably in the right place. The appropriate screen for the Westell is shown in Figure 11-18.

Note
If you find an option to enable UPnP on your router, you may want to enable it, save the configuration, and attempt the automatic setup again. Many routers that claim to support UPnP do not have a complete implementation, so Windows Home Server may still fail at setting them up properly.

Now you must set up three ports to forward to your Windows Home Server. The first two required ports are fairly standard and these port types are often predefined. Port 80 is also known as *HTTP*, *WWW*, or *Web Server*. Select this protocol from the drop-down list and click Enable. When you are prompted whether this is a host or dynamic service, as shown in Figure 11-19, select host. If you are given the option of TCP or UDP, select TCP for all three ports that are being forwarded.

Chapter 11: Remotely Accessing Files and Computers

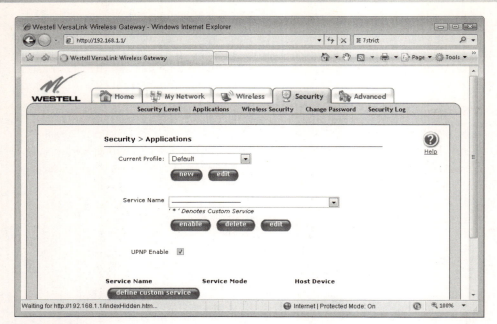

Figure 11-18

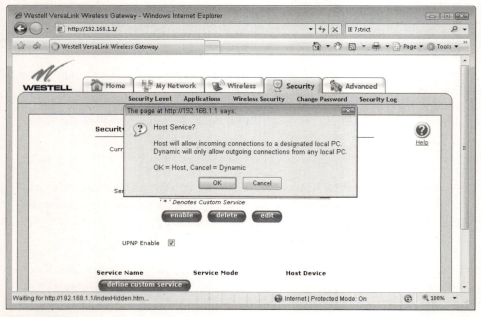

Figure 11-19

Chapter 11: Remotely Accessing Files and Computers 203

You will now be prompted to designate to which device the inbound traffic should be directed. Most routers will allow you to designate a target based on the host name, so you can select the host name of your Windows Home Server machine (usually `server`, as shown in Figure 11-20) and click Done.

Note

If you are unable to select your home server by its name, you must enter the server's IP address. A simple way to find this is to open a command prompt on one of your client computers and type ***ping server*** and press Enter. You should see four lines that say Reply from followed by an IP address. This address is the local private address of your server that is needed by the port forwarding configuration.

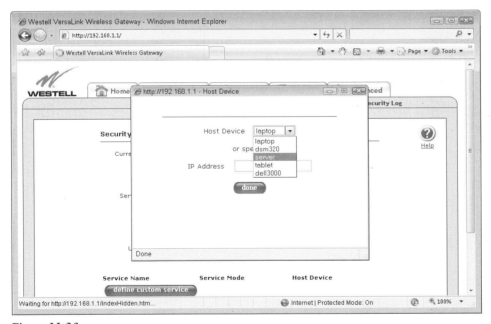

Figure 11-20

Repeat the process for port 443. This port is commonly known as *HTTPS*, *Secure WWW*, or *Secure Web Server*.

The one nonstandard port that Windows Home Server Remote Access requires is port 4125. This port is not currently listed as a standard port in most routers, but may be added to them in the future. If you find a service or port labeled Windows Home Server Remote Access, this may be the right port, but for the Westell 327W, you have to manually configure a port. To do this, click the define custom service button. The first window prompts whether you want to define a port forwarding service or a trigger service, as shown in Figure 11-21.

204　Chapter 11: Remotely Accessing Files and Computers

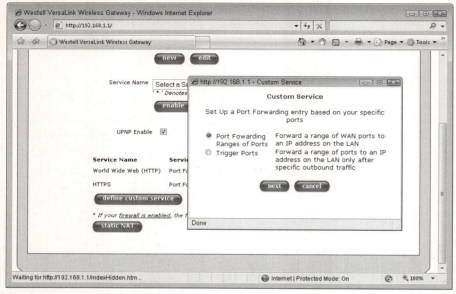

Figure 11-21

Select Port Forwarding and click next to continue. In the following screen, shown in Figure 11-22, enter **4125** as the start and end of the port range, and as the base host port. This basically tells the router to map the port directly from the router to the home server. Add a friendly name for the service, like WHS Remote Access. Confirm that TCP is selected as the protocol and click Next.

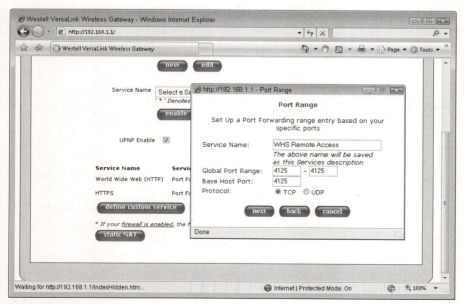

Figure 11-22

Chapter 11: Remotely Accessing Files and Computers

The next screen shows a summary of the selections you have made, as shown in Figure 11-23. Click Close. You can now select this protocol just as you did the standard protocols for ports 80 and 443 by selecting its title from the drop-down list. Add your newly created service and designate your home server as the destination for the traffic.

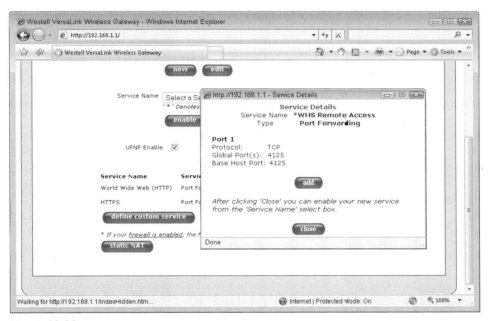

Figure 11-23

Your service listing should now include entries that relate to each of the three inbound ports, as shown in Figure 11-24. (See the following table for a summary of the ports and their services.) On most routers, these changes take effect immediately.

Summary of Required Port Forwarding

Port	Service Name	Purpose
80	HTTP	Provides the regular web interface
443	HTTPS	Provides the secure web interface, used for accessing File Shares
4125	WHSRA	Used for Windows Home Server's remote access proxying that allows remote access to desktops and the Windows Home Server Console

Figure 11-24

Once you have port forwarding enabled for each of the three services, your home network router is ready to pass traffic from the Internet to your Windows Home Server.

Testing your configuration is a little bit more difficult than the earlier steps. Many home routers do not properly route traffic back to themselves. For example, if you configured your server to use the http://whsbook.homeserver.com URL, it works properly when you access it from the Internet, but when you try to access it from your home network, the connection fails. The best way to test this is to try to access your custom homeserver.com URL from a network other than your home network. This could be at a neighbor's house, at work, or at an Internet café. If you access your home server with the HTTP protocol, you should be shown a screen similar to Figure 11-8. Because of past Internet worms that used port 80, many ISPs block this port on residential Internet connections. If this is the case, you may be able to access your server with the HTTPS protocol instead. Just type **https://yourdomain.homeserver.com** into the address bar of an Internet browser, replacing *yourdomain* with the custom domain that you have selected. Again, the resulting screen should be similar to Figure 11-8 (shown earlier). For further information about the success of your configuration, click the Details button on the Remote Access settings page, as described earlier in this chapter.

Considerations for Your ISP's Terms of Service

You should be sure that you understand how your Internet Service Provider's (ISP's) Terms of Service (TOS) might affect your ability to make use of Windows Home Server's Remote Access features. Many residential ISPs have restrictions about running server software on the Internet connection that they provide. Windows Home Server's Remote Access features utilize a Web server running on port 80 and/or 443, and also use port 4125 for remotely accessing your home computers.

Some ISPs have restrictions only in their TOS, and others actively block some or all of the restricted protocols. If the ISP blocks the port, even if you have configured everything properly, remote access from the Internet will not function.

Perhaps more troublesome is that even if the ISP is not blocking the ports, if you choose to set up and use Windows Home Server's Remote Access features, you run the risk of your ISP shutting down your account, or charging you for a more expensive business-class plan.

The details of each ISP's TOS will be wildly different, so if you don't know or don't understand if running Remote Access is acceptable to your ISP, your best option is to call and discuss the matter with your ISP's technical support department. Explain that the server will only be used by you and your household to access your home network when you are away from the house, and that it only requires inbound traffic on ports 80, 443, and 4125. You may also have to explain that Windows Home Server does *not* require a static IP, and that it will work just fine with the dynamic addresses that most ISPs use. The result of this discussion may be that you can use Windows Home Server as you please, or your ISP may ask you to upgrade to a more expensive Internet plan in order to enable this functionality. Many ISPs offer relatively inexpensive Home Office/Home Business grade plans that allow remote access, and may offer greater speed as well.

As Windows Home Server is adopted by consumers, ISPs will realize that many of their Terms of Service are incompatible, and they may choose to offer special consumer packages that will allow remote access, or they may modify their current TOS to allow inbound connections. Just be mindful of the fact that your current network provider may disallow, block, or have a policy against making use of inbound connections, so you should research the issue so that you understand it and how things can be made to work.

Connecting to Windows Home Server Shares

Now that everything is configured, it's time to actually make use of the Remote Access features of Windows Home Server. From outside your home network, begin by opening Internet Explorer and entering your custom homeserver.com URL in the address bar. You should see the same home screen shown earlier in Figure 11-8. First click the Log On button in the upper-right corner. You will be presented with the logon screen as shown in Figure 11-25.

Enter a username and password that has been granted remote access through the Windows Home Server Console. After you have successfully logged in, you will be presented with a welcome screen similar to Figure 11-26.

To access your Windows Home Server shared folders, click the Shared Folders tab at the top of the window. You will be presented with a browse interface that will let you navigate through the folders and upload or download files or directories. An example of the browse interface is shown in Figure 11-27.

208   Chapter 11: Remotely Accessing Files and Computers

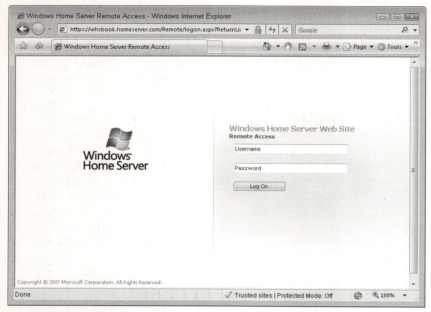

Figure 11-25

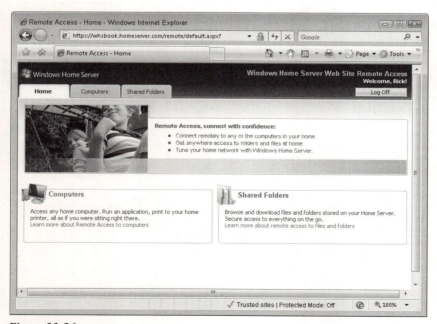

Figure 11-26

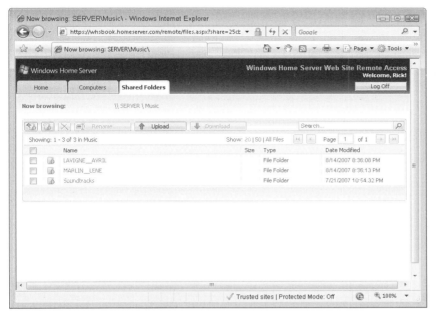

Figure 11-27

The shares that a user can access remotely are exactly the same as the shares they have access to when on the local home network. Access permissions and restrictions still apply in the same manner. For more details on setting permissions, see Chapter 6.

Enabling Remote Desktop Access on Home Computers

To enable remote connections to your home computers, you must configure the system and security settings for those computers to allow the connection. Remote Desktop is only supported on the following operating system editions:

- Windows XP Professional or Tablet Edition with Service Pack 2 (SP2)
- Windows XP Media Center Edition 2005
- Windows Vista Ultimate, Vista Business, or Vista Enterprise

These editions are only needed if you wish to remotely access your desktop computers. They are not needed to support remote access to files stored on your Windows Home Server.

Enabling Remote Desktop Access

To enable Remote Desktop on your system, you have to go to your computer properties. To do this, open the Control Panel, open the Systems and Maintenance subfolder, and then click the Allow Remote Access task under the System heading. After agreeing to continue through the User Account Control prompt, you will be shown a screen similar to Figure 11-28.

Figure 11-28

You have to select the option to Allow connections from computers running any version of Remote Desktop in order to enable Windows Home Server to act as a gateway for remote access to the local computer. (Because the Remote Desktop proxying software is based on earlier versions of Windows, it does not support Vista's enhanced security model.) By default, only user accounts that are in the administrators group are allowed Remote Desktop access. If you wish to allow other users Remote Desktop access, click the Select Users button to add them.

Configuring Your Firewall to Allow Remote Desktop

Different firewalls handle this in different ways, but most have a predefined setting that will allow Remote Desktop Connections to pass through. The process for Windows Live OneCare is as follows:

1. Open Windows Live OneCare by double-clicking the OneCare icon in the system tray.
2. Click Change OneCare Settings in the task pane on the left.
3. In the resulting dialog box, select the Firewall tab.
4. Select the Advanced Settings button from the Firewall tab to display the Windows Live OneCare Firewall Advanced Settings dialog box.
5. Select the Managing and sharing tab in this dialog box, and you should see a screen similar to Figure 11-29.

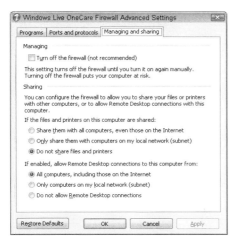

Figure 11-29

6. Select the option to allow Remote Desktop Connections from All computers including those on the Internet in order to enable remote connections.

Other firewall programs may just have an option to enable or disable Remote Desktop Connections. This may also be labeled as RDP, or Remote Desktop Protocol. Once you have enabled this setting on your firewall, your computer should be ready for remote connections through Windows Home Server.

Security Considerations

In the previous sections about setting up port forwarding on your router, and enabling remote access on your computers, it is important to realize that you are making changes to the security mechanisms of your home network. Modern day broadband connections are pretty resistant to inbound attacks because they basically disable inbound connections altogether, and only allow traffic to pass that was initiated by a user inside the home network. Enabling port forwarding basically pokes a hole in this first line of defense, which could make your systems more vulnerable to outside attacks.

Many people think that they don't need to worry about outside attacks because they believe that they don't have anything that hackers would want. The truth is that the overwhelming majority of Internet attacks are automated, and somewhat random. Internet worms generally scan through random sections of IP addresses looking for vulnerable machines, and hackers use automated tools to search across the Internet. The two things that most home users have that the bad guys might want are bandwidth and personal information. Some Internet criminals accumulate large groups of vulnerable machines, known as *zombies*, that they can use to flood other Internet computers with traffic. This type of attack is known as a Distributed Denial of Service attack. Zombie computers are also used as launching points for generating e-mail spam. The other thing home users need to worry about is the introduction of code that will gather personal data or information that might be used in identity theft.

Chapter 11: Remotely Accessing Files and Computers

With all of that said, Windows Home Server is based on the Windows Server 2003 operating system, which has a very good track record with regard to security. By default, Windows Home Server will install updates as they become available, so you will be protected from most attacks.

In addition to the default security of Windows Home Server, it is also a good idea to install a decent virus or malware scanner on your home server, as well as on your other home computers. This acts as a second line of defense in case a new threat emerges too quickly for Microsoft to release a fix, or in case an action that is taken locally on a computer or on the server allows malicious code to run.

The use of security software is discussed at length in Chapter 13. The important point to remember is that opening up your network to the Internet does make you more vulnerable, so it is even more important to be proactive with maintaining up-to-date antivirus software and operating systems updates for your server and home computers.

Connecting to Home Computers

Connecting via Remote Desktop to one of your home computers starts from you home server's website. Connect and log in, just as in the previous section, but instead of selecting the Shared Folders tab, select the Computers tab. The resulting screen lists all of the computers that are currently managed by your home server, similar to Figure 11-30.

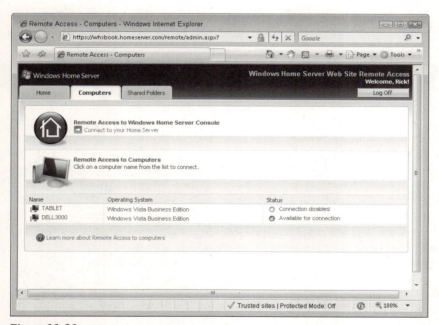

Figure 11-30

Note

The first time that you remotely access a computer through Windows Home Server, you may be prompted to install the Terminal Services ActiveX Client. This control is needed in order to open the Remote Desktop Connection that allows remote access to your home clients. After it has been installed on a particular computer, it should not have to be installed again unless the control is updated by Microsoft.

The listing will indicate which computers are available for connection, and if they are not available it will show a brief explanation. To connect to a computer, click the computer name in the listing. In the following dialog box, shown in Figure 11-31, you can select some options about your connection speed, and you can choose a screen size for your connection.

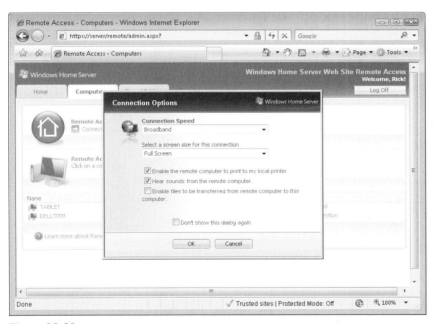

Figure 11-31

Select appropriate options and click OK. You will be asked to log in to the remote machine, and you can do so just as if you were sitting at that machine. Once you log in, you will have access to all of the resources and programs that are on that machine.

One important reminder is that if you connect remotely to a computer, it will lock local users out for the duration of your desktop session. Anyone sitting at the physical computer will see a message indicating that someone is logged on remotely. If the person sitting at the computer logs in, it will kick off the remote user and they will receive a message saying that the connection timed out. Just be mindful of this fact if there is a possibility of both a remote user and a local user trying to make use of the same computer at one time.

Summary

In this chapter, you learned how to make use of Windows Home Server's remote access features. You discovered how to use the Windows Home Server Console to enable remote access features for Windows Home Server, and how to enable specific users to use Remote Access. After learning some basics about networking, you learned how to configure your home routing equipment to forward traffic from the Internet to your home server by configuring port forwarding.

Next you learned how to enable Remote Desktop Connections on your client computers. This involved making changes to both the system configuration, and to the firewall configuration. After reviewing some security considerations, you learned how to access your Windows Home Server shared folders, and how to remotely connect to your home computers from the Internet using Windows Home Server's Remote Desktop features.

Chapter 12

Taking Care of Your Home Server

Your Windows Home Server is an appliance that requires care and maintenance in order for it to provide you with a long life of reliable service. To maintain your server, you need to perform two different types of care. The first broad category is called functional maintenance. This basically means that you have to do certain things in order to assist the server with the functions that it is designed to perform. This includes responding to alerts, verifying that the system is operating properly, expanding or removing storage when necessary. The second category is physical maintenance. Your server is a machine that is built from many different mechanical and electrical devices all working in concert. Keeping your server physically clean is also important to keeping it running and reliable for a long time.

Common Problems and Alerts

Windows Home Server is constantly monitoring the operations of its core functions, like backup, and it is monitoring the health status of its own hardware, as well as keeping track of certain attributes of all of the computers on your home network. Occasionally, Windows Home Server will issue an alert that indicates that some action needs to be taken in order to maintain the healthy operation of the network. These alerts appear on any computer with the Windows Home Server Connector software installed, unless the alerts have been disabled for that machine. This section highlights some of the more common alerts and discusses how to address them.

To enable or disable alerts on a client machine, right-click the Windows Home Server icon in the system tray, and check or uncheck the Display Network Health Notifications option shown in Figure 12-1.

Figure 12-1

This setting is separately configurable for each user account on each client computer. You can set notifications to be displayed for the more technical members of your household, and turn them off for less technically inclined individuals for whom they would just be an annoyance. These notifications will typically pop up as a balloon message from the Windows Home Server icon in the system tray.

Failed Backups

You will receive a failed backup alert, similar to the one shown in Figure 12-2, any time a backup does not complete on any machine in your home network. The alert will show on all computers that have the Display Network Health Notifications option enabled in the connector software. (This option is *on* by default.) This means that you may receive the alert on a different machine from the one that actually has a problem.

Figure 12-2

Failures can occur for many reasons, including system restarts, network hiccups, or user cancellation. You don't necessarily need to do anything to respond to this alert other than be aware that the specific machine that generated the alert missed a day of being backed up. The machine will be backed up during the next backup window. If this is the first day that you are seeing the notification, it's probably safe to just take notice of the fact that the backup failed and wait and see if the computer is backed up during the following backup window. However, if your computer has been showing signs of trouble or if you know you have made recent important changes on the machine, including editing files, you may want to manually initiate a backup. The process for creating manual backups is covered in Chapter 7.

Missing or Disabled Security Elements

Windows Home Server integrates with the Windows Security Center on each of your computers, and it will report problems to the server and to any computers that are configured to display alerts. Some sample alerts are shown in Figures 12-3, 12-4, and 12-5.

Figure 12-3

Chapter 12: Taking Care of Your Home Server   217

Figure 12-4

Figure 12-5

If you see one of these alerts, you should check the respective security element on the machine that is reporting the problem. Sometimes viruses or root kits will disable these security features, so if you cannot find an explanation for why an item is not working, you should run a full system scan with your virus protection software and/or seek the help of a computer professional who understands how to detect and remove advanced malware. Some of these programs can even hide from antivirus packages such as Symantec and McAfee, so if there's evidence of a problem, don't hesitate to ask for help.

Missing or Unhealthy Drives

If one of your drives shows signs that it is beginning to fail, Windows Home Server will display an alert to warn you. Windows Home Server monitors several factors to determine the health of a drive, including S.M.A.R.T. (Self-Monitoring, Analysis, and Reporting Technology) diagnostics if both your server and drives support it. If a drive is showing signs of failure, you will see an alert similar to Figure 12-6.

Figure 12-6

If this happens, your first option is to repair the drive. Sometimes a drive will be marked as unhealthy because it experienced a momentary glitch, such as someone wiggling a USB cable attaching the drive.

You repair a drive through the Windows Home Server Console. Open the console by double-clicking the Windows Home Server icon in the system tray, and then enter your server's administrative password. When the console appears, select the Server Storage tab at the top, and you will see a listing of your drives, similar to Figure 12-7. Right-click the drive that is listed as Unhealthy, and select Repair from the context menu. The repair process will run, and Windows Home Server will report any errors. If the repair is successful, the status column for the drive in question will return to Healthy.

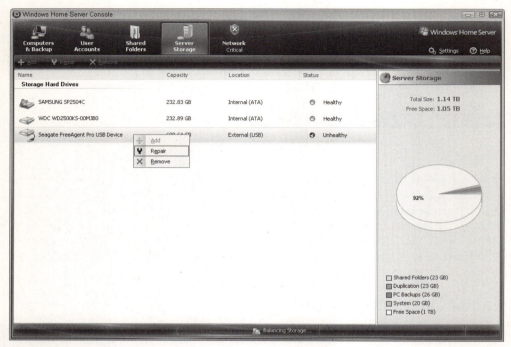

Figure 12-7

Caution

Many computer users are familiar with tools like Chkdsk, Defrag, The Disk Cleanup Wizard, and NTFS compression. Because of the way that Windows Home Server's Drive Extender software works, you should never attempt to use any of these standard disk tools directly on your Windows Home Server. All interaction with Windows Home Server's storage pool should be done through the Windows Home Server Console or through the \\SERVER\ shares. In addition, any tools that interact with the server's hard drives at a low level (like antivirus software) or advanced disk defragmenting programs (like DiskKeeper) need to be specially designed to interact properly with Drive Extender.

If the repair is successful and no further warnings appear, the drive is probably going to continue to function reliably. If a particular drive repeatedly gives you errors, it is time to replace it so that it doesn't cause data loss.

If a drive is powered off, disconnected, or has actually failed, you will see a warning similar to Figure 12-8. If this happens, you should shut down the server and check the power and data cables that are connected to the drive. After powering the server back on, check to see if the drive is still missing from the Windows Home Server Console. If it is, then the drive has failed and you will have to remove it from the storage pool as described later in this chapter.

Figure 12-8

Note
After a non-repairable drive failure, some of your backup sets may no longer be available. You may want to consider recreating any manual backups that you use as a baseline for restoring your computers. Data in folders that were not set to duplicate may be missing. All other data on duplicated folders should be intact.

Low Disk Space

If your Windows Home Server is running low on free storage space, you will see an alert similar to Figure 12-9. If you receive this warning, you have a few options for addressing it. You can either spend some time perusing the shares on your home server, looking for files that you no longer need and can delete, or you can add storage to your Windows Home Server.

Figure 12-9

Deleting files is an easy solution, but it will probably only buy you a few more months before you need to address low storage space again. The better solution is to add additional storage, which is covered in detail in the following section.

> ### Can You Free Up Space by Deleting Backups?
>
> The short answer is, not really. Windows Home Server's backup engine makes very efficient use of space by performing a block-by-block backup of the files on your computer hard drives. When it backs up a file to the server, the blocks that make up the file are compared to the blocks that already exist on the server, and if the block already exists from an earlier backup or from another computer's backup, it does not make an additional copy of the block, but just makes a reference to the existing block.
>
> This means that while the initial backup of a computer may take up a considerable amount of space, each backup thereafter will take a negligible amount of space. Only files that are new or have changed since the previous backup will consume additional space.

Adding and Removing Hard Drives

Windows Home Server's Drive Extender technology makes it easy to increase storage capacity on your server. You don't have to worry about drive letters, partitions, or any of the usual hassles associated with adding drives. You simply install or plug in the additional drive, and then use the Windows Home Server Console to add it to the storage pool.

Adding a Drive

Windows Home Server's storage is designed to grow to keep pace with your needs. You have many options for the type of drive that you add to your home server, depending on the form factor of your server and the expansion options that are included.

Many home servers, such as HP's MediaSmart Server, support between two and four internal SATA hard drives. The process for selecting and installing an internal drive will vary between the different manufacturers, so you will have to refer to your hardware owner's manual for instructions.

The easier option is to add an external hard drive. External drives should be USB 2.0, Firewire, or eSATA in order to keep your server's performance reasonable. All Windows Home Server machines will have several USB 2.0 ports, but you may have other options as well.

The physical setup of an external drive is as simple as locating the drive next to your home server, connecting the appropriate cable, and then if necessary providing power to the drive. Remember that you'll want to hook your drives directly to a port on your home server. Connecting through USB hubs can significantly reduce the speed at which your new hard drive can operate.

After your new drive is physically connected to your home server, you use the Windows Home Server Console to add it to the storage pool. Start by double-clicking the Windows Home Server icon in the system tray, and then enter your home server's administrative password.

Click the Server Storage tab at the top of the screen. You will see a listing of drives that will be broken into two sections, similar to Figure 12-10. The first section labeled Non-Storage Hard Drives should contain your new drive. The other section labeled Storage Hard Drives lists all of the drives that have already been added to the pool. Right-click the new drive, and select Add from the context menu, as shown in Figure 12-10.

Chapter 12: Taking Care of Your Home Server 221

Figure 12-10

The resulting screen, shown in Figure 12-11, shows the Add a Hard Drive wizard. Click Next to begin the process of adding the drive.

Figure 12-11

On the following screen, you will see a message warning you that continuing will erase all existing data on the new drive, as shown in Figure 12-12. This is a very important warning for you to read. The nature of Windows Home Server's Drive Extender technology requires that the new drive be formatted before it is added to the pool. Any data that existed on the hard drive previously will be wiped out! If you need to back up the data, you can select Cancel and then you can move the drive back to one of your client computers to copy the data to a different location.

Figure 12-12

After you read the warning, click the Finish button to continue. Windows Home Server will format the new drive and add it to the Drive Extender storage pool. When the process is complete, the drive will be moved to the Storage Hard Drives section of the display, as shown in Figure 12-13, and you will have more space available on your Windows Home Server!

Removing a Drive

Occasionally you will need to remove a drive from your Windows Home Server's storage pool. This could occur if you need to use the drive for another purpose or if you need to make room for a larger drive. You can also remove a drive that is listed as Failed, Missing, or Unhealthy from the storage pool in this manner. Removing a drive is accomplished through the Windows Home Server Console.

Start the console by double-clicking the Windows Home Server icon in the system tray, and then enter your home server's administrative password. Click the Server Storage tab at the top of the screen. You will see a listing of drives that will be broken into two sections, similar to Figure 12-13 (from the previous section).

Right-click the drive that you wish to remove from the storage pool and select Remove, as shown in Figure 12-14. This will start the Remove a Hard Drive wizard, as shown in Figure 12-15.

Chapter 12: Taking Care of Your Home Server   **223**

Figure 12-13

Figure 12-14

Figure 12-15

Click Next to continue. Windows Home Server will then calculate whether the drive can be removed without losing data, as shown in Figure 12-16. Once these calculations are completed, you will be presented with the confirmation screen shown in Figure 12-17.

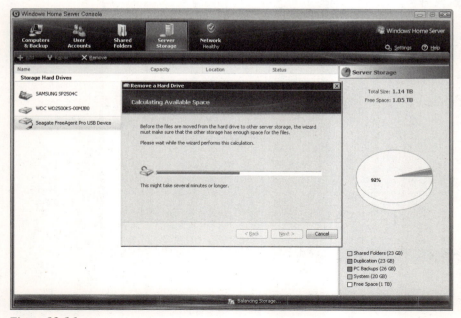

Figure 12-16

Figure 12-17

After you confirm that there will not be any data loss, click Next to continue. Be forewarned that this process can take many hours to complete. During the removal process you will not be able to access any of your Windows Home Server shared folders, and the backup service will be unavailable.

After the removal is completed, if the drive was not previously listed as Missing, the drive will be moved into a section of the list titled Non-Storage Hard Drives, as shown in Figure 12-10.

Monitoring and Preventative Maintenance

As with any appliance or machine, there are things you should do to keep your Windows Home Server in good working order. You should occasionally verify that the functions of Widows Home Server are all working as you expect. You should also periodically inspect your physical home server and work to maintain it in good order.

Monitoring the status of the various functions of your Windows Home Server gives you confidence that it is protecting your data, lets you plan for ways that you can utilize Windows Home Server better, and may allow you to catch problem situations before they become urgent.

Taking care of the mechanical health of your server will enable it to serve a longer, more reliable life as part of your home network.

Reviewing Operations of Windows Home Server

It's a good idea to stay familiar with the operations of your Windows Home Server. The Windows Home Server Console provides several screens that will give you different types of information regarding backups, storage, and network health.

Chapter 12: Taking Care of Your Home Server

To get started, open the Windows Home Server Console by double-clicking the Windows Home Server icon in the system tray of one of your computers. Enter the administrative password for your home server. The console has five tabs listed across the top.

COMPUTERS & BACKUP

The Computers & Backup tab, shown in Figure 12-18, is used for reviewing the computers that are attached to your Windows Home Server, checking on their backup status, removing computers that are no longer part of your network. The process for reviewing backups for a specific computer is covered in Chapter 7.

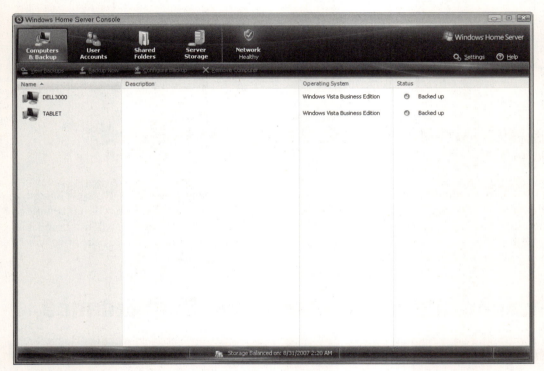

Figure 12-18

You can use this tab to get a general overview of the computers on your network and to verify that they are all being backed up regularly.

USER ACCOUNTS

The User Accounts tab, shown in Figure 12-19, provides a quick review of the users on your home network. This tab is covered more extensively in Chapter 6.

You can quickly confirm that the appropriate accounts are present, and that no extra or unneeded accounts are listed.

Figure 12-19

SHARED FOLDERS

The Shared Folders tab shows a listing of all of the shares that Windows Home Server is currently providing for your network, as shown in Figure 12-20.

You can review how much space each share is consuming, and verify that folder duplication is turned on for the appropriate shares.

SERVER STORAGE

The Server Storage tab lists all of the drives that are connected to the Windows Home Server and their current health, as shown in Figure 12-21.

You can review the health of all of your drives and see a picture of how much space you have utilized on your home server, as well as the amount of free space that you have available.

NETWORK

The Network tab actually opens a pop-up window that lists your home networks' health status, as shown in Figure 12-22. Any warnings or alerts will be shown here.

228 Chapter 12: Taking Care of Your Home Server

Figure 12-20

Figure 12-21

Figure 12-22

Physical Maintenance

Your Windows Home Server contains many electrical and mechanical parts. While these parts are generally reliable, there are extra steps that you can take to extend the reliable life of your server. The primary enemies of computer parts are: heat, dust, electricity, and vibration. This can be a bit troublesome, because these enemies are used or created during the normal operation of the server. They cannot be eliminated, but they can be managed so that your home server can serve a long reliable life.

MANAGING HEAT

Heat is enemy number one for all computers, and especially your home server. Almost all energy that comes into your Windows Home Server through the power cord will eventually become heat. It does useful things along the way, providing power for the processor, spinning and moving the parts of your hard drive, and so on, but eventually it becomes heat.

As long as this heat is continually removed from the server, it will never be a problem. Most home servers are designed with fans to make sure that enough air can be pulled through and pushed out of the server to carry this heat away. Some servers may have *fanless* designs. These servers rely on the case to move heat away without the benefit of large volumes of air moving around the parts. Metal conducts heat well, so these types of servers will sometimes have solid metal bars that connect certain components with the case, and the case will often be designed to include ridges or fins so that it can act effectively as a heat sink.

Retail OEM Windows Home Server machines, or regular computers or computer cases, will be designed with sufficient cooling capacity, so the most important maintenance that you can perform with regard to heat is to make sure that the server can use it's designed heat removal mechanisms.

As a first step in your maintenance, clear any unneeded papers, books, or other obstructions that would block air inlets or outlets. If you have a fanless server, you should also make sure that nothing is stacked directly on or against the server.

You may also want to review the placement of your Windows Home Server, as sometimes the environment that it is in will change in ways that increase the possibility of building up excess heat. Be sure that the server is not in direct sunlight or placed too close to incandescent light bulbs. Other computers also generate heat, so be sure that you are not collocating too many heat-generating devices in one location. (More recommendations on placement of your Windows Home Server can be found in Chapter 5.) You should also check that air conditioning registers and returns are open during the cooling season, and you should make sure that the server is not subjected to excess heat from heating registers, baseboard heaters, or radiators during the heating season.

REMOVING DUST

As you are clearing away any obstructions, you may notice another common problem: dust. Dust is made up from accumulation of various materials that can be found in a home, including dead skin cells from people and animals, pollen from indoor and outdoor plants, and fibers from paper and carpeting. Dust can cause problems in two different ways. The first is that it can obstruct your server's designed mechanisms for removing heat. If dust accumulates on air inlets or outlets or on heat sinks, it can reduce the volume of air that is carrying away the heat that is generated by the operation of your server. Dust is a fairly decent insulator for heat, so it can form a barrier that keeps the heat that is generated inside your Windows Home Server machine from escaping to the surrounding area.

The second way that dust can cause problems is by accumulating on moving parts. The moving parts on your hard drives are sealed, so you don't really need to worry about them, but you should keep an eye out for dust accumulating on fans. In addition to constricting airflow, dust can cause slight imbalances on fans, which will cause the bearings or bushings to wear out prematurely, making the fans noisy, and eventually causing them to fail.

As a general rule, you should not need to worry about cleaning dust from inside your Windows Home Server. The risk of causing damage while the case is open outweighs the benefits of cleaning dust off the internal components. You should do your best to remove dust that is visible on the outside of your home server, paying special attention to any areas that allow heat to be removed. You can remove dust with a dry dust cloth, and sometimes it helps to use a can of compressed air (available at most office supply stores) to clean irregular surfaces or air grates.

You should also review the environment around your server to see if it is being subjected to excessive amounts of dust. Forced air systems for heating and cooling tend to accumulate dust in ductwork and around returns and registers. You should avoid placing your server in the path of this airflow, either near returns or registers, because the moving air tends to carry a volume of dust, some of which is deposited on anything in the path of the airflow.

Additional preventative steps you can take are to keep your home server at least two feet off the ground (especially if the room has carpeting), and to keep it clear of places where dogs, cats, or other pets sleep.

SHOCK, VIBRATION, AND PART FATIGUE

Shock and vibration can slowly shorten the life on the various moving parts in your Windows Home Server, so it should be monitored and avoided when possible. Strong enough vibrations or shocks cause more friction to occur against the bearings in spinning parts. Sometimes the bearings can even be misshapen by outside physical stress. Shock and vibration can also affect the various connectors that tie together the parts inside your home server. Repeated shocks or vibrations can cause connectors to fatigue or wiggle loose, degrading the life of the server or even causing a failure.

You should look at the types of shock and vibration that your Windows Home Server experiences, and then do your best to limit the amount that it is subjected to. Some common sources of vibration and shock include loud music (especially subwoofers), slamming doors, people running up and down stairs, and air conditioning fans. Protect your server as much as possible from shock and vibration, and it will have a longer useful and reliable life.

Can You Vacuum Your Home Server?

When battling dust, many folks decide that a quick and clean way to clean up would be to use their household vacuum. Unfortunately this method could actually cause significant damage to your Windows Home Server. Unless you have a vacuum that is specifically designed to eliminate static electricity, you will be risking the delicate electrical components of your home server.

When a vacuum runs, it obviously is moving a great deal of air. When you add dust to that air and pass it through the plastic tubing of a vacuum cleaner, it can generate a large static electric charge. If this charge is released through contact with your home server, the high-voltage spark can actually cook the insides of an important computer chip.

It is best to stick with manual means for eliminating dust and keep some compressed air handy to dislodge stubborn dust.

MANAGING ELECTRICITY

Electricity is the fuel that your Windows Home Server uses to operate, so it might be surprising to see it in this section, but when you're learning about keeping your home server reliable and healthy, it's important to understand the good and the bad aspects of electricity.

Computers operate best and most reliably when they are given a steady electrical supply. Brownouts can be caused by excess demand being placed on the electrical lines, either within your own home or anywhere in your town. When a system such as an air conditioner suddenly places additional demand on the electrical supply, it sometimes takes an instant for the power company's controlling equipment to respond to the demand. You may notice that the lights in your home flicker just a little when this occurs. For light bulbs this is not really a big deal, but these transient power fluctuations can shorten the life of the components in your home server. In addition, they can cause small errors on hard drives or in your server's memory and those errors can cause other problems.

Power surges can happen any time. Small surges are sometimes caused by a sudden decrease in demand for current on the electrical lines. This might happen when your air conditioner turns off or when an electrical line is broken by a tree falling. Larger surges can be caused by electrical storms.

Surges, small or large, can push more current through the components of your Windows Home Server than those components were designed to handle. When too much voltage is applied, the delicate electronics can be weakened, or they can even melt or boil.

The best way to protect your server from all types of electrical damage is to invest in an Uninterruptible Power Supply, or UPS. A UPS generally conditions and monitors the power that is passing through it, and it can compensate for slight increases or decreases in voltage, in addition to keeping your server running in the event that power goes out altogether. A UPS contains a large battery that it can use to provide power for a short period of time if the power in your home goes out. Smaller consumer UPS units are available for less than one hundred dollars. If you plug your home server into a UPS, you will also want to connect any external drives. It can also be useful to connect your Internet router and, if separate, your networking devices as well. Doing this will allow you to use a laptop with a battery or another home computer that has its own UPS to access your server or the Internet even when the power is off.

If you aren't ready to invest in a UPS, you should at least keep your Windows Home Server connected through a surge protector. While these generally don't do much for the smaller transient power problems, they will protect against the larger more damaging surges that can occur from lightning strikes on the power lines, or the surges that sometimes occur when power is restored after an outage.

Some additional steps you can take to protect your home server from power damage include:

- If your entire network is going to be unused while you are away from your home for a period of time, turn off and unplug your Windows Home Server and any other computers or networking equipment that are connected via wired Ethernet.

- If a power outage occurs, either turn off at the surge protector or power strip, or unplug your home server and computers until after power is restored and is stable. Power surges and brownouts often occur within the first few minutes of power being restored.

- Install and maintain a humidifier in your home during the winter. Extremely dry air in the winter can cause static electricity to be generated quite easily. Keeping a humidifier running can reduce or eliminate this problem.

- When you are cleaning your Windows Home Server, keep it plugged in so that it will have the benefit of being connected to your home's electrical ground. Whenever you first touch the home server, especially after walking on carpet, touch a metal part of the case that is away from any connectors. This will help keep static electricity away from the inside of the computer.

MAINTAINING YOUR SERVER FOR A LONG LIFE

The frequency of maintenance for your home server will depend very greatly on the environment that you place it in. A little bit of dust won't cause immediate damage; you just need to remember to occasionally check on your server's physical environment to make sure that it is allowed to operate as designed. If you take care of your home server's environmental needs, it is more likely to serve reliably for a long time to come.

Summary

Just like a car or any other machine, your Windows Home Server needs to be monitored and maintained in order to make sure that it stays reliable. Part of this process involves responding to the various errors and alerts that Windows Home Server can generate.

This chapter covered some of the more common alerts so that you will understand what they mean, and you will know what action you need to take if you encounter them. You also learned how to add and remove drives from Windows Home Server's storage pool, so that you can expand your home server's storage if needed, or remove a drive that has failed or that you need to use for another purpose. Next, you reviewed the various sections of the Windows Home Server Console and what information you can gain from them. Lastly, this chapter covered the physical maintenance that you can perform in order to protect your home server from damage from heat, dust, or electricity.

Your Windows Home Server is designed to be a reliable machine; take care of it properly, and it will take care of your data for a long time.

Chapter 13

Security and Your Home Server

Bringing a Windows Home Server machine into your home network brings both new tools and responsibilities for keeping your network secure. By integrating with the Windows Security Center on your client computers, Windows Home Server makes it easier to keep track of updates, virus and malware protection, and firewalls.

Keeping your Windows Home Server secure provides unique challenges. Because it is built on Microsoft's server architecture, many consumer security tools will not run on Windows Home Server. It will take some time for all of the security tool vendors to come out with consumer class (affordable) security solutions that will run on Windows Home Server. For now you will have to select from a limited number of options to keep your network safe.

How Windows Home Server Helps with Security

Windows Home Server does not address all aspects of security for your home network. The things it does, it does well, but it is not a comprehensive solution for security conscious users.

Windows Home Server's primary benefit for security is that the connector software integrates with the System Security Center on your client computers. The security posture of your home computers is then integrated into the network health monitoring that Windows Home Server performs. This means that you will get notifications of problems through the connector software on any computer that is configured to Display Network Health Notifications. Examples of problems could include out-of-date antivirus software or a disabled firewall.

The list of things that Windows Home Server does *not* do is much longer. Windows Home Server does not act as a firewall. Business users of Windows Home Server's cousin, Windows Small Business Server, may see this as an oversight. In addition to the added complexity that this brings to the product, Windows Home Server is meant to be integrated into your network in a way that makes it unsuited to be a firewall. For a firewall to be effective, it must sit between your home network and the Internet. Most consumers already have a firewall that is part of the home router or modem that their Internet Service Provider required. In addition, having a Windows Home Server act as a firewall would require it to be connected to the Internet in a way that might actually make the home server more vulnerable to compromise.

The current version of Windows Home Server is designed to be used behind a consumer firewall, and it should be connected in the same manner as a client computer would be connected. For more details on how your Windows Home Server should be connected, refer back to Chapter 4.

Another feature that is related to firewall functionality is web proxying. Web proxying allows a server to monitor Internet traffic for malicious or unwanted traffic. Many businesses use this feature to limit access to illegal or undesirable websites. Some tech-savvy home users have found ways to set up proxy servers at home in order to keep track of children's Internet usage, and to block inappropriate content. Like the firewall function, proxying is also best done at the edge of your network, and is most effective when it is integrated into the same device as the firewall function. There are also additional challenges for using proxying that require locking down configurations of different browsers, or configuring properties on a firewall to make sure that users can't simply bypass the proxy server. These challenges make enabling proxy functionality on Windows Home Server a non-trivial exercise.

Microsoft's current offering for server firewall and proxying is called Internet Security and Acceleration Server, or ISA Server. ISA Server is sold as a standalone product and it is also integrated into Microsoft's Small Business Server operating system. The full version of ISA Server is way more powerful and more complicated than any home network should require. In the future, a slimmed down version of ISA Server may be integrated into Windows Home Server, but until then, users will have to rely on client-based tools like WebWatcher (www.webwatcherkids.com/) or NetNanny (www.netnanny.com/) if they require this functionality.

Monitoring and Managing Home Network Health

Windows Home Server simplifies monitoring of the health of your home network. Every computer that has the Windows Home Server Connector software installed will report to the server on a number of security related settings and features. Windows Home Server does not check these features itself, but rather relies on integration with the client computer's Windows Security Center, a feature of Windows Vista, or Windows XP Service Pack 2 or above.

The Windows Security Center monitors several security-related aspects of each of your client computers. It keeps track of whether your computer has a firewall program installed and operating. It monitors whether you have Automatic Updates enabled. It monitors whether you have active and up-to-date virus and malware protection. Lastly, it keeps track of whether your Internet and local security settings are set to recommended levels. An example of the local view of Windows Security Center is shown in Figure 13-1.

By default, Windows Vista and XP include Firewall protections through Windows Firewall, and Automatic Updates are turned on by default (with user agreement). Virus and Malware protections are typically provided via third-party software, although Microsoft has entered this space with its Windows Live OneCare security suite covering virus and malware (spyware) protection, and Windows Defender offering a standalone malware protection solution. Microsoft also offers business-class solutions with its Forefront Client Security offerings.

Chapter 13: Security and Your Home Server   237

Figure 13-1

While there are certainly differences among the various security offerings, the only requirement for making the most of your Windows Home Server's monitoring capabilities is that the security solution that you use integrates with Windows Security Center so that the proper status can be reported to your home server. Other tools may in fact function properly, but if they do not integrate with the Windows Security Center, you will receive unnecessary alerts. If your preferred tools are not integrated, see the sidebar later in this chapter titled "What if WHS Doesn't Recognize Your Security Tools?" for instructions on suppressing unnecessary notifications.

Most current antivirus and security products have been updated to work well with Windows Security Center. Commercial offerings from Symantec and McAfee seem to be some of the more popular products, but smaller vendors such as AVG have also done a good job of making their products work well with Windows' built-in monitoring. Look for labeling that indicates that the security product that you are purchasing works with Windows Vista. This labeling generally indicates that they have done the work necessary so that their products accurately report to Windows their current status so that Windows Security Center can monitor them properly.

Free Antivirus?

With more and more households maintaining two or more computers, paying for up-to-date antivirus subscriptions for each machine can seem like a daunting prospect. Many folks assume that they will have to pay for each machine if they want functional antivirus protection for their home computers. While this is sometimes the case, there are many avenues for protecting your computers without it costing an arm and a leg.

The first option is to check with your employer to see if they have any agreements that will allow you to get antivirus and security software for free or at a reduced cost. Many employers, especially larger companies and organizations, have negotiated licensing deals with antivirus vendors that allow their employees to use corporate antivirus products. This makes great sense because people often work on projects from home, and thus protecting the home computers of the employees is an important aspect of protecting the corporate network. If you are unsure if your company has a similar arrangement, check your company intranet, or contact your IT department or company helpdesk.

If you do not have the option of getting discounted or free antivirus from your employer, there is still an option. A company called Grisoft has been offering a free version of their AVG product to consumers for many years. The features of this version of the software generally lag behind their commercial offering by a version, and it doesn't include some of the more advanced security features, but the virus definitions are kept up to date just the same. The free version of AVG can be downloaded from `http://free.grisoft.com/`. There are restrictions on the use of the free version, so read the license carefully.

Understanding Security Suites

One of the most confusing aspects of securing your home network is that most security tool vendors have adopted the notion of a security *suite*. What this means is that instead of selling discrete tools, such as a firewall or an antivirus scanner, they want to provide all of this in an integrated package.

The benefit of the security suite to the user is that they get a certain level of *defense in depth* by installing a single software package. The benefit to the software company is that they get to sell you more software, albeit in a single package.

The downside to the idea of a security suite is that it uses a one-size-fits-all approach, and each piece of the suite uses a certain amount of resources on the computer where it is installed.

The key to the security suite puzzle is understanding. By understanding what each aspect of the suite provides, you can make good decisions about installing and configuring the tools.

Most security suites include three main features: antivirus, antispyware, and a firewall.

Antivirus

Antivirus is responsible for keeping your computer free of viruses. A computer virus is basically any computer code that is able to replicate, or make copies of itself, without requiring the permission of the person using the computer. Viruses replicate in different ways. Older viruses would alter the contents of hard drive and floppy disk boot sectors in order to spread. Some viruses would search for executable programs on the computer and modify those programs by adding a copy of the virus code. Most modern viruses find ways to spread over the network using vulnerabilities in operating systems, or even hijacking a user's e-mail to send copies to a person's contact list.

Besides replicating, many viruses do other malicious things. Some install additional code that let hackers use your machine remotely. Others install logging capabilities that look for usernames, passwords, credit card numbers, or other information that can be used for identity theft. Some delete or alter files or even erase the contents of your entire hard drive.

Antivirus software stands between a system and the user, and monitors the actions that the user takes to make sure that they don't accidentally infect their computer. The antivirus engine monitors the hard drive and removable storage, and if it finds a virus, it attempts to quarantine the virus so that it cannot do any damage. Most antivirus programs include something called *real-time* protection, which means that they scan every program that is accessed on the computer to make sure that nothing matches the signature of any of the viruses that are in the vendor's database.

Antispyware

Spyware is a category of software that keeps track of the actions of a user, and reports those actions back to some entity. Over the past decade, there was a sort of gray market for spyware, where seemingly legitimate companies would try to exploit technology in order to better track user's actions so that the data could be sold to advertisers.

Determining whether a certain software package is spyware is not as cut and dry as it would seem. Many legitimate businesses use similar tactics in order to provide users with features and advertising that suits them. Most of the programs that have been labeled spyware were add-ons that were bundled with other software that users might actually want. Often this software provided something that would entice the user to install it, but the value of the feature was rarely worth the privacy and computing resources that were surrendered.

Some spyware would actually get a user's permission to do what it did on their computer, but this was usually buried deep in a legal agreement known as an End User License Agreement (EULA) that would display when the software was first installed. Other spyware programs would forgo this formality.

Current thinking is that a program should be labeled spyware if the collection of data is not necessary for the features that are provided, or if the user is not clearly and properly notified and given the option of opting out of data collection.

Like antivirus, antispyware software functions by maintaining a database of signatures that can be used to identify offending programs. This functionality is often bundled with antivirus software, because the mechanics of each are similar.

Firewall

The term *firewall* is used to describe any hardware or software that provides a virtual barrier to keep unwanted network traffic from passing through. Firewall appliances are often used by corporations to protect their internal networks at points where they are connected to the Internet. Your Internet modem or router probably acts as a firewall, either through basic Network Address Translations (NAT), which disallows inbound traffic, or through more advanced filtering features that are available on some models. The firewall that is included in a software security suite is more often called a *personal* firewall, and this distinction just means that it is a software firewall that protects a single computer.

The basic idea behind a firewall is that it should block any traffic that is not authorized. A working firewall should not allow strangers to connect to your computer, should not allow viruses or Internet worms to probe your computer for unpatched vulnerabilities, and should not allow malicious code on your computer to send data to the Internet without your knowledge and consent.

Other Features

Many security suites include other features as well. A common addition to a security suite is to offer monitoring of backups or integrated backup capabilities to keep your data safe. Other suites will monitor your operating system and other software and manage the installation of important security updates. Some solutions will also help with e-mail security by monitoring and removing unwanted messages, often called spam.

Defense in Depth

The multiple layers of security, including the security features of your operating system, your home network, Windows Home Server, and any additional security software that you run, are all part of a strategy known as *defense in depth*.

In the realm of security, making a system that is 100 percent secure is accepted to be prohibitively expensive. Because of this, computer users are encouraged to build systems that have multiple layers of security. If a weakness happens to be found in one layer, another layer will likely stop the exploitation of the vulnerability. Instead of striving for 100 percent in any one layer, you can get very reasonable security by stacking many layers that are each *very good*, blocking 95 percent or so at each layer.

Trade-offs

Keeping in mind the idea of *defense in depth*, you should understand that every piece of software that runs on your computers will use resources. I have seen many computers that become almost unresponsive when they are loaded down with all of the features of a *full* security suite. Most security suites will allow you to select the features that you want to install, and they will let you enable and disable features any time.

For each computer in your home network, you can customize the options that you enable. You should consider both the way that a machine is used and how it is connected to the network when you do this.

If you have a laptop that you frequently connect to public networks, such as at the airport or library, then you probably want to include the best firewall technology that you have available. On the other hand, if you have a desktop computer that is connected via wired Ethernet to your home network, you may decide that the built-in firewall in Windows is sufficient, because it uses fewer resources than most third-party firewalls. Likewise if a machine is rarely used for e-mail or Internet access, you might choose to use the free Windows Defender from Microsoft (www.microsoft.com/defender) instead of opting to pay for a spyware solution.

There is also value in having an identical setup on each of your computers, and many security suite vendors offer licensing that allows installation on multiple home computers. Keep this all in mind as you decide how to best protect your home computers.

Chapter 13: Security and Your Home Server   **241**

What if WHS Doesn't Recognize Your Security Tools?

If the Windows Security Center, and therefore Windows Home Server, doesn't recognize the security tools that you have installed, you can disable the warnings using the Windows Security Center on the computer where the software is installed.

To do this, open the Windows Security Center from the computer's Control Panel. Open the Control Panel by clicking the Start orb, and selecting Control Panel from the right column. Under the Security heading, click Check this computer's security status. If you have a security tool that is not recognized by Windows, the screen will look similar to the following figure.

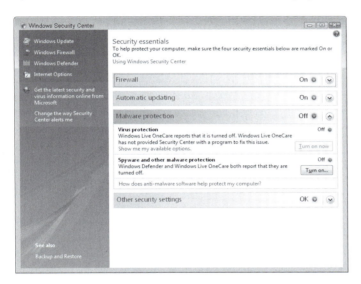

Under the heading for the specific type of software that is not recognized (Firewall, Malware Protection, or Automatic Updating), select the Show me my available options task. The resulting dialog box is shown in the following figure.

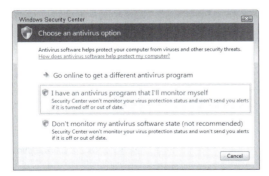

Select the option to indicate that you have a solution you will monitor yourself, such as the "I have an antivirus program that I'll monitor myself" option shown in the previous figure, and Windows Security Center and Windows Home Server will no longer alert you regarding the status of that security feature.

Antivirus for Windows Home Server

Now that you have looked at security for your client computers, it's time to address the security needs of your Windows Home Server. Your home server has unique requirements when it comes to security software. As a headless box, you will never use common Internet tools such as a browser or e-mail program from the Windows Home Server's desktop. Likewise, you will probably never run any software on it that is not packaged as an add-in, and thus the likelihood of accidentally running virus code on your home server is diminished. Because the server is not supposed to be utilized as a general-purpose computer (as your client computers are), antispyware protection is not as necessary. Also, the built-in Windows Firewall that is included with Windows Home Server is more than adequate for most users, and the fact that it is integrated and tested with the rest of the Windows Home Server setup means that it won't interfere with any of Windows Home Server's features.

Security experts like to talk about experiments where they place unpatched systems on the Internet to see how long it takes before they are compromised by viruses. The time for older operating system releases such as Windows 2000 and the original Windows XP without service packs is usually measured in minutes, or just a few hours. Because Windows Home Server is based on an up-to-date Windows Server 2003 architecture, it is leaps and bounds ahead in terms of security, but you should be aware that the security of an Internet-connected server will constantly be tested.

As part of your defense in depth strategy, you should employ antivirus software on your Windows Home Server so that it will be better protected from malicious software. When a new vulnerability is discovered, it is often a race between the operating system vendor and hackers. The operating system vendors try to develop, test, and release a patch before the hackers can develop code that exploits the bug. Antivirus software vendors can release new detection signatures much more quickly. Many antivirus software vendors release updates on a daily basis, so that even if the hackers beat Microsoft in the race, the antivirus software can detect and stop the threat.

With all of the security benefits that are gained by using Windows Server 2003 as a basis for Windows Home Server, there is at least one drawback. Many consumer antivirus tools are specifically designed to run on consumer-class operating systems such as Windows Vista or Windows XP, and they will refuse to install on Windows Home Server.

The best solution is to use antivirus software that is specifically designed for Windows Home Server. At press time, there was only one company on record as having a solution in the works that would be designed for Windows Home Server. In May 2007, F-Secure announced that they would be developing a data security product for Windows Home Server, and the press release indicates that it would include protections against viruses and other threats. As Windows Home Server adoption increases, the other security vendors will most likely release products that are specifically designed for Windows Home Server.

If you can't find a Windows Home Server–specific solution that meets your needs, you can make use of any antivirus product that is designed to be used with Windows Server 2003. This greatly increases the field of possible solutions. During the beta testing program for Windows Home Server, users reported successfully running Corporate Editions from McAfee, Symantec, and Alwil software.

To install standard antivirus software to your Windows Home Server, you must log in to the desktop running on the home server. This process was outlined in Chapter 9 as part of the process for installing a printer. You can log in to your home server's desktop in order to install antivirus software in this same manner. If your Windows Home Server does not have a CD or DVD drive, or if you have downloaded installation files, you can copy the installation program for your antivirus software to your server's software share at \\SERVER\Software.

To conserve processing and memory resources on your server, you should pay attention to the installation program and decline any options that do not make sense for your server. You should allow installation of features that enable real-time file system protection and scheduled scanning and updates, but you should opt not to install or enable features such as e-mail protection, antispyware, and any web-related features. These features are designed to protect the computer when a user is actively using the machine by reading e-mail or browsing the Internet, which as a general rule you should not be doing directly on your Windows Home Server.

If Windows Home Server Has a Desktop, Can You Use It?

Many folks will be tempted to use Windows Home Server's desktop as an extra client computer. For retail OEM machines that lack a keyboard and display, this temptation will be low because it requires logging in through remote desktop, but for home-built or system builder machines, the temptation to hook up a keyboard and monitor is there.

The short answer is that while you *could* use your home server as an extra client machine, you should *choose* not to do so.

The key purposes of your Windows Home Server are to provide a stable and reliable backup solution for your home computers and for it to keep your data safe and accessible. If you choose to use Windows Home Server as an extra client computer, you are exposing your server to additional risks, and this undermines its purpose as a reliable keeper of your important data.

Additionally, because Windows Home Server is not intended to be used as a desktop, security tools that protect against threats related to desktop use, specifically AntiSpyware and more customizable third-party client firewalls, will not be available for Windows Home Server. Security vendors will focus on providing tools that are appropriate for Windows Home Server's role as a server, such as server-grade Antivirus.

The safest course is to only use a local keyboard and display or the Remote Desktop Connection to your Windows Home Server for installing software that cannot be installed via the Windows Home Server Console, and you should limit this software to programs that are designed and tested for use on Windows Home Server.

Patches and Updates

Software, and specifically operating system software, will always have bugs. Companies such as Microsoft strive to reduce the number of these bugs that their software has, but developers are human, and humans make mistakes. Microsoft has gotten very good at eliminating the obvious mistakes with automated code analysis tools, but hackers and virus writers are always innovating and have found ways to exploit even the most secure systems. When vulnerabilities or bugs are found, software vendors have to build, test and release updates to keep their customers' software running properly and securely.

Automatic Updates

One of the best things you can do to ensure the security of your home network is to enable automatic update installation on all of the machines on your network. In the past many folks took more of a *wait and see* approach to patches, and many businesses opted to only install patches if there was an obvious problem with how the software was working. This mindset was reinforced by some hiccups that occurred with some patches that were covered under early automatic update efforts, which broke some computers when the patches were installed.

It has been a long time since Microsoft released any patches that caused problems on more than a handful of computers. Microsoft's patch testing regimen has improved greatly over the years, and it is now common practice to just let Windows install updates as soon as they are available.

Another facet that has emerged in recent years is that hackers now reverse engineer any patches that are released by software vendors. They use special tools to highlight the files that have changed, and to analyze the vulnerability that has been patched. They can then use this information to develop viruses and tools that can exploit the vulnerability, even if it is one that was patched without any disclosure of the details of the vulnerability. It is a bit of a catch-22 that the patches can be used as a roadmap that helps hackers discover more about the vulnerability that is being patched. This makes it even more important to install updates as soon as possible, so that you can avoid being caught off guard by opportunistic hackers that are hoping to infect computers before they are patched with new updates.

Enabling Automatic Updates on Client Computers

Many computers are now shipped with automatic updates enabled, but you should confirm that this functionality is turned on for all of your computers to be certain that your network is as secure as possible.

To check your computer's Automatic Updates settings, open the Control Panel by clicking the Start orb, and then selecting Control Panel from the right column. Click the Security heading to open the Security submenu. Next, click the Turn automatic updating on or off action under the Windows Update heading, as shown in Figure 13-2.

Figure 13-2

Chapter 13: Security and Your Home Server   245

The resulting screen, shown in Figure 13-3, allows you to enable or disable updates. You can select a time for updates to be installed, or you can change the frequency of when your computer will attempt to update itself.

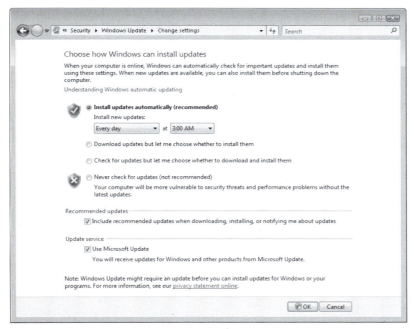

Figure 13-3

In addition to enabling Windows automatic updating, there is an option to enable additional services known as Microsoft Update, under the Update Service heading toward the bottom of the screen. Enabling this feature will make it so that in addition to downloading updates for Windows, the update process will include security updates and bug fixes for other Microsoft products as well. It is a good idea to turn this on as well, so that programs like Microsoft Word and Outlook can be patched. Because these programs are Internet-enabled, they can also be used to spread viruses, so it is just as important that they are updated as well.

Keeping Other Programs Updated

Many software vendors, including Adobe, Google, Apple, and even the Mozilla Foundation (makers of the Firefox Web browser) include update functionality when you install their software. The level of automation varies considerably between vendors, but most options are very user friendly.

The more Internet-centric software is, the more important it is that you keep it up to date. When software asks for permission to install updates, try to make the time to allow it to check for and install updates. While many viruses simply target Windows as a common denominator, new threats are emerging all of the time. As the operating systems become more secure, hackers and virus writers are beginning to target third-party software as a means for infecting computers.

Automatic Updates and Your Windows Home Server

In the default configuration, Windows Home Server is set up to automatically install updates when they become available. You can check this setting through the Windows Home Server Console. To open the console, double-click the Windows Home Server icon in the system tray. Enter your home server's administrative password, and then you will see a screen similar to Figure 13-4.

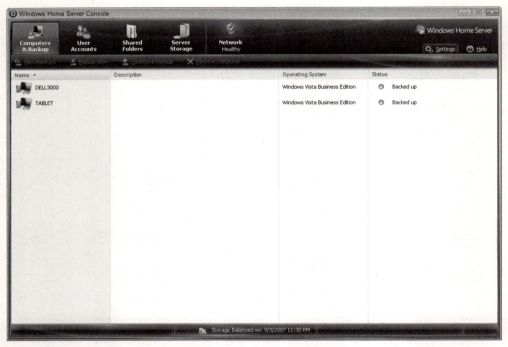

Figure 13-4

Click the Settings button in the upper-right corner of the console window to open the Windows Home Server Settings dialog box. The settings dialog box defaults to the General section, and looks similar to Figure 13-5.

Under the Windows Update heading, you can see that there is an option to turn Windows Update on or off. There is no schedule configuration available. Windows Home Server simply adds the update task to the list of things it will do during the nightly backup window. (For more details on changing your backup schedule, see Chapter 7.) This allows Windows Home Server to schedule the updates to occur at a time when they will not interfere with computer backups, storage balancing, backup cleanup, or other maintenance tasks. Once you have confirmed your settings, click OK to save any changes.

You should also confirm that any antivirus solution that is installed on your Windows Home Server is configured to automatically download updates so that you will be protected from any new viruses and Internet worms. You should also check occasionally to make sure that the antivirus updates are actually being updated.

Figure 13-5

Feature Overlap Between Windows Home Server and Windows Live OneCare 2.0

It's worth noting that Microsoft and other vendors' security suites are starting to include features that solve some of the same problems that Windows Home Server solves. The latest version of Windows Live OneCare offers a comprehensive computer backup solution, and also enables monitoring of the health and security status of all computers that are part of your OneCare *circle*.

When asked about the feature overlap, a Microsoft representative explained that OneCare is intended to be an all-in-one solution for consumer desktops and laptops and while they are working to ensure that consumers can simultaneously use both OneCare and Windows Home Server, they did not have any further integration plans to announce. Basically, Windows Live OneCare will recognize Windows Home Server as a valid backup solution and will give you the option of relying on Windows Home Server for backups, or it will allow you to still use the OneCare backup service as well.

The coming years should yield some interesting developments in home network security. The availability of a centralized resource such as Windows Home Server should enable innovative methods for making home networks more secure and more usable.

Other Backup Tools

Some people may have other backup tools available, such as the ones included in Windows Live OneCare 2.0 or in the various editions of Windows Vista. If one of your other backup options provides additional coverage for scenarios that Windows Home Server does not cover well, then it makes perfect sense to use the solutions in parallel. For example, you can use OneCare to automatically back up digital photos from your client computers to an online storage space. If you are not already backing up your home server to an online service (two such services are covered in Chapter 14), then you might consider using OneCare's features to provide extra protection for your photos.

If you do use more than one backup tool, make sure to set the schedules so that they operate at different times. Each tool will operate more efficiently if it does not have to contend with other tools for access to disk, CPU, and network resources.

Summary

In this chapter, you learned that bringing a Windows Home Server into your home network provides tools for maintaining your network better, and introduces challenges. You now understand how Windows Home Server integrates with the Windows Security Center to report the security posture of all of your networked computers as part of an overall network health. This chapter also discussed several security features that Windows Home Server does not perform, for which you would have to rely on third-party solutions. Next you learned about how client security suites can help protect your computers, what is required for them to integrate properly with Windows Home Server, and how to evaluate the various features to see what aspects of the security suite you need to install and enable on your various computers.

Next, this chapter covered the importance of installing antivirus software on your server, and discussed the difficulties associated with finding a compatible solution for a new platform like Windows Home Server. Also discussed were the options for installing antivirus software if you cannot find a solution that is specifically designed to be used on Windows Home Server.

Lastly, you learned the importance of keeping your systems and software updated so that you will be protected from newly discovered vulnerabilities. You learned how to check to make sure that automatic updates are configured properly for both your client computers and your Windows Home Server.

Chapter 14

Expanding Your Windows Home Server

Windows Home Server has been developed primarily to serve several key functions on your home network. Its primary roles are to provide reliable and consistent backups for your home computers, and to provide universal access to your data both from within your home network, and when you are away from home. While this may seem like a pretty short list, getting these features right and making them easy enough for all home users was a major challenge.

In the future, Microsoft may decide to add features to Windows Home Server to fill in the gaps that some customers perceive, but until then they have done something even better. Microsoft is working to develop a healthy third-party software ecosystem around Windows Home Server. Because it is based on Windows Server 2003, Windows Home Server is able to run software that is built in just the same manner as traditional Windows applications. Commercial software companies, hobbyist developers, and other third parties can use the tools they already know in order to expand the functionality of Windows Home Server.

The main difficulties in developing *add-ins* for Windows Home Server stem from the fact that home servers usually have no keyboard, mouse, or display attached. Along similar lines, there is no desktop session that will be run. This means that all interactions with users have to take place through either the Windows Home Server console or the Remote Access web interface.

The solution to these problems was provided by Microsoft in the form of a Software Development Kit (SDK) that allows programmers to build solutions that interact with the core elements of the Windows Home Server software. Using the SDK, software can add its own user interface in to the Windows Home Server Console or Remote Access website so that it can be accessed and controlled just like the built-in functions of Windows Home Server. The SDK also allows software to interact with the core features of Windows Home Server in order to enhance and augment existing functions.

The Sky Is the Limit

Microsoft released the SDK to Independent Software Vendors (ISVs), partners, and hobbyist developers during the public beta testing period for version one of Windows Home Server. Currently there is not a great number of add-ins available, but there has been a good deal of speculation about the types of solutions that could be integrated with Windows Home Server.

Media Hub Enhancements

As you saw in Chapter 9, Windows Home Server already has many features that make it an ideal hub for all of your digital media. Several companies (such as SageTV and Electric Pocket) are looking at taking this functionality further by integrating Windows Home Server with additional content sources, such as TV tuners and Digital Video Recorder (DVR) software. In addition to bringing more content in, other solutions will allow you to push content out, sharing pictures and videos through services such as Flickr, YouTube, or even allowing you to stream content from your home network to remote computers and mobile devices.

Security and Home Automation

The idea of using your Windows Home Server as part of a *Smart Home* has been talked about since the public announcement of the product back in January 2007. Windows Home Server provides a secure website interface, and when tied to computer integrated automation and security technology, it opens up a whole new world of possibilities.

Currently, two companies (Embedded Automation and Lagotek) are developing home automation solutions that will integrate with Windows Home Server. Hobbyists who enjoy tinkering with programming and home automation may choose to develop their own solutions that can be integrated with Windows Home Server in the meantime. Other people will likely choose to wait until packaged solutions come to market. Either way, there are many exciting possibilities for integrating home automation with Windows Home Server.

Imagine being able to log in to your Home Server's website while you are away on travel, and check the status of a home security system. You can verify that the system is properly armed, and check the status of the various sensors. If you need to alter the alarm schedule so that a friend or worker can gain access to the house, this could be done remotely. With the proper equipment, you could even make it so that you could lock and unlock the door through the secure website, allowing you to open the door for home contractors or a child or spouse who had lost his or her key!

You could even include computer-connected cameras in your home security setup. This might allow you to check on your pets during the day, or just have more peace of mind that your home is safe while you are away.

On the automation front, a Windows Home Server connected home might allow you to remotely turn lights on or off, change thermostat settings, or open and close electric blinds. A great deal of possibilities for home automation can be found via web retailers such as www.smarthome.com, and the utility of almost any of these solutions could be multiplied by integration with Windows Home Server. Many currently available home automation packages include APIs that can be used to develop a solution that integrates with Windows Home Server. In the near term this integration will be limited to those who understand how to program, but as demand grows, more consumer-friendly packages should become available.

Personal Publishing

The last big thing that Windows Home Server can enable is the sharing of our digital lives with others. Many folks have extended families that span the country, and keeping everyone up to date can be tough. As part of Windows Home Server's Remote Access features, the server includes a full-scale web server. This web server is the same technology that runs sites like Microsoft.com, so it is more than capable of running your Windows Home Server remote access as well as any other personal publishing tasks that you have. You can put together a website such as a Web log (blog), a photo sharing site, or pretty much anything else, and run it in addition to the Remote Access website that is included with Windows Home Server. (Adding websites to Windows Home Server without breaking the existing Remote Access website is a challenge, but the Whiist add-in discussed later in this chapter makes this process a breeze!)

Data Security and Information Sharing

While Windows Home Server's base functionality goes a long way toward protecting your data, there are still scenarios where it will still fall short. If your server is stolen or severely damaged, you may not be able to recover your data.

Many vendors, including KeepVault and JungleDisk, are looking at integrating their online storage and backup services with Windows Home Server. This will provide an extra layer of protection for a user's data, and many services will also let you access your files remotely and optionally share certain files with others.

If your ISP does not allow Windows Home Server's Remote Access features, this might be another option for making your data available remotely, in addition to protecting your data in the event of a disaster.

Installing Add-ins

Some add-ins may have unique installation requirements, but for the most part the process will be fairly similar. These general guidelines will usually apply.

Buying or Downloading the Software

The first step toward installing an add-in is getting the software onto your Windows Home Server's hard drive. For add-ins to be available, they need to be placed into the \\SERVER\Software\Add-ins folder. You can download the files to, or place the installation disk in any of your client computers, and then copy the .MSI file to the \\SERVER\Software\Add-ins folder on your server, as shown in Figure 14-1. A proper add-in is always copied to this location as a .MSI file. If you have a .ZIP file or .EXE file, it probably needs to be run or extracted on one of your client computers first.

Installing an Add-in

Once the code is copied to the correct location on your home server, you install it using the Windows Home Server Console. Open the console by double-clicking the Windows Home Server icon in the system tray on one of your client computers. After you enter the password, you should see a console screen similar to Figure 14-2.

Chapter 14: Expanding Your Windows Home Server

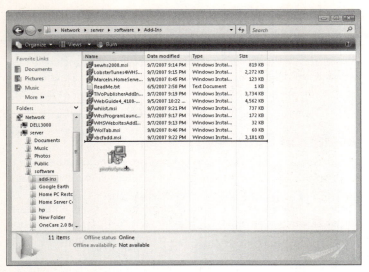

Figure 14-1

Figure 14-2

The initial screen shows the add-ins that you have already installed, so if this is your first time installing add-ins, the list will be blank. To see the add-ins that are available to be installed, select the Available tab at the top of the main panel.

Chapter 14: Expanding Your Windows Home Server

Select the Settings action in the upper-right corner of the console window. In the dialog box that opens, select Add-ins from the left panel, and you should see a screen similar to Figure 14-3.

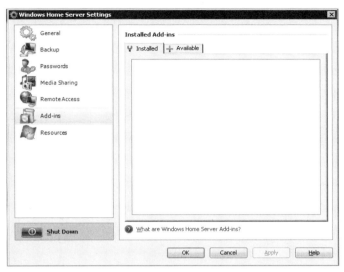

Figure 14-3

Figure 14-4 shows the resulting screen, and you can see the listing of add-ins found in the `\\SERVER\Software\Add-ins` folder. From this screen, locate the add-in that you wish to install, and click its Install button.

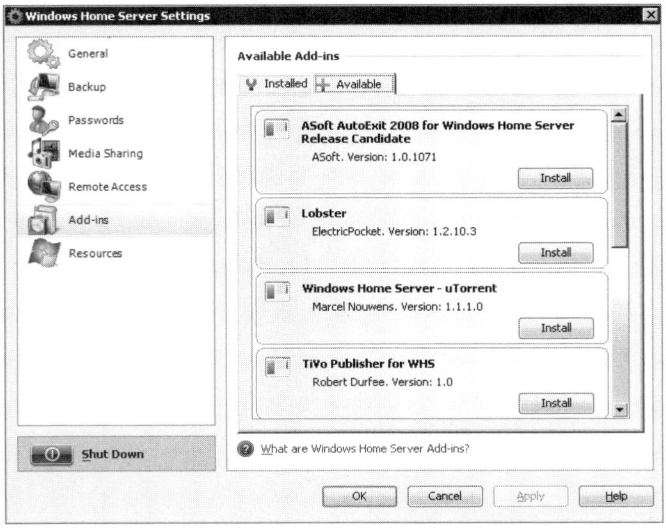

Figure 14-4

Most add-ins will require you to restart the console after they are finished installing, as shown in Figure 14-5. Before you click the OK button to restart the console, be prepared to see an error message. Don't panic. As you will soon see, everything is fine. Click the OK button to continue.

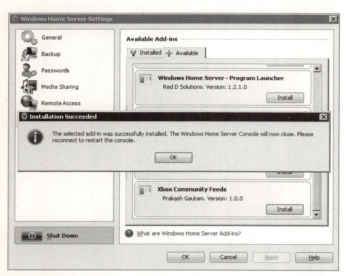

Figure 14-5

When the console is reset, you should see an error message similar to Figure 14-6. Although this message looks like an error, it should actually be expected at this point. This is just a consequence of the way that the Windows Home Server Console communicates with the client computer. The portion of the console that runs on the client computer can't differentiate between a console reset and an actual loss of connectivity, so the same error is presented.

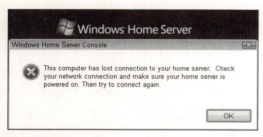

Figure 14-6

Chapter 14: Expanding Your Windows Home Server   255

After you click OK the error message, you will be returned to the Windows Home Server Console login screen. Most add-ins are configured through the console, so you will probably want to log in to explore whatever functionality you have just added. Some add-ins add a new tab to the main console interface, others add a section to the Settings dialog box, and some actually add to both areas.

Add-ins bring new functionality to your Windows Home Server, and because their interfaces are usually added into the interfaces that you normally use to work with the other features of your home server, they tend to blend in very well. If at some point in the future you decide that you no longer want a particular add-in installed, the following section will show you how to remove it.

Uninstalling an Add-in

If you decide that you no longer want a particular add-in installed on your home server, follow these steps to remove it. The process is very similar to the installation process.

Open the Windows Home Server Console, click the Settings action, and select Add-ins, just as you did during the installation process. The dialog box should look similar to Figure 14-7, with a listing of any currently installed add-ins showing in the main panel.

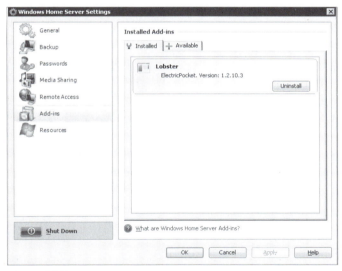

Figure 14-7

Find the entry for the add-in that you wish to remove, and click the Uninstall button. There is no confirmation for the uninstall action, so once you click the button, the add-in will be uninstalled immediately. When the uninstall process completes, you will be prompted to restart the console, as shown in Figure 14-8. Click OK to continue. You will see the error message from Figure 14-6 again, but you can disregard it. If you are done working with the Windows Home Server Console, there is no need to log back in. You can simply close the console window.

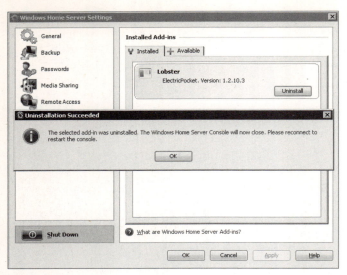

Figure 14-8

Finding Add-ins

The process of finding add-ins can be a little hit and miss if you don't know where to look. Microsoft may start maintaining some sort of listing in the future, but until then your best bet is to visit a blog site called *We Got Served*, published by Terry Walsh. Terry does a phenomenal job of keeping up with the current news around Windows Home Server. You can find his current list of add-ins by clicking Windows Home Server Add-ins on the menu at www.wegotserved.co.uk. Other resources for researching add-ins can be found at this book's website, http://whsbook.com, and Microsoft's Windows Home Server Forums, http://forums.microsoft.com/windowshomeserver.

Current Add-ins

In the short time that the SDK has been available, several add-ins have been published that are beginning to show the potential of the Windows Home Server platform. Some of these add-ins are simple tools that serve a basic purpose. Others fill perceived gaps in the feature set of Windows Home Server. Still others are built on existing products that have been modified to support integration with Windows Home Server.

ASoft AutoExit 2008 for Windows Home Server

AutoExit adds a tab to the Windows Home Server Console that allows you to remotely manage the computers on your home network in a variety of ways. You can shut down or restart computers, and if they are connected via wired Ethernet adapters that support the Wake On LAN (WOL) feature, you can even turn on computers that have been powered down. The AutoExit 2008 console interface is shown in Figure 14-9. Note that an additional tab has been added to the console between Server Storage and Network Healthy. Many add-ins will add a tab in this manner.

AutoExit is available at www.asoft.be/prod_autoexitwhs.html.

Figure 14-9

ElectricPocket LobsterTunes

LobsterTunes lets you leverage the media and Internet connection available on your Windows Home Server by streaming content to your Windows Mobile phone or connected handheld device. Using LobsterTunes you can play MP3 files from your home server, view saved television shows or video, or even use LobsterTunes to connect to Internet radio stations and have them converted to a stream format that will work with your mobile device.

LobsterTunes is available at www.lobstertunes.com/.

KeepVault Windows Home Server

KeepVault fills in a vital link in a total protection plan for your digital life. KeepVault offers a service that will allow you to backup your Windows Home Server's shared folders to a remote service. If you ever lose your Windows Home Server to fire, burglary, flood, or any other calamity, your data will still be backed up and available.

You can run the installation file for KeepVault on any client computer. It will prompt you to enter the location where the .MSI file should be placed. Direct it to \\SERVER\Software\Add-ins and it will extract the necessary files, and provide you with instructions for completing the setup.

KeepVault adds a new tab to the Windows Home Server Console called Internet Backup. The first time you open this tab, you will be prompted to create a KeepVault account, as shown in Figure 14-10.

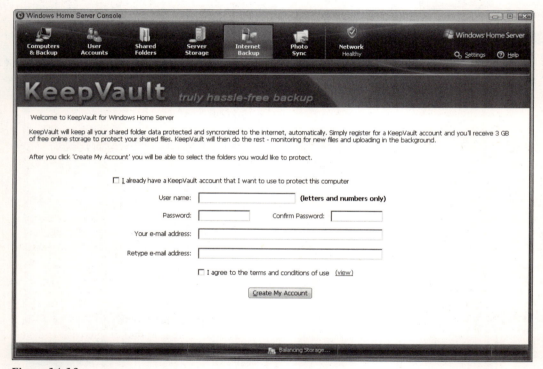

Figure 14-10

After you create an account and follow the instructions to verify your e-mail address, you are presented with a screen that will allow you to configure the online backup settings for all of your shared folders. Each shared folder can be configured separately, and the interface will provide an updated display showing how much space each share consumes, and how much space you are using on the KeepVault service, as shown in Figure 14-11.

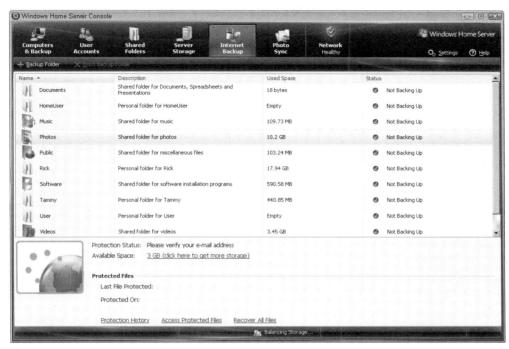

Figure 14-11

It is worth noting that KeepVault specifically allows for the backup of the Windows Home Server's shared folders, but that it does not allow you to save your computer backups online. This means that only data that is stored on the server's shares would be backed up and recoverable in the event that you lose both your server and your client computers at the same time, like in a fire. This is another good reason to keep your important data on the server.

KeepVault is available at www.keepvault.com/.

Jungle Disk for Windows Home Server

Jungle Disk is another online backup program with some very unique features. Jungle Disk is developed by Jungle Tools, and instead of providing servers themselves, the developers have integrated Jungle Disk with Amazon.com's S3 Storage service. S3 is a pay-as-you-go service that allows anyone to store information on Amazon.com's datacenter servers. The data is backed up and stored continually on multiple servers in different geographic locations.

To use Jungle Disk for Windows Home Server, you have to purchase the software from Jungle Tools, and then you have to sign up for an Amazon S3 account. The Jungle Disk software provides links and instructions for signing up for S3. There is no subscription cost associated with Jungle Disk itself, but you must pay Amazon.com each month (they set up automatic billing) for whatever amount of data storage and data transfers you are using. While this variable cost may seem a little intimidating, rates for storage on S3 generally run much lower than comparable rates at dedicated online backup services. Jungle Disk for Windows Home Server is available at www.jungledisk.com/whs.shtml.

Be Aware of What You Store Online

Online backup services can play an important role in protecting your data, but you should be aware of what data you are storing online, and you should evaluate whether you can trust the service providers that will hold the data for you. The two online services here, Jungle Disk and KeepVault, both utilize encryption in order to help keep your data safe, but encryption is not perfect. There may be weaknesses in the system that malicious individuals could exploit to access data.

Be reasonable about who you trust with your data. Use reasonably strong passwords for the accounts that these providers require, and carefully consider what data you want to backup online, weighing the risk of loss against the risk of accidental exposure or theft of the data.

PhotoSync for WHS

PhotoSync was one of the first and most popular add-ins to be published for Windows Home Server. PhotoSync allows you to designate a folder to be synchronized with the Flickr.com photo-sharing site. Any photos that are copied into the specified folder will automatically be uploaded to your Flickr account, allowing you to share them easily with friends and family.

Flickr requires you to authorize programs that want to interact with your account, but the PhotoSync add-in makes it very easy. After the add-in is installed, you are presented with a familiar browser window where you can log in to your Flickr account. You will then be prompted to authorize the connection, as shown in Figure 14-12.

Figure 14-12

After the initial setup, you will be prompted with a settings screen similar to Figure 14-13. You will probably want to modify the Photo Sync Folder option, because the default setting will have it synchronize your entire \\SERVER\Photos shared folder to Flickr. A good alternative is to set it to use a folder like \\SERVER\Photos\Flickr, so that you can select which photos to share, and copy them to that folder.

PhotoSync is available at www.edholloway.com/.

Figure 14-13

Whiist Website Management Plug-in

Whiist allows users to add links and additional websites to their Windows Home Server. This useful tool provides a simple interface and handles all of the complexity of adding settings and files to Windows Home Server's web server.

Whiist adds a Website Management tab to your Windows Home Server Console, as shown in Figure 14-14. You can manage links and websites from this interface, and Whiist provides a wizard that will step you through the process of creating a link or website, and even includes options to generate a default content page or a simple photo album. The default content page is shown in Figure 14-15, and an example of the photo album is seen in Figure 14-16.

Chapter 14: Expanding Your Windows Home Server

Figure 14-14

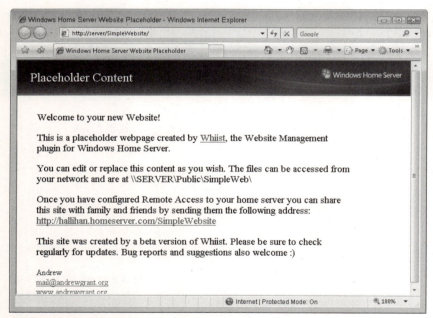

Figure 14-15

Figure 14-16

Whiist is available at www.andrewgrant.org/whiist/.

Windows Home Server Program Launcher

The Program Launcher add-in allows you to exploit the fact that the Windows Home Server Console is actually built on top of the Remote Desktop Protocol. Usually when you log in to the console, your actions are constrained so that only actions that are built-in to the console are available.

The Program Launcher add-in allows you to enable almost any program to be launched and run from the Windows Home Server Console. These programs execute directly on the server and the interface is displayed to the client through the Windows Home Server Console window.

Once installed, the Program Launcher add-in provides a new tab in the Windows Home Server Console and includes some default shortcuts, as shown in Figure 14-17.

You can add a shortcut to any program that is loaded onto your Windows Home Server, as shown in Figure 14-18. Just use the controls to browse and locate the program's .EXE file and then give it a friendly name.

After the shortcut is set up, you can launch it anytime from the Program Launcher tab of your Windows Home Server Console. In Figure 14-19, you see an example showing Notepad running on the server.

264 Chapter 14: Expanding Your Windows Home Server

Figure 14-17

Figure 14-18

Chapter 14: Expanding Your Windows Home Server 265

Figure 14-19

The Program Launcher add-in can be used to enable easy access to programs that are not designed specifically to run with Windows Home Server. Basically anything that runs properly under the Remote Desktop Connection will work under Program Launcher. Some programs may appear to hide the Windows Home Server Console by bringing up the Desktop. If this happens, simply click the Start button in the console window and select Log Out. This will reset the console session and will allow you to reconnect.

Caution

This add-in allows you to run pretty much any program in your Windows Home Server. While this may be a convenient way to provide access to a needed program, Microsoft does not recommend using the Windows Home Server for general-purpose computing such as browsing the Internet or word processing.

Program Launcher is best suited for running programs that are useful in the context of managing your home server. You should never use it to access low-level utilities such as the Disk Management console, because using these tools can corrupt the data stored on Windows Home Server.

Program Launcher is available at www.danno.ca/.

Windows Home Server Website Manager

The Website Manager add-in allows home users to easily add links to the remote access web pages that are part of the Windows Home Server Remote Access functionality. With this add-in installed, users can go to the Website tab in the console to add and remove links that will be displayed whenever someone connects to the remote access web interface on their server. The console interface for adding links is shown in Figure 14-20, and Figure 14-21 shows the resulting web page being served by the home server.

Website Manager is available at `www.vanhorn.net/addin/`.

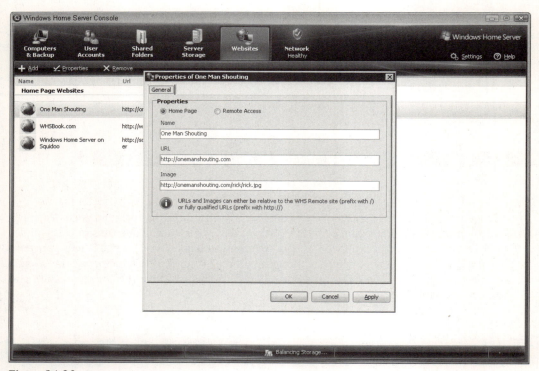

Figure 14-20

Xbox Community Feeds

Xbox Community Feeds is a general-purpose RSS Aggregator that downloads blog posts, podcasts, or vidcasts and converts them into a format that can be displayed on an Xbox. If you don't have an Xbox 360 but you do have another Media Connect device, you can still make use of the Xbox Community Feeds add-in.

This add-in provides the user with the capability to set up a list of feeds through the Windows Home Server Console, as shown in Figure 14-22.

Chapter 14: Expanding Your Windows Home Server 267

Figure 14-21

Figure 14-22

For each feed that you include in the list, Xbox Community Feeds will download all content. Text content is formatted and the add-in generates an image that can be displayed on the Xbox 360 or any other Media Extender via the Media Connect interface. An example showing my blog feed is shown in Figure 14-23.

Figure 14-23

Xbox Community Feeds is available at `www.xbstream.com/`.

Interested in Building Add-ins Yourself?

If you are a professional or hobbyist software developer, building add-ins is a relatively simple exercise that can allow you to tailor your Windows Home Server to provide new features and solve new problems. A properly packaged Windows Home Server add-in can be shared with the community or even sold if it's good enough!

The process of developing an add-in is well outside the scope of this book, but if you are interested, there is a great deal of online resources available to help you get started.

The first and most official resource is the Software Development Kit (SDK) documentation on Microsoft's MSDN (Microsoft Developer Network) website. It can be found at `http://msdn2.microsoft.com/en-us/library/aa496121.aspx` or you can simply search for Windows Home Server in the search box at `http://msdn.microsoft.com`.

Another great resource for developers of any experience level is the Developers subgroup at the Windows Home Server Forums. Just point your browser to `http://forums.microsoft.com/windowshomeserver` and select the Developers group from the list of forums.

Evolving Add-ins

Windows Home Server is an exciting new product. Consequently, there is a lot of energy and activity happening around it. People are constantly announcing plans for new tools, add-ins are being developed, and early versions of products are being released. Some of the emerging add-ins are presented here. Of course, new ideas are being introduced all the time.

> **Note**
>
> Like you, I am excited about all of the new developments around Windows Home Server. Go to http://whsbook.com periodically to find information on new add-ins, to ask questions, and to become more engaged in the growing Windows Home Server community.

Diskeeper Corporation's Diskeeper 2008

Windows Home Server's Drive Extender technology makes it so that many currently available hard disk tools will not work properly. The commitment from Diskeeper to provide a compatible solution means that users will have a reliable option for keeping their Windows Home Server hard drives operating properly and efficiently.

More information is available at www.diskeeper.com.

Embedded Automation mControl for Windows Home Server

Embedded Automation has announced that they are producing a version of their mControl home automation product that will integrate with Windows Home Server. This will enable users to integrate Windows Home Server into their home automation solution, including controlling lighting, security, and pretty much any aspect of their home security and automation setup.

More information is available at www.embeddedautomation.com.

Lagotek Corporation's Home Intelligence Platform

Another Home Automation vendor, Lagotek, is integrating Windows Home Server with their Home Intelligence Platform. Like Embedded Automation, Lagotek enables access to climate, lighting, and security features of your home. Lagotek focuses on making Automation easy to use, and their solutions enable users to easily build profiles that enable them to quickly select a new state for the house that will adjust many different aspects of the home.

More information is available at www.lagotek.com.

SageTV for Windows Home Server

SageTV takes the ability of Windows Home Server to act as a media hub and expands it to the next level. SageTV can bring content in through tuner cards and other devices, and with the optional hardware SageTV Media Extenders, you can make use of all of your content anywhere in your home. The Media Extenders are inexpensive devices that let you use content from the SageTV server on televisions throughout your home.

Instead of being a central storage point from which you can download media files, SageTV actually streams data to your different devices. This means that the media can begin playing almost immediately without having to wait for a lengthy download to complete. Streaming from SageTV does require a special media player or an extender device.

More information is available at www.sagetv.com/whs.

Summary

In this chapter you learned how you can enable your Windows Home Server to handle more than backups and data access by installing add-ins. You learned that the basis for Windows Home Server's expandability is the fact that it is built on top of Microsoft's Windows Server 2003 platform. This chapter discussed how Microsoft has made an SDK available to Independent Software Vendors and hobbyists alike, so that everyone could create solutions that would integrate with Windows Home Server.

You learned how to install add-ins by first placing the software onto the Windows Home Server, and then utilizing the Windows Home Server console to enable the add-in. You also learned how to remove add-ins that are no longer needed.

Next, the chapter covered several of the initial add-ins that have been released to the public, and then covered several of the add-ins that are being developed.

Overall, you should now have a better understanding of how you can make your Windows Home Server into an integral part of your home network, not just serving its core functions, but as an expandable platform that is able to fit into a variety of roles including home automation and security, personal publishing, and an advanced media hub.

Appendix A

Finding More Information

These resources will help you find more information about Windows Home Server, Home Automation, and protecting your home and your data.

Windows Home Server Communities

Online communities offer people a forum for asking questions and discussing products. Communities often rely on the participants to answer questions, but can be a great resource for finding help because you can often find other people who have already experienced the same problems.

Microsoft's Windows Home Server Forums

Located at `http://forums.microsoft.com/windowshomeserver/` (see Figure A-1).

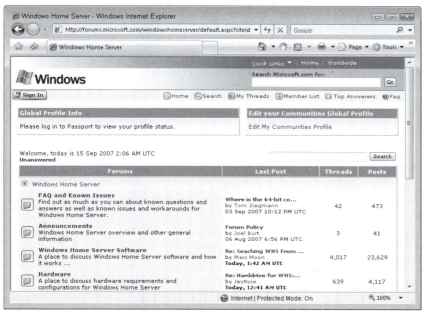

Figure A-1

Appendix A: Finding More Information

Microsoft started the Windows Home Server Forums site during the public beta testing period for version 1 of Windows Home Server. This is a fairly active community, and new questions are generally answered in less than a day. The community is divided into sections that focus on the Windows Home Server Software, Hardware, Developers (focusing on third-party add-in development), and Suggestions.

Most questions on the forums are answered by community members, but members of Microsoft's Windows Home Server team often stop through to answer some of the tougher questions.

WHSBook.com

Located at `http://whsbook.com` (see Figure A-2).

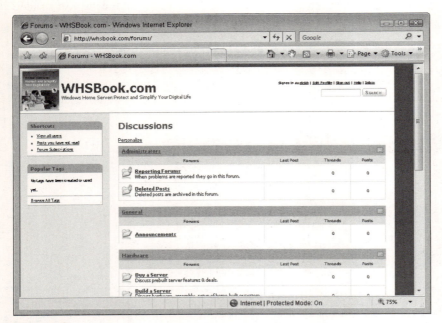

Figure A-2

WHSBook.com was started as a community site to give readers a place to discuss the topics covered in this book. There are forums focused on buying a prebuilt server, building your own server, troubleshooting and maintaining a server, organizing your digital life, securing your home network, using remote access, working with backups, and using third-party add-ins.

I frequently monitor this site, so it's a great place to ask questions about the topics in this book or about Windows Home Server in general.

Blogs

The term *blog* was originally derived from the term web log, and it is used to describe a website that periodically posts new information in the form of *posts* or *entries*. Some blogs are like personal online diaries that the world can read, but they can also be a great way for people to communicate and share information about technology.

In addition to providing a regular web view that can be visited using an Internet browser such as Internet Explorer or Mozilla Firefox, most blogs also offer a feature called a *feed*. A feed is a special file, usually in the RSS or Atom format, that allows a reader to subscribe to the blog using a feed reader like NewsGator Online (http://newsgator.com) or Bloglines (http://bloglines.com) or a client-based reader like FeedDemon (http://feeddemon.com) or RSS Bandit (http://rssbandit.org). Once a user subscribes to a feed, they no longer need to continually visit a site to check if new information is posted. They can simply open their feed reader, and any new content from any of their subscribed feeds will be shown.

Microsoft's Windows Home Server Blog on TechNet

Located at http://blogs.technet.com/homeserver/ (see Figure A-3).

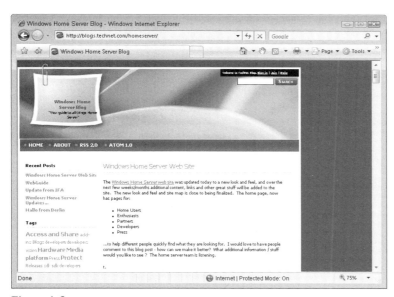

Figure A-3

Several members of Microsoft's Windows Home Server team post announcements and other useful information to the Windows Home Server blog on Microsoft's TechNet. This is a great place to get official updates from Microsoft regarding Windows Home Server. They also post helpful tips for making use of Windows Home Server's various features, and link to other blogs and news sites that have interesting information relevant to Windows Home Server.

Charlie Kindel's Blog—cek.log

Located at `http://kindel.com/blogs/charlie/` (see Figure A-4).

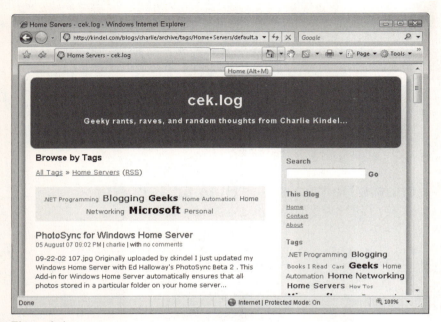

Figure A-4

Charlie Kindel is the general manager at Microsoft in charge of Windows Home Server. Cek.log is Charlie's personal blog, and he often posts interesting information related to Windows Home Server, in addition to a great deal of other random topics.

We Got Served

Located at `http://wegotserved.co.uk/` (see Figure A-5).

We Got Served is a blog published by Terry Walsh that covers many different aspects of Windows Home Server. Terry seems to be the first to find out about many of the hardware and software developments around Windows Home Server. This is a great blog to subscribe to if you want to keep up to date with the latest news.

In addition to keeping on top of the latest news about Windows Home Server, Terry also maintains a list of how-to articles, a list of third-party add-ins that have been published for Windows Home Server, and a catalog of the retail Windows Home Server machines that are available to be purchased by consumers.

Figure A-5

MS Windows Home Server

Located at http://mswhs.com/ (see Figure A-6).

Figure A-6

Published by Philip Churchill, this MS Windows Home Server blog tracks news and information related to Windows Home Server. Phillip stays on top of the news related to Windows Home Server and posts frequent updates on this blog. There is also a WHS Jargon Explained section that explains some of the more technical terms and acronyms that are related to Window Home Server.

Home Automation

Home automation is one of the more interesting possible expansions for Windows Home Server. If you want to get started with automating your home, the following sites can help.

Embedded Automation

Located at `http://embeddedautomation.com/`.

Embedded Automation produces a software product called mControl that interfaces between computers and a variety of automation technologies. Embedded Automation has committed to releasing a version of their mControl software that will run as an add-in for Windows Home Server.

Lagotek

Located at `http://lagotek.com/`.

Lagotek focuses on providing wireless home automation solutions, including both hardware and software. This is a good approach to take if you are trying to automate an existing home without trying to retrofit wiring. Lagotek has committed to supporting the Windows Home Server platform as part of their automation solutions.

Smarthome Home Automation Superstore

Located at `http://smarthome.com`.

In addition to being an online source for purchasing a wide variety of home automation solutions, the Smarthome website hosts a wide variety of tutorials and other information that will help you make sense of the variety of automation options that are available. Check out their Getting Started and Learning Center sections.

Other Information

Some other information that is useful in the planning of your home network and the protection of your home network can be found in the following sections.

Underwriters Laboratories Consumer Section

Located at `www.ul.com/consumers/`.

In addition to keeping your data backed up with Windows Home Server, another major step you can take toward keeping your data safe may also help keep you and your family safe! The

Underwriters Laboratories maintains a site that covers a wide variety of topics for consumers including how to prevent fires, protect your family from carbon monoxide, and how to protect your home with smoke detectors.

While you are focusing on protecting your digital life, take some time to think about other ways you can reduce risks in your home by visiting the Underwriters Laboratories website.

Other Questions?

If you have other questions or comments about the book or about Windows Home Server, feel free to drop me an e-mail at author@whsbook.com.

Index

A

accounts. *See* user accounts
Active Directory, Windows Home Server, not included in, 8, 93
adapters, 51–52
    installing, 51
    speed of, 35
    wireless, 51
add-ins
    add-ins, installing/uninstalling, 251–256
    AutoExit, 257
    building add-ins, 268
    future add-ins, 269–270
    KeepVault, 258–259
    LobsterTunes, 257
    PhotoSync, 260–261
    Program Launcher, 263–266
    sources for, 251, 256
    Website Manager, 266
    Whiist website management, 261–263
    Xbox Community Feeds, 266–268
administrative password
    data recovery, 164
    importance of, 83
    Remote Desktop Connection, 143
    setting, 75–76
    versus user password, 75, 81, 102
Always Available Offline, 15
antivirus software
    automatic updates, 244–246
    for computers, 238–239
    free software, 238
    for Windows Home Server, 242–243
Application Programming Interface (API), 7
authentication
    cryptographic, 79
    user accounts, 79–80
AutoExit, 257
automatic login, setting up, 90–91
automatic updates, 70, 244–246
AVG software, 237–238

B

backup(s), 99–120
    Backup Configuration Wizard, 113–117
    cleanup process, 104–107
    copying to hard drive, 168
    data recovery from, 164–168
    disabling/reenabling, 109–112
    excluded files, 100, 113, 116–117
    hardware limitations, 2
    manual, steps in, 122–124
    for mobile computers, 117–118
    network congestion during, 101
    online backup service, 8, 122
    opening, 164–167
    schedule, setting, 101–104
    in Sleep/Hibernate mode, 100–101, 119
    time frame, default, 99, 101
    time required for, 101
    volumes, 112–113
    and Windows Vista, 2
backup retention, 104–109
    backups to save, marking, 105–106
    decision-making about, 107–108
    schedule, setting, 99, 104, 108–109
    unkept files, 104–105
Backup Time, 103
BIOS
    and boot from Restore CD, 176–178
    setup utility, 61
blogs, Windows Home Server blogs, 256, 273–276
boot
    DVD, booting from, 61–62
    from Restore CD, 176–178
bridge mode, 51, 198
broadband
    network setup. *See* network connections
    service options, 42

C

cable(s)
    crossover cables, 50
    Ethernet, 50
cable Internet service, 42
cable modem, 40–41
cache files, client-side, excluded files, 100, 113
central processing unit (CPU), context switch, 33
channels, wireless connections, 55
Charlie Kindel's Blog, 274
chronological organization, photos, 19–21
clients. *See* server(s)
Connector Software. *See* Windows Home
    Server Connector
    installing, 75–77
crossover cables, 50
cryptographic authentication, 79
Ctrl key, files, multi-select, 131–132

D

data collection, 129–137
    moving files, 131–135
    search, 130
    staged folders, use of, 129
data recovery, 163–185
    from backups, 164–168
    from hard drive. *See* hard drive failure
    passwords, 164
    shared folders, restoring files to, 169–172
deleted files, restoring. *See* data recovery
digital rights management (DRM)
    copying files, restrictions, 156
    media files, 156
    moving files, caution, 24
Diskeeper 2008, 269
documents, organizational methods, 23–24
domain name
    remote access settings, 199
    for server, 190–191
Drive Extender, 34, 68, 104
driver(s)
    loading, 63–64
    network adapter settings, 51
    printers, 142, 145, 147
drives. *See* hard drives
DSL modem, 40
DSL service, 42
dust problem, 59–60
DVD, booting from, 61–62
Dynamic Host Configuration Protocol (DHCP)
    IP address, 50
    network connections, 50–51
    routers, 41
    and wireless connection, 50–51

E

edge routers, 198
e-mail, Windows Home Server, not included in, 8
Embedded Automation, 250, 269, 276
End-User License Agreement (EULA), 66, 75, 239
entertainment
    organization of media, 22–23
    See also media sharing library
error reporting, 71–72
Ethernet. *See* network connections
expansion options, 249–270
    media hub, 250, 269
    online backup services, 251, 258–260
    publishing, personal tasks, 250–251
    for servers, 36
    smart homes, 250, 276
    and Software Development Kit (SDK), 249
    Software Development Kit (SDK), 268
    and switches, 43

F

Fast User Switching, 91
FAT, versus NTFS formatting, 77
files
    excluded in backup, 113
    referencing, 124
    sorting, 131
firewalls, 239–240
    NAT, 198, 239

Remote Desktop, configuring for, 210–211
Windows firewall, 236
Flickr, 260–261
folder(s)
excluded files, 113, 115–117
manual search, 130
organizing. *See* organization of digital information
permissions, changing, 96–97
referencing, 124
subfolders, creating, 127–128
unsorted folders, 129
folder duplication
benefits of, 122
multiple drives requirement, 122
Full access, avoiding, 127

G

gaming
speed requirements, 35, 44
Xbox 360 access, 157–161
Gigabit Ethernet, speed, improving with, 43–44
granular control access, 90
guest accounts, 93–95
enabling/disabling, 94–95
functions of, 93
passwords, 94–95
security issue, 93–94

H

hard drive(s)
adding to Windows Home Server, 5, 15, 34
backup files, copying to, 168
crashing. *See* hard drive failure
FAT versus NTFS formatting, 77
formatting, 68
multiple, and folder duplication, 122
partitions. *See* volumes
reliability measures, 34
speed, 34
hard drive failure, 173–185
boot from CD, 176–178
causes of, 173

recovery, same computer requirement, 173
recovery CD, starting process, 175–178
Restore Computer Wizard, 178–185
heat, excessive, caution about, 59
hibernation
backups during, 100–101
enabling, 100
file, excluded in backup, 100
functions of, 100
home automation. *See* smart homes
home computers, remote access. *See* Remote Desktop Connection
home network. *See* network connections
Home Network Health, functions of, 5–6
HP MediaSmart server, 36

I

images
metadata, 16
speed requirements, 44
See also photos
input devices, 58
installation. *See* setting up Home Server
Internet Explorer, versus Firefox, 197
Internet service
cable, 42
satellite, 42
Internet Service Provider (ISP), remote access restrictions, 206–207
IP address
finding, 49, 200
functions of, 197
standard/private addresses, 197
iTunes, moving files, caution, 24

J

Jungle Disk, 259

K

KeepVault Windows Online Backup Service, 15, 258–259
keys, for WEP/WPA security, 54

L

Lagotek, 250, 269, 276
LobsterTunes, 257
logon name, creating, 82

M

MAC Filtering, 54
mControl, 276
mean time between failures (MTBF), hard drives, 34
Media Connect, 155, 157
media files, digital rights management (DRM), 156
media hub, 250, 269
    SageTV, 269–270
MediaLounge, accessing media from, 161–162
media sharing library, 155–162
    digital media receivers, 155
    MediaLounge access, 161–162
    setting up, 155–157
    Xbox 360 access, 157–160
memory. *See* random access memory (RAM)
metadata
    basic concept, 16–17
    search by, 17, 26
    sort by, 131
mobile computers
    backup tactics, 117–118
    media streaming add-in, 257
    Vista, settings for, 118
modems
    connectors, 40
    for port forwarding, 198
    setting up, 49
    types of, 40–41
moving files
    with digital rights management (DRM), 24
    files not to move, 137
    multi-select options, 131–132
    process of, 133–135
    search for files, 135–137
    select all files, 132
    staging folders, use of, 135
    wireless, speeding process, 133

Mozilla Firefox
    versus Internet Explorer, 197
    remote access problems, 197
My TabletPC, 117

N

Network Address Translation (NAT)
    as firewall, 198, 239
    functions of, 197–198
    routers as NAT device, 41, 49, 198
network connections, 39–57
    broadband options, 42
    Connector CD, 75–77
    device lights, 58
    Dynamic Host Configuration Protocol (DHCP), 50–51
    Ethernet cabling, 50, 58
    Gigabit Ethernet, improving speed with, 43–44
    high-speed needs, 35, 44
    home network, connecting Home Server to, 75–77
    home network configuration, 45–47
    modems, 40–41, 49
    network adapters, 51–52
    old buildings, influencing factors, 47–48
    placement of equipment, 48
    port forwarding, 198–207
    routers, 41, 49
    server requirements, 35–37
    speed, 43–44
    subnets, 50–51
    switches, 42–43, 50
    unconnected computer warnings, 109–110
    wireless, 44–45, 52–55
network interface card (NIC), 43
    installing, 51
noise level, servers, 60

O

Offline Files, 15
online backup service, 8, 122, 251, 258–259
    Jungle Disk, 259
    KeepVault, 258–259

organization of digital information, 13–27
    basic requirements, 14–15
    categories/subcategories, creating, 17–18
    centralized storage, 15
    data collection, 129–137
    documents, 23–24
    entertainment, 22–23
    flexibility, need for, 26
    folders/categories, 17–18
    organizational plan, writing, 139
    of photos, 19–22
    shortcuts, 137–138
    subfolders, creating, 127–128
    unsorted categories, 18
    user-defined shares, 125–127

P

parental control, Windows Home Server, not included in, 8
passwords, 91–92
    administrative password, 75–76, 81, 102
    authentication, 79–80
    basic precautions, 184
    changing on PC, 91–92
    data recovery, 164
    for family members, 90–91
    guest accounts, 94–95
    remote access, 193, 195
    Remote Desktop Connection, 143
    setting at installation, 70, 75
    strong, character types in, 97–98, 193, 195
    user accounts, 87–91
    for Windows Home Server Console, 81, 83
patches, security, 243–244
permissions, 96–97
    folders, changing, 96–97
    guest accounts, 95
    remote access, 97–98
personal shared folders, 25–26
photos
    categorical organization, 22
    chronological organization, 19–21
    devices, accessing media from, 162
    PhotSync and Flickr photo sharing, 260–261
    tagging, 21–22
PhotoSync, 260–261
Port 80 (HTTP/WWW/Web Server)
    ISP blocking of, 206
    remote access settings, 201–203
Port 443 (HTTPS/Secure WWW/Secure Web Server), remote access settings, 203
Port 4125, remote access settings, 204–205
port forwarding, 198–207
    and edge routers, 198
    manual set up, 200–206
    troubleshooting, 199
    UPnP router set up, 198–199
power down, versus Sleep mode, 100, 119
power requirements, 57–58
    surge protector, 48, 58
printers, 141–155
    adding printer, 145–152
    central, benefits of, 141
    client connection to, 153–155
    connecting to server, 143
    direct connect, avoiding, 153
    drivers, 142, 145, 147
    limitations with Home Server, 142
    log into Home Server, 143–145
    log off Home Server, 152–153
Program Launcher, 263–266

R

random access memory (RAM)
    increasing, 35
    server requirements, 34–35, 37
    thrashing problem, 35
Read access, 127
recovery of files. *See* data recovery
referencing files/folders, 124
remote access, 187–213
    benefits of, 3
    defaults, 145
    enabling/disabling, 82, 97–98, 193

and ISP terms of service, 206–207
passwords, 193, 195
Port 80 (HTTP/WWW/Web Server), 201–203
Port 443 (HTTPS/Secure WWW/Secure Web Server), 203
Port 4125, 204–205
port forwarding, 198–207
publishing, personal tasks, 250–251
Remote Desktop, 143–144, 209–213
router IP address, 200–201
search capability, 26
security, 211–212
setting up, 187–193
Shared Folders, accessing, 207–209
testing access, 196, 206
troubleshooting, 143, 199, 206
user accounts, configuring for, 193–197
web server, 250–251

Remote Desktop Connection
computers, connecting to, 212–213
enabling, 210–211
firewall, configuring for, 210–211
home server, logging in, 143–144
operating systems for, 209
Remote Desktop Protocol (RDP), 143
troubleshooting, 143

reorganizing data. *See* spring-cleaning
residential wireless, 42
Restore Computer Wizard, 178–185
retention of backups. *See* backup retention
routers
edge routers, 198
functions of, 41
IP address, 49, 200
as NAT devices, 41, 49, 198
and remote access. *See* port forwarding
setting up, 49–50
switches, 43
wireless security options, 52–55

Run Disk Manager, 180

S

SageTV, 269, 269–270
schedule for backups. *See* backup(s)
search
by metadata, 17, 26
methods, 26, 135
remote capability, 26
via Windows Explorer, 130
via Windows Vista, 135–136
security, 235–248
and administrative password, 83
antispyware, 239
antivirus software, 238–239, 242–243
basic precautions, 184–185
defense in depth, 240
firewalls, 239–240
and guest accounts, 93–94
Home Server benefits, 235–236
and NAT, 198
non-recognition by Home Server, 241
online backup service, 251
patches/updates, 243–247
remote access, 211–212
user-defined shares, 125–127
Windows Security Center, 236–237
and Windows Vista, 84
wireless connections, WEP/WPA, 52–55
zombie computers, 211
server(s), 29–37
backup(s), 36
building server, 31–33
chassis/expansion options, 36
cost factors, 32
CPU of, 33–34
domain name, 190–191
environmental concerns, 59–60
functions of, 1
hard drives, 34
home network configuration, 45–47
installation/support, 30
multiple on home network, 40
network connections, 35–37, 39–57

OEM/retail equipment, 30–31
RAM, 34–35, 37
System Builder program, 29, 30
setting up Home Server, 61–77
    drivers, loading, 63–64
    DVD, booting from, 61–62
    End-User License Agreement (EULA), 66
    hard drive formatting, 68
    home network, connecting to, 75–77
    localization options, 65
    with OEM/retail equipment, 73–74
    password, setting, 70, 75–76
    server name, 66
Shared Folders
    files, restoring to, 169–172
    permissions, changing, 96–97
    personal shares, 25–26
    predefined, 25
    Read versus Full access, 127
    referencing, 124
    remote access to, 207–209
    subfolders, creating, 127–128
    user-defined shares, 125–127
    Volume Shadow Copies, 169, 171
Shift + Select, files, multi-select, 131–132
shortcuts
    creating, 138
    naming, 138
    usefulness of, 137
Sleep
    backups during, 119
    enabling, 119
Smarthome Home Automation Superstore, 276
smart homes
    future options, 250
    Internet resources, 276
Software Development Kit (SDK)
    functions of, 249
    web site for, 268
sort
    files, 131
    by metadata, 131
    unsorted categories, 18
    Windows Explorer options, 131
Soundbridge devices, accessing media from, 162
speed
    hard drives, 34
    network connections, 43–44
    and wireless, 44–45, 133
spring-cleaning, 121–140
    data collection, 129–137
    pre-cleaning backup, 122–124
    shortcuts, 137–138
    subfolders, 127–128
    user-defined shares, 125–127
spyware, antispyware, 239
staged folders
    functions of, 129, 135
    unsorted folders, 129
storage
    centralized, pros/cons, 15
    expansion of, 5
streaming video, speed requirements, 35, 44
subfolders, creating, 127–128
subnets, 50–51
surge protector, basic requirements, 48
Suspend to Disk. *See* hibernation
switches
    DSL modem, 40–41
    functions of, 42–43
    routers, 43
    setting up, 50
Sync Center, 15
System Builder
    features of, 30
    license for, 29
system file page, excluded in backup, 100, 113

T

tagging, photos, 21–22
TechNet blog, 273
temporary files, excluded in backup, 100, 113
Temporary Key Integrity Protocol (TKIP), 54
Terminal Services ActiveX Client, 213
thrashing, 35

U

Underwriters Laboratories Consumer Section, 276–277
Universal Naming Convention (UNC), referencing files/folders, 124
unsorted folders, functions of, 129
updates
    automatic, 70, 244–246
    importance of, 245
    Update Password tool, 91–92, 98
UPnP, port forwarding set up, 198–199
USB connections
    and expansion of system, 36
    functions of, 40
    printers, 143
    USB adapters, 35, 51
    USB hubs, 36
    wireless adapter, 51
user accounts, 79–91
    authentication, 79–80
    automatic login, setting up, 90–91
    creating on Home Server, 81–85
    creating on PC, 86–89
    for family members, 90–91
    granular control access, 90
    guest accounts, 93–95
    logon name, 82
    matching accounts, 80
    passwords, 87–91
    permissions, changing, 96–97
    remote access, 97–98, 193–197
    User Account Control (UAC), 84–89
user-defined shares, 125–127
    creating, 125–126
    Full access, avoiding, 127
    security, 125–127
username, authentication, 79–80

V

video, streaming, speed requirements, 35, 44
video adapter, for initial installation, 37

viruses
    operation of, 238–239
    See also antivirus software
volumes, 112–113
    in backup configuration, 112, 114
    defined, 104, 112
    excluded files, 112
    including in backups, importance of, 113
    new, creating, 181–182
    NT file system and backup, 115
Volume Shadow Copies, 169, 171

W

web server, 250–251
Website Manager, 266
We Got Served blog, 256, 274–275
Whiist website management, 261–263
Wi-Fi Protected Access (WPA), wireless set-up, 53–55
Windows Explorer
    manual search, 130
    sort options, 131
Windows Home Server
    Application Programming Interface (API), 7
    backups, 99–120
    blogs on, 273–276
    data recovery, 163–185
    desktop as client computer, 243
    digital life, organizing. *See* organization of digital information
    direct connect, avoiding, 153
    expansion options, 249–270
    features not included, 8–10
    functions of, 1, 9
    guest accounts, 93–95
    Home Network Health feature, 5–6
    input devices, 58
    Internet Explorer versus Firefox, 197
    Live OneCare overlap with, 247
    media sharing library, 155–162
    network connections, 39–57
    Online Backup Service, 15

permissions, 96–97
power requirements, 57–58
printers, 141–155
remote access, 3, 97–98, 187–213
Restore CD, 178–185
search feature, 26
security, 235–248
server, choosing, 29–37
setting up. *See* setting up Home Server
Shared Folders, 25–26
shortcuts, 137–138
spring-cleaning, 121–140
storage, expansion of, 5
system requirements, 36–37
use, rationale for, 2–7
user accounts, 79–91
web site for, 275–276
Windows Home ServerBook (WHSBook), 272
Windows Home Server Connector
    backups, opening, 167
    installing, 75–77
Windows Home Server Console
    accessing, 81, 96, 102
    passwords, 81, 83
    screen, size and viewing, 165
Windows Home Server Forum, 271–272
    Developers group, 268
Windows Live ID, 189
Windows Live OneCare, 247
Windows Vista
    Always Available Offline, 15
    automatic login, setting up, 90–91
    backups, 2

mobile PC settings, 118
Photo Gallery, 22
search, 135–136
security features, 84
sort options, 131
Sync Center, 15
tagging, 21
User Account Control (UAC), 84–85
user accounts, adding, 86–89
Wired Equivalent Privacy (WEP),
    wireless set-up, 53–55
wireless connections, 44–45
    in apartment buildings/dense areas, 55
    in bridge mode, 51
    channels, 55
    client connections, checking, 54–55
    Dynamic Host Configuration Protocol (DHCP) and set-up, 50–51
    home network configuration, 47
    moving files, speeding process, 133
    residential wireless, 42
    security, 52–55
    speed limitations, 44–45, 133
    USB adapters, 51

X

Xbox 360 access, accessing media from, 157–160
Xbox Community Feeds, 266–268

Z

zombie computers, 211